D0952961

"In today's turbulent business environment, decision-makers in global companies, particularly financial institutions, need a clear vision, effective strategies and state-of-the-art execution. In this book, Alain Martin provides thought-provoking analyses, a practical framework and concrete examples of how to develop the business intelligence required to support these three major challenges. Highly-recommended reading before taking action."

André Bérard, Chairman of the Board
National Bank of Canada

"Information in the past tense is never as valuable as information in the future or present tense. How often do we hear that 'the signs were all there.' Martin has created a framework and processes that anyone or any organization can adapt and use to create information and intelligence that will prevent or reduce unpleasant surprises in their lives or work."

Professor William J. Bruns, Jr., Henry R. Byers Professor of Business Administration, Emeritus, Harvard Business School Visiting Professor, Graduate School of Business Administration Northeastern University

"This book is crisply written, offering a conceptual framework to tie together technical tools and practical wisdom. It is a must-read for Chief Intelligence Officers and others focused on moving to the forefront of their industry or shaping the next competitive arena."

Professor John S. Carroll, Sloan School of Management
Massachusetts Institute of Technology

"Alain Martin integrates strategic planning, competitive analysis, and risk management tools into a powerful framework that provides valuable theoretical and practical approaches to strategy formulation and business risk management. His trenchant advice to "use competitive intelligence as both a sword and a shield" is particularly relevant in today's competitive marketplace. More importantly, Martin shows how the ethical and responsible use of competitive intelligence can prepare an organization for unprecedented changes in the external environment. This practical book is well worth the busy executives' time."

Dr. Peter B. Corr, Senior Vice President, Science and Technology
Pfizer Inc

"Alain Martin provides many up-to date examples, in a concise format that allows the reader to put the concepts to use immediately. I got ideas from the "*Intelligence Insights From The Battlefield*" regarding competitive intelligence cases in the public domain that I am already using to obtain competitive information."

Daniel B. Cunningham, President & CEO
Long-Stanton Manufacturing Co.

"This book is a useful guide on frameworks to enhance intelligence gathering and strategic planning in business."

Holger G. Demuth, Managing Director
Credit Suisse, Zurich

"Alain Martin provides great insight into the competitive intelligence function. Vivid examples from multiple industries bring the book alive. The framework and tools are practical. They would have broad applicability across our company from guiding R&D decisions to developing strategies for our sales representatives."

Denise Dickson, Director, Global Competitive Intelligence
Eli Lilly and Company

"Executives that are just becoming aware of the untapped intelligence potential within their organizations need to absorb this book. Martin's prescription for enhancing traditional market research information with intelligence activities will provide managers with the key to strategic advantage. Martin shows how to exploit the untapped competitive power in day-to-day intelligence. He presents ethical methods of collection and usage of intelligence and shows how all types of organizations can identify, monitor, and exploit early detection signals. If anticipating your competitors' next move is what keeps you up at night- start here."

Dr. Paul Dishman, President
Society of Competitive Intelligence Professionals
Associate Professor, Brigham Young University, Marriott School

"Alain Martin delivers a powerful message that the most vital determinant of a company's future performance is not reflected on its balance sheet. Rather, it's the knowledge that's retained within the organization. Martin's latest publication is a richly-resourced guide for the intelligence gathering practitioner, replete with compelling examples of successful applications. And, in the process, Alain presents a wonderful panoply of methodologies for understanding people – and their cultures."

Archie W. Dunham, Chairman, President and CEO
Conoco Inc

"All too frequently the information coming into a company about its suppliers, competitors and customers is passive, ad hoc and fragmented. In this book, Alain Martin provides a structure for organizations of whatever size to assemble and collate the vital signs of change and proactively and ethically search for corroborating material. The section on exploiting the power of Search Engines typifies the extensive research input into this book."

John Fletcher, Global Change Advisor
Shell International B.V., The Netherlands

"Alain Martin's new work is the perfect combination of practical advice and theoretical frameworks for building effective, far-sighted strategies. It is an easy-to-read reference source that will prove a valuable tool for strategic planning."

Tina Georgeou, Vice President, Business Development - Publishing Meredith Corporation

"This book cites pertinent reference materials and explicit examples that substantiate Alain Martin's methodology for assessing competitive intelligence, formulating strategic plans, and mitigating inherent risks. It provides a formidable and useful framework for a way forward in our dynamically changing business environment."

Amy M. Gepes, Vice President, Business Development & Planning MasterCard International Incorporated

"I have used the framework described in this remarkable book successfully for several years, first, to orchestrate the turnaround of North America's fastest growing casualty-insurance company, and subsequently, to craft a vision and strategic direction of a $75 billion financial institution."

John Harbour, Former President and CEO, Desjardins Casualty Insurance Group, and President & COO, Desjardins Confederation

"Alain Martin has created an easy-to-read primer filled with clear examples of intelligence, counterintelligence and decision making in large organizations. This book is highly recommended."

Fred Hassan, Chairman and CEO, Pharmacia Corporation and Chairman of the Board Pharmaceutical Research & Manufacturers of America

"Alain Martin has produced a very useful guide for strategy formulation that should be of interest to any general manager."

Professor Emeritus Samuel L. Hayes Harvard Business School

"Alain Paul Martin has produced a book that allows decision-makers to improve their ability to understand how intelligence professionals link the dots between collection, analysis and interpretation."

Ray R. Henault, General and Chief of the Defence Staff Canadian Forces

"Decision-makers who carefully read this remarkable book will improve their ability to connect the often-neglected dots between intelligence collection, analysis and interpretation. Alain Paul Martin's framework and road maps are excellent."

Paul Hession, Chief Information Officer Fisheries and Oceans Canada

"This impressive book forces us all to rethink the role of intelligence in organizations. It is an essential encyclopedia of knowledge about why intelligence gathering is vital for businesses and it also shows how it can be carried out successfully".

Robert J. Jackson, Fletcher Jones Professor of Government
University of Redlands, California

"This book is worthwhile to read. The intelligence framework it presents helps executives reshape their own model to better focus on mission."

Jean-Peter Jansen, CEO and Chairman of the Executive Board
Lufthansa Cargo AG

"Productive corporate governance, dynamic strategic planning and focused risk analysis are inextricably bound together. They are driven by the rigorous conversion of information into intelligence, the identification of threats and opportunities and a foundation for proactive management in an environment of constant change. *Harnessing Intelligence, Counterintelligence and Surprise Events* is a pragmatic blueprint for this essential process."

H. Earl Joudrie, Director of Abitibi Consolidated, ATCO,
Conoco Canada Resources, Canadian Tire and Zargon Oil & Gas

"Competitive intelligence is one of the key prerequisites to develop a robust and deliverable set of strategies. I found this book very appropriate to my business and I recommend it to decision makers who must secure high performance, particularly at a time of rapid change."

Werner Jung, Vice President, Finance, Strategic Planning & Legal
SAAB, Sweden

"A must read for senior executives. Alain Paul Martin built his concepts very cleverly with thought-provoking examples and jogs the minds of the readers to ponder deeper into the power of intelligence! This is a grand slam by Martin."

Professor Sunder Kekre
Carnegie Mellon Graduate School of Industrial Administration

"At present, one of the most important strategic management challenges is understanding and enhancing the process of transforming vast amounts of information into useable knowledge. Alain Martin's book is an excellent guide to meeting this challenge. He provides a structure and format that enhances our understanding and creates useable knowledge. I highly recommend that all managers and leaders read this book with a view to gaining informational insights and practical knowledge that can be applied to either everyday or crisis situations."

George Kolisnek, Director Strategic Intelligence
Department of National Defence

"Alain Martin has presented several important concepts within a single volume which will be beneficial whether utilized together or separately. The first is a strategy, structure and sources for the critical task of actionable strategic intelligence gathering and analysis, which is vital in the fast moving, highly competitive world of global consumer products. The second part is a framework for creating the circumstances in which things can happen, not just as result of new intelligence, but for any necessary change in business. This book should be compulsory reading for senior executives."

Howard Mann, President and CEO
McCain Foods

"Mining intelligence is a tall order. To tackle this formidable task, Alain Paul Martin delivers sensible advice, rich in practical ideas and real-life examples."

Douglas McCracken, CEO
Deloitte Consulting

"This is an extraordinarily thoughtful and well written book on a topic of great contemporary importance. Its advice is detailed, practical and completely on target."

F. Warren McFarlan
Albert H. Gordon Professor of Business Administration
Harvard Business School

"This book is well researched. It stimulated my thoughts on the importance of competitive analysis and provides excellent examples of not only "how to", but also the consequences of failing to try to understand your competitors' strategies and actions."

Thaddeus T. Moore, Director - Missile Defense
Washington Operations, Boeing

"Must Reading... Alain Martin proposes a solid contemporary vision of risk management, with a rigorous method that is simple, practical and very effective, regardless of the size and current situation of the firm. Today, no organization is immune to surprises or perturbing events. We must learn how to promptly decipher the meaning of these events in order to manage their impact. Martin's framework is equally useful to effectively plan and manage strategic change involving stakeholders with various vested interests. I recommend this excellent book to those who must lead their organization to the cutting edge, or simply wish to be equipped to better manage uncertainty."

Gilles Morin, Vice-President, e-Business
Export Development Canada

"Alain Paul Martin starts the book with a quote from Napoleon and ends it with one from Sun Tzu. The book tries to be something to all people, which is normally a doomed endeavor. Paul Martin succeeded in doing so by a clear mission definition, a wealth of information sources and practical modeling to real-life applications. This book is highly recommended to everybody in the business field with a need for change."

T. Nakagawa, President
ExxonMobil Chemical Japan

"Competitive intelligence is one of the key antecedents for successful marketing strategy formulation. This book outlines the pertinent issues in conducting competitive analysis and provides an extremely useful tool for the practicing marketing strategist. As such, Alain Martin's book is a timely as well as important contribution."

Professor Werner Reinartz, INSEAD, Fontainebleau, France

"This groundbreaking book is invaluable to decision-makers who plan for emergencies and important risks. My fear is that most may read it after rather than prior to a major incident when it can really help save lives and property."

Jeff Robertson, President and CEO, CML Emergency Services Inc.

"Alain Martin has compiled an excellent compendium of tools and examples which define the "why and how to" of corporate intelligence. This book is highly recommended for anyone wanting to acquire an overview of this very complex subject."

Professor Dennis G. Severance, Accenture Professor of Computer
and Information Systems, University of Michigan Business School

"Alain Martin's book provides a clear insight and a new perspective on risk and opportunity identification with an abundance of actual business cases. His book goes beyond the subject of competitive intelligence and addresses such wide subjects as strategy formulation, risk management and governance. It is a must read for senior executives."

Hiroaki Shigeta, Chairman of the Board
Nippon Roche

"I sincerely hope incumbent members of the Defence Department will read this book, and that it be used in the instruction of all at military staff colleges, so that application of its guidance will assist all levels of national defence management in "harnessing" the powerful intelligence factors. Not only will the lessons be instructive for all, but also, the book will be an invaluable resource for its research references."

Brigadier-General Lloyd Skaalen, Formerly Director General, DND
NORAD Regional Deputy Commander (retired)

"This book takes us beyond the rhetoric by setting out a bold plan of action for hitch-hiking on surprise events. The combination of useful examples and a theoretically grounded approach to navigating turbulence makes this book worth reading - and using!"

Cathrine F. Stene, Vice President, Human Resources Corporate Scandinavian Airlines Systems, SAS, Sweden

"Few executives have a systematic, theoretically grounded, and practical management approach to navigate turbulence. This book fills that need with powerful management advice on how to turn intelligence into practical value."

Dr. John Sviokla, Vice-Chairman, DiamondCluster International Former Professor, Harvard Business School

"In today's fast changing global markets where money and information flow at the speed of light, intelligence tasks should feature prominently on the daily agenda of every manager. For an innovative provider of application software like LBS, this book describes a proven method to implement an ethical and far-reaching intelligence program."

Tugrul Tekbulut, President and CEO Logo Business Systems, Turkey

"This book - well structured, excellently documented and easy to understand - represents a great step in mastering this extremely difficult subject. What fascinates me is that Alain Martin not only encourages to improve your management skills but awakes in you a strong desire to do so. He also shows insight stressing the difference between human capabilities and supporting tools. With this book you can conduct your business according to the French saying "Diriger c'est prévoir". Bravo!"

Jean-Claude Theurillat, Vice President Schindler Management Ltd, Switzerland

"Alain Martin has deftly incorporated, adapted, challenged, and complemented the insights of Fuld, Porter, Sun Tzu, and others to achieve a superb practical guide to the strategic and tactical management of institutional information."

Dr. Mark Thompson, President, Equity Resources Group Inc. Former Professor, Harvard School of Public Health

"*Harnessing the Power of Intelligence, Counterintelligence & Surprise Events* provides pragmatic tools to tackle the uncertainties associated with risk assessment between R&D and new product development. The methodologies provided by Alain Martin are instrumental in diagnosing, prioritizing and deciding between technical and commercial factors. The book is lively and its scope is both deep and broad in applicability."

Dr. L.F. Vega, Manager, Technology Development Alcoa

"This serious book is breaking new ground in intelligence production and strategic risk management. It is well worth reading by decision-makers on both sides of the Pacific Rim."

Professor Tak Wakasugi, University of Tokyo
Also concurrently Co-Director, Mitsui Life Financial Research
Center, and NTT Program of Asian Finance and Economy
University of Michigan Business School

"I found this book interesting and thought provoking. As Alain Martin clearly indicates, running an honest and ethical business does not mean that one should not do everything to understand and anticipate market and competitive activity. I have found over the years that these activities can and must be conducted fully consistent with the highest business principles. I found Martin's Factional Scale an interesting tool, as well."

Group Chairman, Major Pharmaceutical Company

HARNESSING THE POWER OF INTELLIGENCE,
COUNTERINTELLIGENCE & SURPRISE EVENTS

Harnessing The Power of

Intelligence
Counterintelligence
& Surprise Events

A Proven Framework and New Tools for
- *Predicting Threats and Opportunities*
- *Analyzing Stakeholders (F-Scale)*
- *Selecting Reliable Allies and Teams*
- *Building a Culture of Intelligence*
- *Hitch-Hiking on Surprise Events*
- *Mining Virtual Communities*

Alain Paul Martin
Pioneered the Management Road Maps:
Harvard University Global System™
First Author on Proactive Thinking
Architect HUMINT™ Contact

Special Collaboration
Dr. Brian Morrissey

Executive.org

Library of Congress Control Number: 2002093491

National Library of Canada Cataloguing in Publication Data
Martin, A. P. (Alain Paul)

Harnessing the power of intelligence, counterintelligence and surprise events: a proven framework and new tools for predicting threats and opportunities, analyzing stakeholders (F-Scale), selecting reliable allies and teams, building a culture of intelligence, hitch-hiking on surprise events, mining virtual communities / Alain Paul Martin

Includes bibliographical references and index.
ISBN 0-86502-924-5 (bound).—ISBN 0-86502-296-8 (pbk.)

1. Business intelligence–Management. 2. Intelligence service. 3. Psychographics. 4. Risk management. 5. Strategy. I. Title.

HD38.7.M368 2002   658.4'7   C2002-900108-0

The Professional Development Institute PDI Inc. (PDI) publishes Executive.org books. "Executive.org" and the logo on the cover with arrows pointing 45° northeast in a square are trademarks of PDI. For details, visit: www.executive.org. All trademarks are the property of their respective owners. Printed in Canada.

Published simultaneously in the United States and Canada.

Published by Alain Paul Martin

For the latest list of publications in English and other languages, visit www.executive.org

1. Books & Monographs

1. Harnessing the Power of a Clear Mission
   Vision, Values, Goals & Priorities (June 2004)
2. Focus on Accountable Leadership with Competence,
   Commitment and a Conscience (Sept. 2004)
   This book includes: (i) Shifting Gears to Matrix and
   (ii) Overhauling UNESCO and Strengthening its Essence
3. Strategic Thinking Simplified with Harvard Road Maps (2005)
4. Bringing Time to Life: 120 Practical Tips for Managing Your
   Time and Enjoying Life
5. Think Proactive: New Insights Into Decision-Making
6. Recent Developments in Multi-Project Management:
   Crafting a Work Breakdown Structure with the Global Method
   (Out of Print)
7. La genèse de la valeur par l'intelligence, le contre-
   renseignement et les évènements surprise

2. Harvard University Global System™:
Management Road Maps

1. Turning Strategy into Value – Executive Checklist
   This master road map integrates mission setting, strategy
   formulation, business planning, implementation, progress
   control and impact evaluation. It vividly illustrates the intricate
   relationships between these tasks and the ongoing functions of
   management including leadership, intelligence, negotiation,
   communication, building and retaining talent and customers,
   and managing time, conflict and values.
2. Risk Management Road Map
3. Thriving on Quality Time: The Complete Road Map for
   Managing Your Time
4. Building a Great Nation – Executive Checklist
5. The Complete Project Management Cycle (June 2004)
6. Intelligence & Counterintelligence Road Map (March 2004)

Executive.org
Cambridge MA, USA Ottawa ON, Canada

This book is dedicated with love to
Alexandra and Jackson Baker
and June Madeen

Table of Contents

i

FOREWORD

Up-to-date intelligence has been at the center of the most effective policies and decisions advanced by agile enterprises, governments and the military. Its absence has led countless national and business leaders to defeat.

Even so, most organizations today remain vulnerable to and driven by surprise events. And many are beyond rescue because they neglected intelligence and counterintelligence throughout their value chain – from strategic thinking, hiring, contracting, security, research, engineering and IT to marketing, communications, sales and customer service. Yet, the cost of investing in intelligence is negligible when compared to the long-term dividends it yields and the risks it mitigates. Building an intelligence culture is vital, as never before, in a business environment characterized by seamless connectivity, ubiquitous competition, inter-company collaboration (sometimes with direct competitors), speed, chaotic trade, rising tensions, and a trend to letting more workers operate virtually anywhere without supervision, frequently within the reach of a wide-spectrum of adversaries. Good intelligence also helps to forge and maintain a healthy web of allies that nurtures creativity, cooperation, synergy and progress.

Years before the tragedies of September 11, I frequently asked chief intelligence officers and managers to think of a chaotic universe with ten families of generic scenarios including the "unthinkable" in order to predict serious risks and opportunities. Applying the Global Method[1] with clients, we built scanners and "social radars" to capture the earliest signs of incubating threats and opportunities. Boeing, Bombardier, the Royal Bank and defense establishments were among the first to recognize the merit of the framework. An early adopter of Proactive Thinking, Canada's Communications Security Establishment (CSE), went on to adopt the Global Method and its road maps (now Harvard University Global System) as its standard method for managing intelligence projects.

There are several excellent books about intelligence and counter-intelligence. My favorites are by Chun Wei Choo, Leonard Fuld, Michael Porter and Sun Tzu. A list of recommended readings has been included at the end of this publication. This book complements existing literature by providing new knowledge, proven tools and a practical road map for decision-makers. The original content was applied in business and government to mobilize talent and manage intelligence and counterintelligence teams. In that form, it would have been inaccessible to many readers. It has therefore been streamlined for a wider audience. Our objective remains to help managers improve strategic planning and decision-making and carry out their missions expeditiously while mitigating risks by getting to know the players, understanding realities of the twenty-first century and instilling an intelligence mindset in every member of their team.

Considered primarily the domain of the military and the state, intelligence has had a growing impact on the business world, especially with the advent of the Internet and the emergence of global markets. It is fast entering mainstream management as a discipline in its own right, as this book's extensive bibliography and list of references suggest. The unprecedented interest in intelligence collection and analysis in the wake of the sudden downfalls of Enron and WorldCom and the 9-11 tragedies will ultimately translate into further research and heated debates creating the conditions for in-depth education, cutting-edge publications and continuing growth in new directions. With this mind and relying on the help of clients, partners and readers, I intend to keep an up-to-date bibliography in www.executive.org.

I sincerely hope this book series will help you acquire useful knowledge to improve your strategic and operational activities, and support progress in your career and personal life. Your feedback, via www.executive.org, would be greatly appreciated.

Alain Paul Martin
New York, December 2002

ACKNOWLEDGMENT

First, I wish to thank from the bottom of my heart the people who have graciously and generously volunteered their precious time to diligently review the book and provide candid and well-thought out comments, despite their demanding workload and family obligations. These include François Auger, Vice-President, Engineering, Bombardier Transportation; David Baird, President and CEO, ISS Integrated Security Solutions Inc.; André Bérard, Chairman of the Board, National Bank of Canada; Wilbrod Bourget, Director of Business Development, National Bank of Canada; Professor Emeritus William Bruns Jr., Harvard Business School; Dan Cunningham, President & CEO, Long-Stanton Manufacturing Co.; Professor John Carroll, MIT Sloan School of Management, Dr. Peter Corr, Senior Vice President, Science and Technology, Pfizer Inc.; Holger Demuth, Managing Director, Credit Suisse, Zurich; Denise Dickson, Director, Global Competitive Intelligence, Eli Lilly and Company; Dr. Paul Dishman, President, Society of Competitive Intelligence Professionals and Associate Professor, Marriott School, Brigham Young University; Archie W. Dunham, Chairman, President and CEO of Conoco Inc.; John Fletcher, Global Change Advisor, Shell International; Tina Georgeou, Vice President, Business Development, Publishing, Meredith Corporation; Amy Gepes, Vice President, Business Development & Planning MasterCard International Inc.; Fred Hassan, Chairman and CEO, Pharmacia Corporation and Chairman of the Board, Pharmaceutical Research & Manufacturers of America; Professor Emeritus Samuel Hayes, Harvard Business School; Ray R. Henault, General and Chief of the Defence Staff, Canadian Forces; Paul Hession, Chief Information Officer, Fisheries and Oceans Canada; Professor Robert Jackson, University of Redlands, California; Jean-Peter Jansen, CEO and Chairman of the Executive Board, Lufthansa Cargo AG; Earl Joudrie, Director of Abitibi Consolidated, ATCO, Conoco Canada Resources, Canadian Tire and Zargon Oil & Gas; Werner Jung, Vice President, Finance, Strategic Planning & Legal, SAAB, Sweden; George Kolisnek, Director Strategic Intelligence, Department of National Defence; Professor Sunder Kekre, Director, Center for

E-Business Innovation, Carnegie Mellon Graduate School of Industrial Administration; Douglas McCracken, CEO, Deloitte Consulting; Professor F. Warren McFarlan, Harvard Business School; Howard Mann, President and CEO, McCain Foods; Thaddeus T. Moore, Director, Missile Defense, Washington Operations, Boeing; T. Nakagawa, President, ExxonMobil Chemical, Japan; Professor Werner Reinartz, INSEAD, France; Jeff Robertson, President and CEO, CML Emergency Services Inc.; Professor Dennis G. Severance, Accenture Professor of Computer and Information Systems, University of Michigan Business School; Hiroaki Shigeta, Chairman of the Board, Nippon Roche; Brigadier-General Lloyd Skaalen, Formerly Director General, DND Current Policy and NORAD Regional Deputy Commander (retired); Cathrine F. Stene, Vice President, Human Resources Corporate, Scandinavian Airlines Systems, SAS, Sweden; Dr. John Sviokla, Vice-Chairman, DiamondCluster International and Former Professor, Harvard Business School; Tugrul Tekbulut, President and CEO, Logo Business Systems, Turkey; Jean-Claude Theurillat, Vice President, Schindler Management Ltd, Switzerland; Dr. Mark Thompson, President, Equity Resources Group Inc. and Former Professor, Harvard School of Public Health; Dr. L.F. Vega, Manager, Technology Development, Alcoa; and Professor Tak Wakasugi, University of Tokyo, and Co-Director, Mitsui Life Financial Research Center, University of Michigan Business School.

I am also fortunate to have inspiring and helpful friends and family members and wish to thank them along with clients, students, PDI staff and my Harvard Business School Professors: By Barnes, Norm Berg, Bill Bruns, Sam Hayes, F. Warren McFarlan, Ben Shapiro, Bruce Scott, Bob Simons, John Sviokla (now Vice-Chairman of DiamondCluster International) as well as Roger Fisher, and Bill Ury of Harvard Law School, Larry Suskind and Arnold Barnett at MIT, all of whom have contributed to sharpening my knowledge of competitive intelligence, pattern matching (construct validity), leadership, negotiation and strategic thinking. I owe an immense debt of gratitude to my altruistic and inspiring mentors Herb Shepard and Richard Beckhard of MIT, both of whom died too early. Their diligent coaching and seminal ideas about cognitive behavior, attitudes and managing in a turbulent environment have not been forgotten.

I am very grateful to the leading professionals in the competitive and national intelligence communities, who graciously provided practical insights in the early stages of manuscript's development. In particular, I wish to acknowledge the invaluable feedback of my clients Gilles Morin, Vice-President, e-Business, Export Development Canada, and John Harbour, retired President and Chief Operating Officer of Desjardins Federation, who for over 10 years, gave me the opportunity to apply the framework in large-scale multi-billion dollar initiatives, and Stewart Woolner, who took the time to meticulously review the last draft. Mr. Woolner led CSE and recently retired after a 37-year distinguished career in national security.

I also owe much to the caring, incisive comments and long-standing support of my dear friends Dr. J. Brian Morrissey, Former Assistant Deputy Minister, Research Branch, Agriculture and Agri-Food Canada, who prepared the case study on the evolution of vCJD and related policy reform in the UK (see Appendix of Chapter 7); Mark Kohout, who is currently leaving a senior-executive position for an MBA at INSEAD, and Pierre Fournier, Senior Issue Manager, who has provided ongoing feedback while applying the framework in several agencies in the Government of Québec. I also wish to thank the SRI Consulting Business Intelligence team, in particular Patricia Breman and Kristen Thomas, for generously providing valuable ideas, copyrighted materials and case studies on VALS™. For providing thoughtful comments and suggestions to improve the content of the book, several executives deserve credit, in particular Eva Kmiecic, Deputy Commissioner – Strategic Direction of the Royal Canadian Mounted Police (RCMP), Gerald M. Ostrov, Company Group Chairman at Johnson & Johnson, and Dr. Michael D. Langan, a retired senior official of the U.S. Treasury, currently a senior policy advisor in Corporate Security for AOL Time Warner.

My interest in intelligence collection and analysis began early in my career, when I was working on the GD Nuclear-Boat program. It became a vocation while overseeing a major contract for the CF18 Program. In the process, I have been fortunate to work on strategic and operational risk management with remarkable NATO and DND leaders like Bernie Hough of the Operational Research and Analysis Establishment (ORAE) and Brigadier-General Lloyd Skaalen (cited above).

I am especially grateful to PDI team namely Marc Beaudry, Syd Bosloy, Aziza Bouchahda, Jeanine Chateauvert, Hahn Do Doan, Denis Duguay, Simon Gingras, Isabelle Glazer, Claudette Goudie, Linda and Richard Goudie, Roger Lafleche, Paul Leduc, Azadeh Manoussi (now back to California), Helene Martin, Rick Martinelli, Lou Perel, Serge Royer, Marc Sabourin, Maurice Sabourin and Shouan Wang for their integrity, professional talent and candid feedback and for always going the extra mile to exceed our client expectations in every assignment. A warm thank you to Jan Fedorowicz and Karen Markle, who took the time to review the final version and made a valuable contribution to the content. I also wish to thank Mathew Blackwell and André Potworowski who read the first draft. Any errors of omission or interpretation, however, are mine alone.

Last but not least, I wish to thank Bill Sweet, whom I was privileged to meet in Berlin at the 2000 Alumni Reunion of the Harvard Business School. Bill went to Harvard during the depression and learned lessons that guided him to this day. His knowledge of Portuguese led him to a U.S. military assignment in Brazil where he became an entrepreneur. For nearly 70 years, his interests took him from aerospace to construction. His recently acquired bottling venture is now the best performing in Coca-Cola's network. When the NASDAQ was nearly at its peak in February 2000, Bill warned friends and allies in a letter titled *New Economy: A Reality or Fantasy?* With considerable evidence, anchored on ageless business fundamentals and market psychology, Bill predicted a sharp downturn and stressed the importance of a highly diversified portfolio with limited exposure to technology. Bill told us in Berlin that NASDAQ will burst below 2000 within a year and it did! At the 2001 Cleveland Reunion, he explained why North-American recovery could take at least twelve months. So far his timing was exacerbated by Enron-WorldCom scandals and 9-11 tragedies. But more than anything else, Bill's sharp insights into human intelligence and counter-intuitive ways of piecing together scraps of fuzzy information are inspiring. Bill, I just wish I had met you earlier!

PART ONE

-

INTELLIGENCE AND COUNTERINTELLIGENCE:

MISSION, ORGANIZATION AND LEADERSHIP;

COLLECTION SOURCES, PLATFORMS AND TOOLS

War is 90 percent information...
There are but two powers in the world, the sword and the mind.
In the long run the sword is always beaten by the mind.

Napoleon Bonaparte

Competitive intelligence may share the basic theory with governmental
intelligence, and a subset of tools (applied mainly to collection and
dissemination), but it has developed its own set of professional
techniques and models (especially for analysis), organizational
paradigms and areas of applications, which make it
more of a business discipline.

Ben Gilad and Jan Herring
The Fuld-Gilad-Herring Academy of Competitive Intelligence

CHAPTER 1

MISSION-CRITICAL INTELLIGENCE, VITAL GOALS AND INSIGHTS FROM THE BATTLEFIELD

1. What Is Intelligence?

In this book, intelligence is defined as the ability to ethically acquire, validate, interpret and apply actionable knowledge about current and potential events, technologies, products, distribution channels and stakeholders to formulate strategy and support all activities necessary to accomplish a corporate mission by legal and ethical means.

Here, *a stakeholder* is defined as anyone with a vested interest in your mission, business, products or issues. With a wide spectrum of vested interests, the stakeholders comprise, on one extreme, those who perceive you as vital for their survival, and on the other end of the spectrum, your worst adversaries, those whose vested interests include systematic obstruction regardless of the consequences, including self-destruction. Many of your competitors, those who behave in a rational adversarial way, are to be found somewhere between these extremes.

Since all knowledge is perishable, the focus is to acquire and act on intelligence before it can be learned through the media and other communication means. Note that knowledge exists in two forms: explicit and tacit. Explicit knowledge comprises what has been documented and shared. Tacit knowledge resides in the heads of staff, clients and other partners. It includes the informal and unrecorded individual experiences, ideas, perceptions and values. Tacit knowledge can be accessed through interpersonal communication and virtual collaboration. Even in the best-run companies, most in-house (corporate) knowledge is tacit. Sharing tacit knowledge can have a significant impact on the bottom line as indicated in the Nippon Roche case below.

2. Your First Line of Defense and Attack

- ### The New Landscape Demands Agility

Business and government increasingly operate in an environment characterized by borderless trade[2], accelerating discontinuity, perishable technologies, a volatile economic environment, a shorter product life cycle, overcapacity, price erosion, fragmented markets demanding more customization, and changing regulations (retroactively at times). Taken together, all of these factors result in intense asymmetric competition and a huge pressure on margins. Organized advocacy, regionalism and a growing number of hostile and predatory actors, ranging from anti-business activists and terrorists to foreign intelligence agents, are also having a profound impact on the conduct of business and on our daily lives. Organizations armed with insufficient knowledge about the combined effects of these forces face the greatest threats, not only because risks and uncertainty are not readily apparent to them but also because the situation is dynamic and will continue to change at an alarming rate.

Without a compass to navigate the uncharted waters ahead, short-run decisions are bound to lead to abrupt changes in direction, personnel cutbacks, restructuring, and further turmoil, resulting in an enormous drain on resources. Poor understanding of emerging markets or the international environment can lead to staggering losses. Many regions and organizations have already paid a heavy price in terms of human and financial dislocation.

- ### A Powerful Weapon in Every Business Function

In this fierce environment, actionable and timely contextual intelligence is more mission-critical than ever. It allows managers to understand reality in vivid relief before they are called upon to respond to it. It is an integral part of the intellectual capital[3] of the organization and a vital component of every business function starting with mission setting and strategy formulation. At the working level it can yield immediate results in terms of improving quality, productivity, customer acquisition and retention.

At the heart of decision-making, real-time contextual intelligence (sometimes called inferential intelligence) aims at shortening the interval between detection and acting on selected targets. It is an integral part of a manager's early warning system, allowing for

4

the anticipation of opportunities ahead of competitors and the identification of risks that can impede operations, goals and valued relationships.

- ## Human Intelligence (HUMINT) in Context

There are several intelligence-gathering and processing platforms, all of which have finite capabilities. Our journey centers on human intelligence or HUMINT in the parlance of the intelligence community. Contextual HUMINT is the organization, tools and culture of gaining insights into the mindset of *stakeholders* by legal and ethical means from all sources including classified and open-source intelligence (OSINT).

Imagery, signals and signature intelligence, HID and INTELNET infrastructure are beyond the scope of this open-source publication.[4] Where the stakes and uncertainty are high, it is wise to use more than one intelligence-collection platform to overcome the inherent limitations in each. For example, satellite imagery, hot-air balloons and other non-military platforms can provide sensitive information that is otherwise unavailable to tactical-reconnaissance missions on the ground.

Human intelligence relies on two sources of data. Primary data sources are generated by customized surveys and focus groups, interviews, questionnaires, photography and direct observation. Secondary sources include public-domain open-source material (Internet and other publications) as well as proprietary data in corporate intranets, archives, correspondence and application systems supporting R&D, engineering, order processing, billing, customer relationship management (CRM), supply chain management (SCM), production scheduling and enterprise resource planning (ERP), project tracking and other decision-support functions.

- ## Mapping Our Unconventional Journey

This book consists of two parts with six chapters each. Part I addresses the mission of intelligence, its organization and leadership as well as intelligence collection sources, platforms and tools. In Part I, it may be helpful to remember two key functions of intelligence. Firstly, let's call intelligence's offensive role your *sword,* the topic of Chapters 1 through 5. Secondly, consider intelligence's defensive posture as your *shield.* This is primarily fulfilled by counterintelligence, the subject of

Chapter 6. These six chapters will help you collect, validate and manage intelligence and structure resources for both functions.

Part II focuses on intelligence analysis and interpretation. In Chapters 7 and 8, we focus on the incubation of value, threats and opportunities. We shall see why major missions, goals, policies and capital projects are rarely the product of cool-headed choice and logical thinking. Rather, their genesis follows a path driven by surprise events that is similar to the biological process of pregnancy and childbirth. But this reality is frequently unforeseen, and thus, neglected by most organizations. Without understanding the intricate reality of value incubation, the intelligence exercise suffers. Armed with our intelligence arsenal and real-life illustrations, we will learn to identify value, seize opportunities and anticipate threats before they appear on the intelligence radars of others.

Building on this, the remaining chapters will focus on the most important aspect of intelligence analysis and interpretation: the knowledge of clients, staff, influential actors and other constituencies with a vested interest in your endeavors.

Without prompt action and accountable leadership, intelligence is useless. Indeed, without the commitment of a nucleus of competent and influential actors playing complementary roles and scripts, too many important ideas, intelligent trails and even great goals and missions either languish on the drawing board or crumble in the face of resistance. In this context, Chapter 9 examines the power, status and role of the catalysts of innovation and change, i.e., the people necessary to act on valuable intelligence and make a smooth and beneficial transition from the present to an optimal future.

Since perceptions are reality in the eyes of the beholders, Chapter 10 introduces the *Factional Scale*^{TM}, an important tool for examining perceptions before formulating strategy. Chapter 11 outlines additional means of gaining further understanding of your target audience and other stakeholders. It features VALS^{TM}, a flagship product of SRI Consulting Business Intelligence and a unique system for shedding insights into the forces that drive behavior of consumers and other stakeholders.

Chapter 12 provides a final word on the lessons learned and goes beyond the realms of business and government to examine intelligence collection and analysis at the personal level.

The book concludes with a detailed index, an extensive reference bibliography and a list of recommended readings and web sites.

3. Mission-Critical Intelligence: Ten Vital Goals

Charting a clear way of focusing on the levers that drive value incubation, creation and harvesting is the first task in making your organization accountable and cost-effective in its business intelligence endeavors. This is accomplished by providing the means to accomplish the following objectives.

1. Mobilize, empower and retain the very best talent in terms of employees and suppliers to the organization. Thoroughly assess their integrity and commitment. Lead by example. Motivate, inspire and reward risk-taking, success, fast learning, sound effort and teamwork. Terminate unsatisfactory relationships gracefully. Validate relentlessly.

2. Understand your current and potential customers, their power structure and emerging issues. Assess their strategies, needs and credit worthiness by gaining insights into their operations, market segments and supply chains. What are their online and offline activities (products, partners, customer profiles, target audience, distribution channels, brand reach, unoccupied territory)? Track other stakeholders, including current and potential competitors and suppliers. Anticipate the moves of key stakeholders using legal and ethical means. Monitor their actions (staffing, product launches, marketing efforts, new orders, acquisitions, price changes). Assess their strategies (successes and failures), strengths and weaknesses, opportunities and risks. Scan for early warnings of disruption or delays in your supply chain. Use Michael Porter's framework to continually update your intelligence on the dynamics of power among stakeholders throughout your industry value chain, including the threats of substitutes and new entrants, and the rivalry among

7

competitors.[5] Pay attention to the actions and timing pattern of your lesser-known but agile small firms.

3. Safeguard your most-valued relationships with clients, user communities, suppliers, staff, joint-venture partners and other allies, both online and offline. Explore ways to strike a balance between trust and self-interest.

4. Protect your brand presence, trade secrets, corporate data and networks from attackers and other hostile forces. Use selective disclosure. Uncover brand threats and bad publicity early and take prompt corrective action.

5. Understand and anticipate discontinuity and other types of change in the legislative and geopolitical environment of your business, in consumer trends and in your marketplace including new materials, tools, technologies, product substitutes, processes and practices, sales channels and supply chains, including online trading exchanges that can positively or negatively impact your future.

6. Know your community, its issues, aspirations and opportunities and the threats it may face.

7. Based on the above, identify new growth opportunities within and outside your core businesses, including time-sensitive targets and high-payoff targets. *Time-sensitive targets* are talent, customers, mergers candidates, alliances and other fleeting opportunities that could fall in the hands of the competition within a year. *High-payoff targets* are customers, market territories, talent or partners currently allied with the adversary and which must be attracted away from the competition by legal and ethical means. Group competitors in three tiers from the most to the least threatening.

8. Use the intelligence acquired above to achieve victory by striking the right balance between direct and indirect attacks.[6] Use strategic creativity, innovation, speed, surprise and unexpected indirect attacks throughout your value chain to surprise and outmaneuver the competition while diverting its attention on direct attacks. Remember Sun Tzu's advice: "Use the normal force to engage. Do the extraordinary to win."

9. Monitor, measure and benchmark your performance against competitors and best practices in selected activities of your value chain. Keep a log of both the *Meantime Between Bad Surprises* (MBBS) and the *Meantime Between Good Surprises* (MBGS). Like the meantime between failures in engineering, these are crude indicators of the agility[7] of your business intelligence and can be great morale boosters, in the long term.

10. Strike a balance between the levers of value incubation (disruptive technologies) , value creation and harvesting.[8] Weed out markets and relationships. Assertively prune dead wood – be it work, products, processes or platforms – in order to build a lean and robust value chain.

In summary, intelligence supports strategic planning and all mission-critical activities. No organization can build an infrastructure that can address the above objectives overnight. It is therefore essential to opt for gradual and selective growth in intelligence assignments using the framework outlined in the book *Harnessing the Power of a Clear Mission, Vision, Values, Goals & Priorities.*[9] The emphasis should be on a balanced portfolio of high-priority projects and pilot experiments, those that permit superior positioning through innovation, productivity, speed and surprise. In this context, John Prescott, Former President of the Society of Competitive Intelligence Professionals, notes: "we used to use the vacuum-cleaner approach, gathering everything anyone would want to know... I am convinced now that competitive intelligence has evolved to the point where we want business systems that are tailored to specific needs and that help managers make better decisions on a project-by-project basis."[10]

4. Intelligence Insights from the Battlefield

Good intelligence does not apply only to state secrets and large companies. Nor is it necessarily expensive. A controversial word in the past, intelligence is emerging as a vital topic on the business agenda of leading agile organizations, regardless of their size. It is the bedrock of today's knowledge-based economy.

While intelligence gleaned from clients cannot be disclosed, a wealth of public-domain examples can illustrate specific points throughout the book.

- GlaxoSmithKline and Bristol-Myers Squibb

Among the competitive intelligence cases in the public domain, the following reported in *CIO Insight* and *Computer World*, illustrates how competitive intelligence provides early warning signals to permit decision-makers to head off an emerging threat.

Following a search of competitors' activities on the Internet,[11] "the competitive intelligence group at SmithKline Beecham Corp. (SKB) found its first 'nugget' buried in congressional testimony on forestry legislation: Competing drug maker Bristol-Myers Squibb Co. was planning to increase 200-fold its harvest of the Pacific yew tree, whose bark is used to produce the experimental anticancer drug Taxol."[12]

SKB "immediately began canvassing conferences and scouring online resources for clues. It tapped into Web sources on the environment and got staffers to work the phones, gathering names of researchers working for Bristol-Myers. It even zeroed in on cities where BM had sponsored experimental trials of the substance."[13]

"SmithKline Beecham found the second nugget in a sharp rise in the number of Bristol-Myers recruitment ads for oncologists in cities where the company had experimental cancer clinics."[14]

SmithKline Beecham's third nugget came from data discovered on financial web sites and in the comments of Wall Street analysts confirming that Bristol-Myers was increasing its spending on its oncology group.[15]

"When the competitive intelligence team at SmithKline pieced together those and other clues, it became apparent that Bristol-Myers was planning to substantially accelerate its development of Taxol. Sure enough, the company filed its application with the Food and Drug Administration 18 months earlier than outsiders had predicted. But by that time, SmithKline had accelerated the development of its own anticancer drug. "Because of the competitive intelligence, our project team was able to respond much more quickly than ordinarily," says Wayne Rosenkrans, who headed competitive intelligence at SmithKline's research and development group at the time. "It meant we didn't lose 18 months"."[16]

• Harnessing Tacit Intelligence at Nippon Roche

Created in Tokyo in 1932, Nippon Roche[17] is a leading health care company in Japan and an important member of the Roche Group of Basel, Switzerland. Facing demanding physicians and a growing domestic and foreign competition, the company was under severe pressure to improve the performance of its medical sales professionals throughout the late nineties. The training programs conducted throughout its industry were adequate in disseminating explicit knowledge but made no serious attempt to provide the tacit knowledge, skills and lessons acquired by experienced sales representatives in the course of carrying on their business.[18] This knowledge ranged from competitive intelligence and product positioning to targeting the right clients and negotiating with difficult people. As part of a larger initiative, Nippon Roche President, Hiroaki Shigeta (presently, Chairman), assigned 24 high-performers in sales to a *Super-Skill-Transfer* (SST) Task Force mandated to promptly distill the knowledge and lessons acquired in selling to physicians. "A skills transfer team of three members visited each of the branches around Japan, distilling this information on a person-to-person, face-to-face basis and passing it on. The net result was a unique sales-force culture that Roche's competitors found difficult to imitate, and a substantial 40% increase in sales productivity."[19]

The success of the experiment led Mr. Shigeta to create an SST Academy to codify the tacit knowledge and build on the ongoing experience of field staff.

• IBM Advanced Scout Rescues Orlando Magic

This time-sensitive case, reported by IBM, illustrates how business intelligence software can penetrate a large quantity of fluid and time-sensitive data that is beyond the ability of human resources in an organization in order to yield valuable clues that are instrumental to the bottom line.

"When the Orlando Magic were devastated in the first two games of the 1997 National Basketball Association (NBA) Finals against the second-seed Miami Heat, the team's fans began to hang their heads in shame. But fortunately, the Magic had another trick up their sleeves. A data mining application developed by IBM and

IBM Business Partner Virtual Gold uncovered a secret buried beneath the layers of statistics collected at every game.

The application, Advanced Scout, is specifically tailored for NBA coaches and statisticians. Advanced Scout showed the Orlando Magic coaches something that none of them had previously recognized. When Brian Shaw and Darrell Armstrong, were in the game, their presence sparked something in their teammate Penny Hardaway – the Magic's leading scorer at that time. As a result of this analysis, Armstrong received more play-time and hence, Hardaway was far more effective in scoring. The Magic went on to win the next two games and nearly caused the upset of the year. Fans everywhere rallied around the team.

Coaches, like business executives, carefully study data to enhance their natural intuition when making strategic decisions. But unlike business, the direct results of coaching decisions are played out under the eyes of millions of fans, and wrong calls can turn a team's fans against it – leading to lower ticket sales and possibly a vacancy in the head coaching position.

Before Advanced Scout, some teams, such as the Orlando Magic, began developing business intelligence software to find patterns in the mountain of game data that the coaching staff collected during play. But with an average of 200 possessions a game and about 1,200 games a year, the sheer volume of statistics was overwhelming, and the applications produced only basic results – the kind of stats anyone could find in a local newspaper."[20]

Orlando Magic is one of the 25 teams using IBM Advanced Scout which, according to Assistant Coach Tom Sterner, "is playing a huge role in establishing incredible fan support and loyalty – that means millions of dollars in gate traffic, television sales and licensing."[21]

- **Amazon, Honda and Other Dark Horses**

Complacency accounts for the inability of countless market leaders to consider smaller and agile new entrants seriously. Barnes & Noble and Borders in North America and their counterparts elsewhere did not make a major move toward selling books online until Amazon, a dark horse, became a household name. The talent and capital devoted to their online ventures barely gave them the critical mass for a presence on the Web.

Likewise, North-American and European automakers have underestimated Honda's core competency in engine design and its ability to grow in the car-making business. They saw Honda as merely a marginal player making construction pumps, motorcycles, generators, mowers, tillers and marine engines. Honda was considered an outsider by Japan's Keiretsu[22] establishment – some pundits even predicted the company's demise just prior to the oil embargo – when it launched its most lethal weapon, the Honda Civic, a leader in low fuel consumption. To its regret, Chrysler did not pay attention to Honda until the energy crisis showed what was really at issue.

While fighting each other tooth and nail in the photocopier market, Kodak and Xerox paid marginal attention to Fuji, Canon, Ricoh and Minolta. Using standardized components and focusing on a narrower range of machines, the agile Japanese dark horses significantly brought down the cost of production. They slipped into the incumbents' turf, each carving a huge niche in global markets.

- Intelligent Organizations in the Third Sector

Even the non-profit sector can become a greater force for good if it uses a potent intelligence system to improve fundraising, financial returns, productivity, visibility, volunteer mobilization, and closer contact with key constituencies. As an illustration, our research indicates that the Salvation Army cannot excel in fulfilling its noble mission without a sound intelligence system to forecast needs, mobilize and harness talent and enlist allies among leaders and policy makers.[23]

In an empirical study of 600 hospitals, it was shown that establishments conducting ongoing intelligence activities, such as scanning external events and stakeholders throughout their value chain, outperformed institutions that do not.[24]

A partner of the American Society for Association Executives[25] (ASAE), *Associationcentral.com* provides many non-governmental organizations (NGOs) like the Salvation Army, trade groups and professional societies with services, including networking events to structure intelligence teams, conducting strategic-thinking exercises, finding the right joint-venture partner and streamlining community-building activities.

13

- **Further Research**

Other case studies can be found at www.executive.org/news. This web page provides useful links to resources and documents on open-source intelligence.

5. Conclusion

Intelligence has two primary functions: it acts as a *sword* and as a *shield*. As a sword, it is the first line of attack. It offers a means of mobilizing the best talent in an organization, spurring innovation, creating new products, entering new markets, encouraging customers to come back, spawning and seizing untapped opportunities. As a shield, intelligence is the first line of defense. It is a means of mitigating risk, protecting corporate assets and thwarting threats.

This chapter outlined the vital goals of mission-critical intelligence and provided insights into the first function with several business illustrations. The next four chapters will discuss organizational frameworks, tools, platforms and sources of intelligence. Armed with this knowledge, readers can move on to Chapter 6, which addresses the second function, namely counterintelligence and intelligence security.

1. Building A Culture of Ethical Intelligence and Critical Thinking

The majority of today's organizations must rethink the role of intelligence if they are to harness its awesome power. They have to reshape the behavior and attitudes of their workforce and allies to bring useable intelligence to the core of their decisions. They must perfect tools, processes and technology to be able to navigate through the labyrinth of opportunities and risks.

Effective leaders work hard to build teams and a corporate culture of inquiry, critical thinking and learning based on valid intelligence and counterintelligence. The goal is for intelligence to become second nature to policy formulation, decision-making and day-to-day operations. In a 1999 report to the President of the United States, "*Science at Its Best, Security at Its Worst*", a special investigative panel stressed that "security must be more than a concept, it must be woven into every aspect of the agency's business and the daily work of every employee."[26]

- ### The Challenges

The challenges encountered in building such a culture are daunting. There is the arduous task of mobilizing talent and assembling the skilled teams and invisible platforms needed to gather actionable intelligence in a complex environment of highly perishable and often fuzzy information. These teams must have the right blend of competencies in risk management, communication and advanced technologies. Their members must also be free of paradigm traps and well versed in the economic, political, religious, ideological, psychosocial and cultural mindset of their target audiences. They must work ethically, under the shadow of media and public attention and frequently under hostile and stressful conditions. They also need to constantly upgrade their skills and tools in order to collect, validate, analyze, integrate and interpret real-time intelligence.

Even the best researchers can become exasperated with the complexity and occasionally inconclusive or contradictory results of intelligence work. They can also be frustrated when they see that the insights they developed do not necessarily lead to prompt action by decision-makers.

- The Framework for a Practical Solution

Addressing the above challenges requires an intelligence culture:

1. Anchored in ethics, transparency, team-building and renewal;

2. Armed with cutting-edge expertise and applying analytical frameworks and tools that can acquire the best knowledge available ahead of competitors and others who have the potential to threaten the organization (see Chapter 6);

3. Nurturing an agile organization that spares no effort to build and preserve intelligence capital (defined in Chapter 3);

4. Designed with an ultra-light structure that is invisible to outsiders but omnipresent where the stakes are high (see *Intelligence-Centric Organization* below).

2. Intelligence-Centric Organization

We have an intelligence-centric organization when:

1. Intelligence is embedded in decision-making with all management tiers deeply committed;

2. Intelligence gathering is used on an ongoing basis to analyze issues, predict trends and events, improve strategic thinking, policy formulation and decision-making in every business unit;

3. Intelligence is targeted and tailored to suit the evolving needs of each business unit;

4. Everyone actively contributes to the intelligence culture through teamwork, systematic scanning and analysis, knowledge creation and intelligence sharing that advance the organization's interests.

- Resources

Under the guidance of the Chief Intelligence Officer, issue managers, monitors, intelligence collectors and professional analysts team up with management and field staff. As partners, they validate, interpret and transform their findings into actionable intelligence to support strategic and tactical management and day-to-day operations.

Monitors work in teams led by a small but permanent secretariat of issue managers who are recruited from their ranks. Issue managers analyze the findings, coordinate the monitors' work and ensure full coverage of target areas, quality assurance, timeliness, efficiency and continuity.

- The Chief Intelligence Officer

The Chief Intelligence Officer leads the overall intelligence and counterintelligence effort by orchestrating intelligence resources, relationships and other assets for collection and analysis. This officer is responsible for:

1. Working with the executive and the corporate board to (a) structure an accountable, effective and ethical intelligence-centric organization; (b) build an intelligence culture and mindset throughout the organization; (c) turn the organization into a powerful magnet of mission-driven intelligence talent; (d) select the best intelligence tools and Enterprise Knowledge Platform (see Chapter 4) to analyze and integrate intelligence findings with intellectual property and facilitate access by authorized staff; and, (e) ensure that strategic planning and decision-making are continuously supported by valid and timely intelligence;

2. Auditing evaluations of threats and opportunities produced by issue managers; validating the scenarios of the most-likely and most-damaging courses of action open to threatening forces;

17

3. Determining time-sensitive objectives for current focus and high-payoff objectives for longer term projects; seeking agreement of senior executives on priorities for intelligence production; arbitrating between competing requirements;

4. Assessing the intelligence capability and the readiness of rivals and others to manipulate customers, staff and valued allies;

5. Building a network of trusted intelligence allies outside the organization; managing related risks; and regularly reviewing intelligence-sharing policies;

6. Evaluating the integrity, progress and impact of intelligence production and the performance of key intelligence professionals and team leaders;

7. Continually pruning the portfolio of intelligence projects to narrow the scope to high-payoff objectives;

8. Reporting to the CEO and briefing the oversight committee of the board of directors on the status of intelligence and counterintelligence. Depending upon the organization, the name of the committee varies from accountability or governance to intelligence, audit, ethics and compliance committee. The committee should mobilize independent external expertise to audit the quality and effectiveness of intelligence production.

As indicated above, structuring the intelligence function is among the first challenges facing Intelligence Officers. Wayne Rosenkrans, Global Intelligence Director at AstraZeneca Pharmaceuticals, spent nine months learning about his company's business environment before turning his attention to the issue of structure. In the process, he discovered that a structure with "tight central control of intelligence... would never survive because nobody would contribute to it... On the other hand, if I set up a completely decentralized intelligence function, I would not be able to pull information together. My final analysis was the need to have a reasonably strong central coordinating function – a "hub" with "spokes" of information contributors in business units. Regardless, the critical first element to setting up any intelligence function is reverse engineering your company –

there's no substitute for sitting down and understanding the way your company collects and uses information."[27]

Procter & Gamble has also gradually adopted the "hub-and-spoke" project-based structure. While emphasizing that competitive intelligence is everyone's responsibility, a corporate intelligence unit at the center (the hub) provides the intelligence framework and tools, integrates the effort of various business units, promotes synergy, risk management, intelligence sharing and economies of scale. It is also alert to standardization opportunities that do not stifle innovation. At the same time, each business unit acts as a spoke bringing and linking with customers and allies, sourcing innovative ideas and scanning for cross-selling opportunities and other intelligence in its field.[28]

Where a full-time position cannot be justified, a top executive in charge of marketing or R&D should be coached for at least a year in order to meet the requirements of a function that gets more complex and challenging every day. Without adequate training and coaching, current incumbents in these roles try to do their best but frequently in vain. The odds are not in favor of those who rely solely on experience and improvisation. Insufficiently alerted to the early signals of issue incubation, many lack the proactive sense of timing and an understanding of the dynamics of power between change-makers that are described in Chapters 7 and 8. Speed and intuition are important but perfect timing, strategic thinking and a cultured mindset[29] are more critical to the success of the Chief Intelligence Officer. While accountability for intelligence starts at the top, few CEOs can devote adequate time to keeping current and directing the function on a daily basis.

Chief Intelligence Officers act as strategists and agents of change. They require the skills, competencies, attitudes, sharp sense of timing and business acumen that are described in an upcoming book in this series.[30] As indicated in *"Science at Its Best, Security at Its Worst"* cited above, longevity in the position and clarity of mission are key ingredients.

- Issue Managers

The day-to-day analysis and management of intelligence requires a formal team with competent resources and effective leadership. Like a war room, the organization must be invisible to outsiders, but omnipresent. It starts with a small nucleus of core users or *issue managers,* experienced and highly motivated people who know your market and business environment intimately.

Issue managers are the business equivalent of the G2 military-intelligence officers who lead intelligence, counterintelligence and intelligence training in the Army. The skills of intelligence collectors described in the next section are among the prerequisites for the job. Issue managers must also have a background in human dynamics[31] and be prepared to challenge their own beliefs and assumptions. Inadequate sharing of tacit knowledge and biases about industry boundaries,[32] substitutes, new entrants, and competition strengths and own superiority are common sources of misperceptions and complacency.

Reporting to the Chief Intelligence Officer in a matrix mode,[33] issue managers work upstream of the scanning value chain to identify information needs as they scan for current and potential threats and opportunities relevant to their business. They direct the intelligence-gathering effort performed by monitors and intelligent software agents. Downstream, they must work closely with information scientists (economists, applied statisticians or operations-research analysts) who can help them analyze and interpret the data collected by searching for new information patterns, recognizing event interdependence and detecting emerging forces or issues.

- **IT Professionals**

IT professionals, with experience in expert systems, also play a crucial role in the partnership. They help design an overall process and architecture, launch the scanning organization and provide it with a secure IT platform and tools (such as software agents) for intelligence gathering, analysis, modeling, reporting and other communications.

The IT scanning system must constitute an integral part of the enterprise information network. In order to ensure interoperability across the organization, it is important to use compatible off-the-shelf equipment and software. There is no point in building a robust intelligence network that is not instantly accessible to the managers and field staff who ought to use it.

- **Monitors, Intelligence Collectors and Other Scanning Resources**

All employees should contribute to intelligence gathering and analysis under the guidance of a network of skilled *monitors* (or intelligence collectors) who form a sort of lookout institution. Jim Thomas considers investigative reporters the ideal model for those assigned this task. "A gregarious individual who is at ease talking with friends and strangers, someone with outstanding telephone skills. An organized person who can learn how to establish a Source data file and keep records of the information they collect. This person must question all information to ensure it is valid and reliable."[34]

Composure is a vital quality for monitors who need the ability to resist manipulation, seduction and coercion and to remain calm when facing threats and opportunities, regardless of the interlocutor. Intelligence collectors must be subtle and alert if they are to extract clues from even the most casual conversation and reconstruct scenarios of what was said, meant, ignored or concealed without tipping off their audience.

Part- or full-time monitors include experts and other end users (executives and field staff) who are trained for the task. They should come from a variety of functions and backgrounds within and outside the organization, regardless of its size.

Ad hoc consultations with outside monitors, reliable partners and competitive-intelligence providers should bring fresh intelligence-gathering ideas. The small nucleus of issue managers should, on a weekly basis, review intelligence-gathering work and provide clear guidance for intelligence analysis and interpretation, under the leadership of the Chief Intelligence Officer.

The network of monitors should be built strategically and supported with software agents that are capable of scanning the World Wide Web continuously in background mode. An inventory of "who scans what" should be kept up to date and subjected to regular reviews. In general, executives are surprised to find out how narrow and uniform their reading menu is. Apart from *The New York Times*, *The Wall Street Journal*, *TIME Magazine*, *Business Week* and *Fortune*, few managers tend to read more than a handful of publications outside their industrial sector or professional field.

In addition to corporate monitors dealing with factors that transcend functional boundaries, teams should be formed within each function to collect both explicit and tacit intelligence. All managers ought to invest half an hour a day to scan for signals relevant to their own business environment. This scanning is part of a learning process aimed at understanding the changing context in which the organization is doing business. Intelligence gathering and analysis are a collective responsibility. Careful planning is required to foster inter-departmental cooperation and to avoid duplication.

- **Critical-Thinking and People Skills for Intelligence Professionals**

The following notes complement the guidelines of the Society of Competitive Intelligence Professionals (SCIP) about the competencies of intelligence professionals.[35]

Profiling people is an exercise fraught with errors. Assessment tools like the Meyer-Briggs Type Indicator (MBTI) are so widely known, used and abused that experienced respondents can manipulate data to fit expectations. Furthermore, people skills can be learned and personal behavior does change over time.

Although intelligence professionals come from a variety of backgrounds, they must have good people skills. With respect to strengths, they should have the flexibility to work under crisis conditions, alternating between altruistic-nurturing, problem solving and leadership traits based on the requirements of the situation. Behaviorally, they should score high on initiating interaction with others, and have a moderate score in terms of both influencing and being open to influence. On the need for affection, the scores may vary widely based on age and ethnicity among other factors but are far less relevant to performance.[36]

In addition to people skills, intelligence professionals require skills in critical and strategic thinking, the subject of another publication in this series.[37]

- **Coaching and Rewarding Intelligence Professionals**

Resource mobilization is a growing challenge after 9-11 and the demand for experienced professionals is at an all-time high. Responsibilities and rewards must be attractive to retain intelligence executives, team leaders, issue managers and monitors characterized by a sense of purpose and direction and the ability to achieve the highest standards of performance and accountability.

Whether they are voluntary or appointed, all monitors should be rigorously coached and directed to avoid loss of focus and skewed monitoring tainted by individual biases. Without training and guidance, most voluntary monitors – including executives – waste an inordinate amount of time while generating rather limited benefits.

Performance evaluation is also imperative for the team and its members. When work is not evaluated, performers are denied a basic ingredient for continuous improvement. Even high achievers reach plateaus!

Team and individual incentives should be explicit. Even though monitors find the process a rewarding experience in itself, inasmuch as it broadens their horizons, they should be rewarded fairly for the task they perform – even if the reward is symbolic.

Intelligence is not a discipline for public trophy seekers. The U.S. National Defense University does sponsor the Sun Tzu Award, a prestigious open international competition on information-warfare research. Despite this, however, there will never be a genuine Olympics for high performers in business intelligence! Exposure can threaten their employer. The best candidates for most positions tend to feature a track record of ethical behavior and high performance (both academic and professional) combined with a low need for public approbation. That is why monetary rewards, commensurate with achievements, can go a long way to establish a fair and equitable incentive as Buckman Laboratories of Memphis (TN) have found out. With a global knowledge-transfer network accessible to every employee, Buckman built high incentives to reward their best informers.

- **Structure: Further Tips to Keep it Simple**

The overall cost of scanning should be commensurate with anticipated benefits and the potential for mitigating risks. In medium-sized companies, monitoring can be relatively inexpensive. Each monitor should devote approximately an hour per day throughout the year. Some Fortune 500 corporations have a small group of professionals assigned entirely to scanning (including counterintelligence and issue management) in addition to *ad hoc* observers and part-time monitors. A U.S. oil company has set up seven small monitoring teams: petrochemicals, transportation industries, intellectual property and law, IT, biotechnologies and other advanced technologies, and counterintelligence. These teams provide the company managers with competitive intelligence and with a daily bulletin considered essential to informed decision-making.

In a leading financial institution, part-time monitors and issue managers are selected through competitions. A brief orientation session on *intelligence collection and analysis* is provided every year to staff. Active participation in monitoring is encouraged. Candidates are then asked to submit *a unique value proposition* detailing their perception of objectives, means, resources, required timeframe and the skills they need to excel. Selected candidates are given a two-day training on *competitive intelligence* and a day workshop on software agents and service providers. The candidates are then assigned to a different intelligence team every year. Issue managers get additional training in strategy formulation and implementation.

With respect to government, Bruce Berkowitz and Allan Goodman "recommend a system that would utilize the private sector – with its access to more capital and its ability to move more quickly than a government organization. At the same time, this system would encourage government intelligence operations to concentrate on the specialized, high-risk activities they are uniquely able to perform."[38]

- **Experience of Southwest Bell**

"Southwestern Bell Telephone in St. Louis illustrates that a healthy intelligence program is always changing… Initially, the intelligence function was centralized, with one data collector and one analyst each dedicated to a separate functional area (marketing, technology, finance, government regulations). When this scheme failed to yield actionable results, the team reorganized by merging the collector and analyst roles and refocusing on such key telecommunications technologies as wireless, cable telephony and the like… Getting information to flow from the sales and line staff to the central intelligence unit was the biggest challenge, according to Karen Wolters, a Southwestern Bell product-development manager who was a member of the original intelligence team. Employees were so busy doing their jobs that it was difficult to get them to take an extra 15 minutes a day to do a core dump of knowledge gleaned from the day's meetings and phone conversations."[39]

- **Orientation Sessions and Ongoing Learning**

In order to learn about basic intelligence tools, methods and opportunities, users should participate in a short-duration workshop covering the *ten vital goals of mission-critical intelligence* (Chapter 1), the intelligence road map, the selected Enterprise Knowledge Platform (Chapter 4), as well as Google and a couple of special-purpose search engines pertinent to the organization's subject matter. Continuous feedback and knowledge sharing is essential on issues, challenges, lessons learned and success stories.

3. Conclusion

In order to yield full benefits for an organization, intelligence cannot be structured in isolation from other business functions. It must be embedded in every phase of the business value chain from mission setting and the formulation of strategy and policy through to project management, day-to-day operations and impact evaluation. It is vital to every function of the enterprise, from R&D, IT, engineering and production to finance, marketing, sales and human resource management. Nevertheless, the overall intelligence exercise must be led and orchestrated in a matrix mode[40] by a senior executive clearly accountable for intelligence effectiveness, productivity and return on investment.

Bill Gates stresses that 'the most meaningful way to differentiate your company from the competition, the best way to put distance between you and the crowd, is to do an outstanding job with information. How you gather, manage, and use information will determine whether you win or lose. Information flow is the lifeblood of your company because it enables you to get most out of your people and learn from your customers."[41] Mr. Gates' statement is even more applicable to intelligence.

This chapter has focused on the elements of an effective and productive intelligence organization. The next chapter provides the road map for building intelligence capital.

1. The Foundation of Intelligence Capital

- Environmental Scanning

Scanning is the ongoing and systematic process by which each organization must tap and intercept, as early as possible, the universe of relevant external and internal signals, events, transactions, best practices, risks and surprise developments. It includes mining internal and external information banks, collecting and extracting relevant events and data, and continually monitoring factors pertinent to the organization in three subject areas:

- Economic intelligence
- Market and competitive intelligence
- Counterintelligence and intelligence security

- Economic Intelligence

Economic intelligence supports policy and decision-making. The goal is to understand the forces that drive growth, competitive advantage and performance from the local to the global. It is the art of researching, collecting, tracking, processing, integrating and extracting valuable knowledge from new and available economic statistics, reports and information about economic activity in any geographic or socioeconomic order. Most economic intelligence is readily available either free or at an accessible cost from syndicated or open sources. As an illustration, Bank Rate Monitor provides free information on "more than 100 financial products including mortgages, credit cards, new and used automobile loans, money market accounts, certificates of deposit, checking and ATM fees, home equity loans and online banking fees."[42] Rate.net ranks the interest rates on savings, mortgage, equity loans and credit cards as offered by ten-thousand financial institutions across the United States. The Economist Intelligence Unit[43] provides a practical perspective on global economic indicators and trends with a focus on Europe and North America.

At a first glance, leading economic indicators (LEI) provide a broad picture of the health of the economy and its potential impact on the top-line growth (i.e. sales) of organizations. Compiled weekly by the Conference Board[44] for several countries, LEI are composite indexes based on consumer expectations, money supply, interest rate spread, stock prices, claims for unemployment insurance, building permits, vendor performance, manufacturing hours, new orders for consumer goods and materials, and orders for non-defense capital goods. In his recent book, *The Message of the Markets,* Ron Insana offers evidence of widely available economic intelligence ranging from how the yield curve can help predict a recession to factors impacting personal investment and mortgage decisions.[45]

Government produces the lion's share of economic intelligence. As an illustration, the Census Bureau's Statistical Abstract of the United States and the Department of Commerce's U.S. Economic Outlook provide a wealth of potentially useful social and economic indicators for strategic planning.[46]

Unfortunately, most of the unclassified and royalty-free material produced by governments is not currently indexed by search engines. This information is part of the Invisible Web[47] not readily accessible without specialized help.[48] More will be said about the Invisible Web later. A valuable reference library on economic and competitive intelligence material is currently available through the U.S. Government search engine.[49] The site is also the best entry point for any firm interested in doing business with the government. A good way to get information on major commercial opportunities in most countries is to use The Department of State links to every U.S. Embassy.[50]

Some government agencies such as the U.S. Department of Commerce and Export Development Canada (EDC) produce economic intelligence geared for exporters.[51] Every business day, they sift through a vast array of global intelligence sources, validate the content and select what is pertinent to their domestic exporters. Using a subscriber password, EDC clients are provided

28

with international market intelligence, economic and political risk overviews by country and briefs on noteworthy events as they occur.

Information at the city level is pertinent to every business, regardless of size. A.C. Nielsen, Census Bureaus, couriers, utilities, postal agencies, telephone companies and local governments and associations possess a wealth of data on cities and their districts.

Consider Ottawa (Canada) where Nortel, Alcatel, Mitel, Corel and other high-tech firms laid off more than 20,000 talented employees in 2001. This amounted to approximately 7% of the permanent workforce in the region. In just a few weeks, most of these people found a job, became entrepreneurs or joined the federal government's workforce. By Christmas 2001, the city jobless rate actually fell, while the demand for skilled labor, housing and retail space continued rising. This occurred at a time when Canada as a whole was experiencing an increase in unemployment.[52] That is why local, rather than national intelligence data is essential for retailers and entrepreneurs as well as for hiring or real estate transactions.

- **Market and Competitive Intelligence**

Building on the seminal work of Michael Porter who provides a valuable framework for analyzing the competition,[53] we see competitive intelligence as practical research focused on maintaining an accurate profile of present and potential competitors, customers and suppliers as well as their likely responses to perceived threats and opportunities. By getting and validating information ahead of competitors, you can construct new knowledge (e.g. ideas, strategies, practices, processes, transactions), discover strengths, spot opportunities, exploit new applications, introduce innovations, avoid surprises, decrease reaction time, and, if feasible, gain first-mover advantage.

Note the difference between competitive intelligence and industrial espionage. Theft, bribery and other illegal espionage activities are off limits to competitive intelligence. The Society of Competitive Intelligence Professionals (SCIP) defines competitive intelligence as "the legal and ethical collection and analysis of information regarding the capabilities, vulnerabilities, and intentions of business competitors."[54]

We also want to keep in mind that in competitive intelligence, the state of the art is obviously not in the public domain. Those who have it don't talk about it; they act! However, even with limited competitive-intelligence know-how, resourceful executives can make remarkable progress. Just asking lost customers what they like about their new vendor can be revealing. Over the years, our clients found out more about their competitors from lost customers than from open sources. Leonard Fuld suggests that "corrugated boxes, box cars, technical manuals, help-wanted ads and even the Yellow Pages can reveal a great deal about your competitor." [55]

In another illustration, Fuld outlines how Bank One gained "invaluable information on competitors' pricing, new products and target markets" by merely asking the bank's staff to systematically gather up and analyze all of the correspondence and direct-mail pieces they receive from competitors.

Today, the Internet provides much of that information online. It even allows you to track the demands of some of your competitors' customers in real time. With the astute use of Web meta-tags, companies can legally divert traffic generated through search engines from your sites to theirs.

Public companies should scan key capital-market players including bankers, traders (institutional and block), analysts, merger-and-acquisition experts and others with a vested interest in the company. On occasion, institutional investors have been alerted to the supply-chain problems of companies in their portfolios earlier than the management of these companies.

- **Counterintelligence and Intelligence Security (IS)**

Counterintelligence is the *shield* that hides your weaknesses from those who, by knowing them, can benefit at your expense and to restrict the exposure of your strengths to those who ought to know them. Chapter 6 will specifically address this topic.

2. Competitive-Intelligence Road Map

Basically, intelligence work consists of planning and direction, which overlaps with sequential iterative production. These tasks are described below.

- Intelligence Planning and Direction

"This is management of the entire effort, from identifying the need for data to delivering an intelligence product to a consumer. It is the beginning and the end of the cycle – the beginning because it involves drawing up specific collection requirements and the end because finished intelligence, which supports policy decisions, generates new requirements."[56]

Specifically, the questions below should be asked by issue managers and frequently revisited as a way of improving the quality of intelligence planning and production.

1. What are the goals and issues (opportunities and threats) worthy of intelligence work?

2. Which current and potential competitors and other stakeholders should be analyzed and why? What are our time-sensitive goals and high-payoff objectives?

3. What do we need to know about these stakeholders and why? How much do we already know? What are the costs/benefits of learning more versus the adverse consequences of waiting? These questions should help refine the list of high-payoff objectives.

4. What are the most promising sources of data including both explicit and tacit knowledge? What is the way to tap into them? How do we ensure validity and reliability of data? How do we identify and discard misinformation, inaccuracies and anomalies?

5. How can we analyze the data to make it relevant for decision-making?

6. Who should have access to what findings and in what format?

7. How should we build our stakeholder and event-monitoring radar? How often should we update the content? What conditions or people merit a permanent or frequent watch? What common platform should we use to support the capture of standardized information, quick access and the relational mapping of intelligence reports against corporate databases, document repositories, Web links and other intellectual capital?

These questions are the basis for identifying the objectives and scope of intelligence projects, assessing their costs/benefits and determining whether to launch a full-scale project or an experimental pilot. Selected projects and pilots should be integrated into the corporate project portfolio with timelines, adequate resources and budgets using the framework outlined in the book *Harnessing the Power of a Clear Mission, Vision, Values, Goals & Priorities.*[57]

- **Intelligence Production**

This operational phase comprises intelligence collection, processing, analysis, evaluation, interpretation, knowledge construction and dissemination of finished intelligence. It consists of seven major sequential and iterative tasks. Taken together, they form a cycle because intelligence production never stops. Not only is the exercise repeated continuously, but there is also frequent overlap between tasks:

– Asking the right questions;

– Broad scanning or screening;

– Focused scanning and information validation;

– Analysis: sketching the forest from the trees;

– Interpretation: advancing to harvest the forest;

– Seeding the future: nurturing the knowledge repository;

– Communicating actionable intelligence;

– Measuring success.

a. Asking the Right Questions

Working in teams, issue managers should review the intelligence needs of their clients and the questions outlined in the planning phase (see above). These questions should drive information collection, validity checks, tacit and explicit knowledge construction, analysis, interpretation and reporting requirements as well as the process of evaluating intelligence activities.

b. Broad Scanning

Any strategy, be it competitive or corporate, cannot succeed without high-quality intelligence collection.[58] The intelligence-collection cycle goes from broad to focused scanning. Both types of scanning include analysis and interpretation tasks as outlined below.

Broad scanning is the foundation of intelligence gathering. Its purpose is to build informed judgments about what should be scanned and how. Brainstorm with trusted intelligence professionals (within and outside your firm) who know your business environment and its constituencies to draft a set of needs, search assumptions and qualification of information sources.

Start with clear goals. Consider *Mission-Critical Intelligence: Ten Vital Goals* defined in Chapter 1 and the questions above as a starting point. Keep an open mind and do not confine the exercise to what you consider significant to the organization. Consider the assistance or coaching of a computational linguistic expert. It is well worth the training time and cost involved. Broad scanning is iterative but should not be open-ended. Experiment with new trails but constantly prune the scope to weed out dead ends.

Unfortunately, this critical exercise is frequently done hastily. It is often skewed by intuition that tends to overlook important information trails, thus yielding misleading results. With globalization and the information explosion, broad scanning is akin to trying to detect low-incidence forms of cancer in a very healthy population or find a needle in a haystack. Yet our mind is set on a narrow range of clusters within that universe.

Starting from a large set of internal and external information sources containing a potentially infinite universe of data and variables, broad scanning aims at narrowing the search by:

- Validating original search assumptions including the protocol for rejecting sources of questionable or misleading value, be they people, Internet web sites or other information sources;
- Creating or revising a set of qualifying attributes for information sources;
- Finding search criteria (key words) that determine the context of each scanning iteration;
- Pre-qualifying sources, topics of interest and embryos of change to be subjected to focused scanning or continuous monitoring;
- Ensuring that the value of scanning outweighs the costs and risks of collection.

33

Rather than scanning newspapers and magazines manually, intelligence collectors should first call on intelligence service providers, like the Williams Inference Center[59], who can deliver the information sought at a small fraction of the cost.

A good part of broad scanning is facilitated by search engines, news aggregators and online news "clipping" services to be discussed in Chapters 4 and 5. The awesome power of this technology is not a substitute for judgment. Broad scanning is interactive and iterative. Each search stream produces a host of information trails that must be evaluated for further analysis.

The acid test in qualifying information is the potential relevance of the source or the meaning of its data to your organization's constituencies and business environment as defined by the brainstorming team. Repeat the process when the outcome deviates significantly from expectations (blind spots) or when you uncover promising trails (intermediaries).

Blind spots with minimum relevance should be subjected to focused scanning. They can turn out to be a valuable piece of the intelligence puzzle under focused scanning, and can uncover an impending event by a competitor or a great accidental opportunity. Consider Johnson & Johnson's baby powder products, introduced in 1921 merely to replace its irritating construction plaster, and which "remain important products and major components of corporate equity"[60]. Keep in mind that 3M Post-it Notes[TM] also originated with an accident.

Check for redundancy and mixing. "Redundancy simply means ensuring that your information can be verified by several different sources. Mixing your sources helps ensure that they are not all simply repeating information from the same primary source. Using multiple sources involves a tradeoff – you can potentially double your effort, but by using several sources you not only have a better chance of finding the information you need, you'll be able to feel more confident in the authenticity of the information. It also helps guard against deception."[61]

c. Focused Inferential Scanning and Information Validation

With focused scanning (or inferential scanning), issue managers assign priorities and narrow the exercise to specific issues from sources that have been pre-qualified during the broad scanning exercise. Monitors gather and validate further information from pre-qualified sources with the help of technology (search engines, aggregators, data mining tools and enterprise knowledge platforms) and feedback from field observations, intelligence providers and professional indexers (or computational linguistics experts).

For printed or electronic news, monitors read the headlines of the pertinent sections, all the while keeping in mind that dramatic headlines tend to stretch the facts and obscure subtleties that make a significant difference to policy makers and investors. Also keep in mind that some important Web postings are "untitled" because the authors have only a limited knowledge of Hypertext Markup Language (HTML) and do not mark the title adequately. Our research also indicates that almost half of the commercial-site titles are either inaccurate or contain inflated marketing slogans. Non-commercial sites (.edu, .mil and .gov) fare much better.

Any story with potential relevance is skimmed. Even if the relevance appears weak, it is best to err on the side of caution. Unlike reading, skimming is characterized by quickly assimilating facts and by skipping over editorials and opinions. Unlike news stories, editorials can usually be assessed for relevance by reading the conclusion first. The resulting data and stories are screened for in-depth reading and analysis by the team. Lengthy stories should be skimmed only as far as needed to select items for in-depth reading.

Use independent and reliable contacts to verify stories, rumors and news, particularly from unknown or questionable sources. Sometimes a couple of phone calls to a third party will do. Internet data can be flawed by accident or intentionally seeded with misinformation. Unscrupulous competitors thrive on exploiting misinformation as a source of competitive advantage. Misinformation can lead to costly decisions and destroy a corporate image. In the public realm, it plays havoc with democracy by breeding dysfunctional behavior, animosity, and in some cases unrest and violence. Subscribe to a news monitoring service like Cyberalert[62] or CCN Newswire.[63] They scan for information and misinformation published about clients and offer focused briefings and valuable advice on how to remove false information from message boards, newsgroups, portals and web sites.

Financial data must also be validated systematically to detect errors, fraud, and information that has been tampered with. There is now inexpensive software based on Benford's Law[64] and fuzzy-set mathematics[65] for this purpose. Benford's Law can also be helpful in spotting hoaxes from adversaries and unknown sources.[66]

d. Analysis: Sketching the Forest From the Trees

This stage requires skill and discipline. The value added lies in combining open-source with proprietary material to address client issues. It can quickly yield surprising insights, even before the team continues further on its intelligence journey.

Keeping its goals in mind, the intelligence team studies relevant events, interviews, stories, field data and previously available intelligence. Background material on competitor moves and personal observations of successes and failures should be updated and further analyzed for shifts in direction and emerging threats or opportunities. Make an attempt to identify the time-to-market option pursued by each of your competitors and the strategy behind it.[67] If the inferential scanning has pointed to an early release of a product or a beta version of a software, the team uses proxies to buy, operate and reverse-engineer the products made by the competitor (or supplier) to explain their performance and estimate their cost structure. As countless companies have discovered, doing this exercise systematically as part of a total competitive-intelligence program opens the door to better products and new markets.

Throughout the analysis, the intelligence team searches for new patterns, event interdependence and emerging issues. Its arsenal of tools ranges from S-curve modeling, cluster and cross-impact analysis[68] to causal modeling, future wheels[69], mapping and development funnels,[70] and value incubation (the framework detailed in Chapter 7).

Beware of linear extrapolations.[71] The path of adoption of some products, technologies and networks tends to frequently follow the classic S-shaped curve – flatter at both ends and with a steeper positive slope in between. Alas, the curve also models our forecasting biases as illustrated by the flawed predictions of the demand for telecom equipment and services. "In the early stages of network evolution, forecasts tend to be pessimistic because the potential of the network is not well understood. However, as the network starts to grow, predictions become overly enthusiastic. This, in turn, sets up a bust when the growth starts to slow... The Internet and the wireless industry show a similar pattern."[72] Like forecasting, innovation and market penetration, intelligence tends to be diffused in a "slow-fast-slow" S-curve pattern. Intelligence diffusion is virtually unnoticeable at the beginning of the incubation of a strategy or an issue as illustrated in Chapter 7. "Not all products follow the classic S-shaped curve. The sales of products, such as skateboards, rise quickly and then die just. Other products seem to defy entering the Decline stage; for example, classic confectionery products and brands such as"[73] Ivory soap bars, which have defied the product life cycle law for over two centuries! For a practical primer and a bibliography on the power of S-curves, visit www.executive.org/s-curves.

The above instruments are not always a condition for screening the future. Sometimes using qualitative judgment and simpler tools (grids, timelines, ratio analysis, decision trees, and scenarios to simulate or shadow the competition) can help in discovering competitive threats and potentially disruptive technologies[74] that tend to elude and ultimately undermine even the best-run companies.

A caveat with respect to business-intelligence software is in order. As indicated by Fuld, "software generally does not analyze, at least in a purely qualitative sense; thus without analysis, there is no intelligence. While some of the reviewed products perform some rudimentary analysis, this analysis is typically based on internal corporate data that inadequately covers the external environment. Furthermore, the analysis is almost purely quantitative. Business reality dictates that much analysis is based on the qualitative – an argument, a phrase, a visual assessment – not just on numbers and statistics. Analysis is a very human process, one that takes place around a conference room table, a grease board, or over the telephone, or even in a chat room. While software can offer help in generating valuable information, it cannot assess the subtleties of a business decision, or offer implications and recommendations. Developing true intelligence requires an investment of time and a creativity not yet extant within a machine."[75]

e. Interpretation: Advancing to Harvest the Forest

Issue managers work closely with monitors, quantitative analysts and subject-matter professionals to integrate and interpret the knowledge produced so far, cast it in the right context and turn it into intelligence capital. They view newly acquired material from multiple perspectives as illustrated in the case below titled *Glainard: Then and Now*. Indeed, sketching the intelligence forest from seemingly isolated events and exploring the ramifications from many vantage points can create competitive advantage.

The possible impact of new intelligence is assessed. *Hitch-hiking* on surprise events is also considered at this stage, particularly for time-sensitive targets. The goal could be to announce controversial decisions or to exploit events as a cover for pursuing other important endeavors.

The team produces two inferential images of each issue at hand. The first image profiles the new intelligence in order to alert users to issues, people and organizations worth monitoring on their radar screen. The second image describes anomalies and what is still unknown (i.e., unfulfilled information needs) and provides new questions for further research.

These findings are debated with monitors, relevant decision-makers and trusted allies. Employees and partners who need to know should be privy to the full findings in accordance with the intelligence security policy of the firm (see Chapter 6).

f. Seeding the Future:
Nurturing the Knowledge Repository

Selected information content is titled and abstracted with clear reference to its source. It is further cross-referenced by issue or target, function, organization, location, people and constituencies. It should be promptly indexed using the selected Enterprise Knowledge Platform (see Chapter 4).

The intelligence database and its links with other enterprise applications should be kept up to date and readily accessible for browsing and further analysis.[76]

g. Communicating Actionable Intelligence

Authorized staff and close allies are alerted by e-mail whenever the new intelligence is pertinent to their stated search criteria or field of endeavor. In the message, each story is summarized, sorted by relevance, listed by title along with links for details, source references and other related content. Stories with content exactly matching preset criteria and designative keywords (or synonyms) are displayed first. Findings with connotative terms and phrases or a partial match follow.

Users are encouraged to post their own comments and interpretations. The goal is to foster a vibrant virtual intelligence community through the company's Intranet.

The intelligence team prepares *Business Outlooks* and *Issue Briefs* in addition to any specific reports requested by users. The Business Outlook is issued at least once per month. It should be readily accessible to a wide audience and should contain references for those interested in digging further. Issue Briefs on major forces or foreseeable issues should also be prepared. Written in a condensed format, the briefs provide alternative projections with best, worst and most likely scenarios. These documents are essential in formulating strategy, which is the subject of another publication in this series.[77]

h. Measuring Success

The tasks of intelligence collection, validation, integration, interpretation, archiving and sharing are not an end in themselves. The acid test is the impact of intelligence sharing on policy and decision-making. It is easy to lose sight of this and produce a vast amount of content of marginal value. Measuring the bottom line (ROI) of intelligence planning and production through a rigorous evaluation of the impact is therefore of paramount importance. If accurate measurement is difficult or prohibitive in cost, assess the largest payback in terms of market share, client and talent acquisition/retention, revenue generation, productivity improvement, risk mitigation and other strategic and operational benefits. Benchmark the process of intelligence management, production and protection. Identify opportunities and clients lost to competitors due to intelligence bottlenecks and untapped tacit knowledge. Question the capacity to capture, personalize and deliver actionable intelligence (e.g., hard-to-spot developments, market shifts and trends) to those who need it in a timely fashion. Act on the findings.

3. Case Studies

* Glainard – Then and Now

This case illustrates how to track a seemingly isolated event, cast it in the right context and turn it into intelligence capital with far-reaching implications for negotiators and decision-makers. It also demonstrates the importance of nurturing discreet alliances among non-competing vendors as an integral part of your intelligence network, in this case vis-à-vis a difficult customer.

The announcement that Dixibond Capital would relinquish its minority holding of Glainard, a global business-to-business (B2B) stationery chain, was viewed by analysts as an isolated event. The news was the trigger that led our client, a dated-product supplier to Glainard, to scan for further clues. In consultation with his accountant, he discovered that Glainard bill payments were falling behind by approximately 30 days. After examining their own receivables, two non-competing vendors confirmed that Glainard payments were in arrears but saw no reason for alarm. Through informal contacts, the client discovered some additional clues suggesting that the adverse consequences of Glainard's recent acquisitions were being underestimated. The new chain was losing more customers than originally expected. A former executive disclosed that Glainard was planning to compete directly with our client's product line by expanding its own in-house printing facility to produce dated products. He also thought that Glainard problems could get worse. The company's CEO was preoccupied with the loss of major customers and Glainard's inability to build a solid online presence. With further intelligence about Glainard's financial strength, our client was equipped to review the relationship with Glainard and other customers including pricing and terms of payment. He knew Glainard might change owners but that it would not disappear entirely. Using a subtle gambit to speed up bill payments, he managed to squeeze more favorable terms. He went ahead of other vendors to strengthen his firm's position in other channels to make up for the potential loss in volume that could result from the new billing terms. His strategy was the envy of other publishers a year later when Glainard was facing a cash flow crunch.

Our client kept Glainard on his radar screen and was among the first to support the takeover of the global chain by a conglomerate known for its long-standing cooperation with its vendors and excellent treatment of its workforce.

• Bell Canada: Translating Intelligence into Front-Line Dividends

Rigorous scanning of early signs of new business development is a way of life for Simon Roy, a professional engineer, formerly with Rolls-Royce, and now Network Manager at Bell Canada. Mr. Roy monitors news, conferences and selected web sites. He contacts architects, engineers, real-estate promoters, municipalities and boards of trade. He is constantly looking for transactions taking place upstream of the value chain of his industry to get a head start on competition. While questioning an industrial-park agent about available commercial land in the Montreal area, he learned that a large property had just been leased for development. A call to another source revealed that the plot of land was adjacent to a taxiing area in Montreal's Mirabel Airport. Since neither interlocutor would divulge the name of the tenant, Mr. Roy's team listed plausible candidates, analyzed rumors and available intelligence and proceeded by elimination to pick Bombardier as the most likely tenant. That is how Bell learned, several months before the public announcement, about Bombardier's intention to build the new plant to assemble the CRJ 700 and CRJ900 regional jets. Through open-source intelligence, Mr. Roy further learned about the delivery schedule of the new Regional Jets.

After exploring several scenarios of Bombardier's telecommunications needs, it became clear that waiting for the client's invitation to tender would disadvantage Bell over competitors who would use overtime and cut margins to get the job. In order to guarantee delivery and secure a competitive advantage, Simon Roy convinced his organization, in January 2001, to immediately order the fiber optics. For other hardware like transport nodes that required up to sixteen weeks lead-time,[78] it was recommended to order standard equipment that could be assigned to other clients if Bell was not selected. Bombardier announced the telecom project in April 2001, giving providers less than two months to deliver. But, Bell was well prepared to face the challenge. It won the contract and managed to beat the odds by finishing on time and within budget.

4. Conclusion

The economy is shifting more power than ever to consumers and newcomers who will continue to challenge established incumbents. Without knowledge, we are flying blind. If we do so, the value-creation cycle will slow down and even turn into a liability. But, knowledge is perishable. It is necessary but not sufficient. Translating knowledge into actionable intelligence depends on the acquisition of the talent needed to tailor information through relentless funneling and assessment based on a dynamic definition of both funnel and toolkit. The key to managing this task lies in correct conceptualization at the outset, followed by effective leveraging of technologies that maximize return on resources to generate superior intelligence.

This chapter has provided the framework for acquiring and processing that intelligence. Its focus was on the intelligence road map, a core instrument in charting the path to excellence. The next two chapters discuss intelligence tools, platforms and sources of intelligence.

Building on the intelligence road map and framework introduced so far, this chapter helps readers formulate online search queries and understand selected search engines and enterprise knowledge platforms. It assumes the reader has a basic understanding on how search engines work. For a practical primer on the topic, visit www.executive.org/engines.

1. How to Formulate Queries

- Simple Navigational Search

Except for this brief opening section dealing with routine searches, the rest of this chapter tends to focus on more elaborate queries.

Simple navigational searches can now be done without knowing much about search engines and Boolean concepts. With Internet Explorer, searching for a web site has never been easier. There is no need to know the precise URL of widely known organizations or to search other engines to get it. Use the Address bar or the Search button to enter the phrase or keywords such as Ford Motors, Sharp, AMR, London Business School or San Francisco Chronicle. MSN search engine gets the web page matching the phrase and lists additional sites with similar keywords. For example, entering the phrase "Alain Paul Martin" yielded 90,000 links with the first link to the author of the book and the second to Paul Martin, former Minister of Finance of Canada. Even government departments and agencies such as the *Canadian Polar Commission* or the *Department of Foreign Affairs and International Trade* can be visited by simply typing the full name.

- Elaborate Queries

Locating and selecting relevant information can be fraught with risks and its complexity is frequently underestimated. Crafting queries for electronic searches is a skill that requires training, coaching and experience. In the absence of a personal trainer, take a seminar or, at least, carefully study Five-Step Search Strategy[79] by Joe Barker at UC Berkeley, currently the best online tutorial on the subject. Also read Gary Price's *Web Search Engines FAQs: Questions, Answers and Issues.*[80]

Do not hesitate to ask for the assistance of professionals who know where to look and how to corroborate the evidence. An illustration of this is offered in the Stem-Cell Migration Case below. Remember that literature search is a core competency for librarians who are relentlessly validating questions that have often been inadequately formulated by their clients.

- **Risks and Time-Wasting Traps to Avoid**

1. Web content is prone to errors, biases, misinformation and inaccuracies. Invest reasonable time to check the facts. Consider multiple sources including electronic searches (search engines, directories, the Invisible Web), calls and field observations (personal visits). Validate the findings.

2. Many Web users also hinder their search by restricting it to one search engine.

3. Another classic trap is to use either a search engine or a directory rather than considering both options. See Section 2 below.

4. Even when a search-engine offers the best approach, casual searchers do not take the time to think through the search string and end up wasting time with irrelevant documents. On this topic, Joe Barker's *Pre-Searching Analysis* succinctly goes straight to the point.[81] The Refine and Resource features of Teoma contextual search engine described in Section 3 below can help users narrow the search to more pertinent pages.

5. There is no perfect ranking. The first web pages returned by search engines and directories may be sponsored or artificially propelled to the top by shrewd owners who can reverse engineer some ranking algorithms. This is particularly the case for commercial content. That is why it is sometimes preferable to aim at, or exclude, selected top-level domains (.com, .mil, .gov, .edu, .uk). Thus, a trainer preparing a

workshop session on systems engineering or team building would get higher quality content by first excluding commercial sites (.com), starting the search with military (.mil), governmental (.gov, .gov.uk or .gc.ca) and educational sites (.edu) using engines such as Google or AllTheWeb.

- ## Spelling Variants, Synonyms, Connotations, Errors and Other Terminology Traps

Both the search query and targeted Web content are subject to spelling variants and errors, in addition to synonyms, connotations and other terminological traps. Most search engines require multiple entries or the use of the Boolean OR even for basic common words with multiple spellings.

Google flags misspelled words in a query. However, at the time of this publication, it neither automatically searches for equivalent words with distinct British and American spellings (center, color or behavior) nor does it take care of multiple forms ("B2B" and "Business to Business" or luggage and baggage) when only one variant is entered. It does not even alert the user to this possibility even though the technology to do so is relatively simple. Furthermore, it is often necessary to search for both the plural and singular of query words in Google and other engines, which also do not permit truncation or alteration as in the case of terms with changing Latin endings like alumnus, calyx and diagnosis.

Exercise caution with respect to personal names and corporate designations. The President of the United States can be recorded as President Bush, George Bush, George W. Bush, G. W. Bush or simply the President. Indeed, most personal names appear under different variations with or without middle names and either the first names or initials appearing before or after the surname. On the business side, Google returned 220,000 pages for the phrase Procter & Gamble, 187,000 for the P&G acronym without spaces and only 19,000 for P & G with spaces between characters. Note that entering any of the three options in Internet Explorer (Version 6) led to the Procter & Gamble home page.

- ## Avoid Web Stress Syndrome

Tutorials are good timesavers for researchers. Pandia has a free search engine tutorial along with a good introduction about query syntax and rules.[82] Anderson School's Rosenfeld Library (UCLA) also offers instructions with excellent examples on searching for online information and selecting the right search engine based on a variety of needs.[83] Also, directories and search engines are continually improving. Revisiting the Help menu periodically is a good investment of time.

2. Search Engines Versus Directories

Scanning of the Web cannot be done without search engines, directories, news aggregators and clipping services.

- Directories

Unlike search engines, which use crawlers to electronically gather Web content, search directories like Looksmart or Galaxy are hierarchical or relational databases indexed by subject category and containing reviewer-approved abstracts or keywords based on descriptions submitted by content providers. Directories vary widely in quality chiefly because their selection protocols range from refereed selections based on rigorous editorial standards (mostly in science and technology) to uncontested listings strictly driven by fees (in communications and media). Most directories are updated less frequently than search-engine catalogs, which tend to provide more current content.

Directories should be considered first for subject or geography-specific searches.

- Google Directory

Although most directories only search approved descriptions rather than their related web site content, they can serve as a lead or a first filter for researchers who need navigational guidance. As an illustration, the Google Directory[84] did provide, in three neat columns, a list of the home pages of 124 universities in England by drilling down the path of Reference, Education, Regional, Europe, UK and England to Universities. Totaling over 2,100, the number of links available to home pages of faculties, institutes or schools within each institution is shown in brackets. Visiting and tracking the links within each site is now only a click away. Thus, a directory can take us to a particular university site but cannot point to the pages citing that institution across the Web. That is the business of search engines.

3. Important General Search Engines

- ## MSN Search Engine

For all but intricate searches, MSN Search Engine has powerful features that are neglected by most users. It powers Internet Explorer and is therefore accessible directly from the address bar of the browser, particularly for simple navigational searches as discussed in Section 2 above. There is no need for links or bookmarks. In working with teenagers, we were able to locate sites for the inventors of electricity, digital storage, the telephone, the Web and even *Total Quality Management* by simply entering the phrase "inventor of..." in the Internet Explorer address bar. The same was done for finding presidents, prime ministers, queens and kings of most countries. One exception is that the Prime Minister of Canada pops up for several lines when the "Prime Minister of the United States" is requested!

MSN Search Engine also provides suggestions for broadening the search. There is more about this in the case study on Stem-Cell Migration below.

- ## Google Advanced Search

Google takes over where conventional search engines leave off. At the time of this publication, UC Berkeley[85] was only recommending Google followed by AllTheWeb. Google is now clearly the most comprehensive search engine available. It has robust features like sub-searching, fuzzy ranking, image searching, drop-down listing of search history and direct access to over 3.5 billion Web documents including images, newsgroups, Microsoft Office (Word, Excel) and Corel files (WordPerfect, Corel Draw!).

"Google does only one thing – search – and does it spectacularly. Whether I'm looking for a home remedy for sinusitis or trying to find a long-lost friend online, it has an uncanny knack for locating what I want. Google ranks search results not by how frequently or prominently the search term appears on a given page but by how often other pages on the Web link to the page with reference to that term. As a safety measure, Google also analyzes the words around the link to make sure they're relevant to the original query."[86]

47

Google has provided law-enforcement agents with occasional nuggets of information about notorious fugitives. It helped the police locate hijacker Patrick Critton, who had been on the run for over 30 years.[87]

Google is also helpful in automated translation and is currently active in perfecting search engines for foreign languages, including Chinese. Google powers the web sites of clients such as AOL, Cisco, Sony and Yahoo.

- **AltaVista and AllTheWeb**

Although it no longer sorts or searches within results, AltaVista makes up for some of Google's drawbacks by permitting nesting, word truncation, words in NEAR proximity of each other and other Boolean-logic variants. AltaVista is also launching its "paraphrase" query system, which draws from the repository of user queries to suggest refinements to the original request. Here, AltaVista is capitalizing on the experiences of the Teoma[88] search engine and AllTheWeb's FAST technology platform, both of which provide suggestions for narrowing Web searches.

The U.S. Government FirstGov portal is powered by FAST Search and Transfer search engine, the enterprise-solution version of AllTheWeb. In addition to an advanced-search capability with handy features like the ten-word filter, AllTheWeb is "indexing up to 800 news stories per minute." It is "updated every 9 to 11 days as compared to 28 days for Google, and 45-60 for AltaVista."[89] Note however that even if Google takes one to four weeks to crawl a new URL, it "can return results even if it has not yet crawled that page. Pages that are known but haven't been crawled can be returned as results."[90]

- **Teoma: A Virtual Community Drill-Down Search Engine**

Acquired by Ask Jeeves and launched in 2002, Teoma[91] is already forcing established competitors like AltaVista to respond. This contextual search engine organizes its responses in three interesting site categories:

- Refine: sites clustered by topic (naturally occurring communities) with suggestions to narrow the search;

- Results: sites listed based on Teoma's proprietary technique, called *Subject-Specific Popularity*[TM], which "analyzes the relationship of sites within a community, ranking a site based on the number of same-subject pages that reference it, among other things."[92]

- Resources: provides links to expert resources related to the search topic.

By offering users more choices, Teoma merits special attention in the intelligence arena. Each of the above three categories can suggest different drill-down pathways into existing or emerging communities not yet on the radar screen of established search engines.

Rather than limiting their search to a single source and risk losing access to valuable intelligence, searchers should capitalize on the strengths of each general search engine and even consider specialized tools like those discussed in the next paragraph.

4. Specialized Engines and Directories

By focusing on specific subject areas, specialized search engines can save time and are less likely to return trivia.

- ### Science, Engineering and Technology

NEC Research Index[93] is a scientific-literature search engine and digital library providing full-text and autonomous-citation indexing, collaborative filtering, context extraction, query-sensitive summaries, graph analysis, and related document computation.[94] SciNet Science Search[95] is an engine and directory covering engineering, technology and sciences from agriculture and medicine to mathematics. CERN Library provides free access to nearly a quarter million documents in physics, engineering and IT, among others.[96] Powered by master.com, PhysLink[97] is a gateway to physics institutions worldwide including laboratories, think tanks, societies, journals, corporations, universities and other learning resources. The NASA Astrophysics Library is hosted by the Harvard-Smithsonian Center for Astrophysics.[98] Private directory providers include Biolinks,[99] Biologie,[100] Chemie,[101] iCivilEngineer,[102] IT, computer science and statistics Research Papers[103] and SciSeek.[104]

- ### Health, Legal and Communications

In the health field, the leaders are The National Library of Medicine directory,[105] the Health On the Net Foundation's

MARVIN search engine,[106] Medical Matrix,[107] and several private directory providers such as HealthAtoZ[108], Achoo[109] and 9-11.com.

Directories in the legal field include the Legal Research Guide,[110] FindLaw[111] Lawyers.com and LawGuru.[112]

Business, communications and multimedia directories include Company Finder,[113] CanadaOne,[114] Ditto Visual Search Engine[115] and Music Robot.[116] Vivisimo Advanced Search permits concurrent retrieval from a variety of engines, business directories and media sources.[117]

5. Intelligence on Stem-Cell Migration Case

- **The Issue**

Invited for a job interview by a research organization specialized in brain stem-cell migration, a CFO required intelligence on cutting-edge research to prepare for the event. The candidate had undergraduate degrees in science and commerce and a Certified-Public-Accountant (CPA) designation. She had learned the basics of cell biology while working at a summer job twelve years earlier in a governmental research lab, but her knowledge was far from current.

- **The Search-Engine Route**

In the first set of queries (center two columns of Figure 4.1), our candidate went the search-engine route entering the exact phrase "stem cells" and the word "brain" in "All Words" row plus either "migrate" or "migration". The first two general lists successively contained a smorgasbord of 4360 and 5,800 web page documents including comics on stem cells! However, thanks to Google's ranking method, the first ten sites were relevant.[118] Entering the phrase both in singular and plural was worthwhile as it led to additional relevant pages among the first ten responses of each query.

Queries with "Stem Cell" Submitted both in Singular and Plural		First Set of Queries "Stem Cells" + Brain + (Migrate OR Migration)		2nd Set of Queries "Brain Stem Cells" + (Migration OR Migrate)	
		Singular	Plural	Singular	Plural
Google Search Engine	All domains	4,360	5,800	36	192
	Only .org	719	918	3	32
	Only .edu	986	1,430	3	29
	Only .gov	245	296	0	6
	.ca + .uk + .au	501	692	2	19
	gc.ca + .gov.uk +.gov.au	29	28	0	1

Figure 4.1 Search Statistics: Stem-Cell Migration Case

Focusing on selected non-commercial domains (.org, .edu, .gov) led to fewer responses but the first ten items were still relevant. Searching the top-level country domains (.ca, .au, .uk) did not yield much more material specifically of interest to our candidate, although the pages could be of interest to oncologists or educators. Here, our candidate realized, after the fact, that searches with foreign-government domains led to negligible responses and tended to be superfluous inasmuch as their addresses were already part of the first-level country domain names that had been searched.

After sifting through several topical pages for hours and noting interesting tips and queues, the candidate thought of including the word "brain" in the phrase, thus embarking on a second set of queries (see last two columns) searching for "brain stem cells". Although the new query brought the number of responses from 5,800 to 192, five responses out of the first ten were similar.[119] The fact that there was no response overlap between the singular and plural searches is worth noticing. The candidate managed to extract further nuggets from the non-commercial domains in the second set of searches. She ultimately scanned nearly 50 documents and read 12. The total search time alone exceeded an hour. In retrospect, she thinks one way to narrow the scope and focus on current stem-cell literature would have been to limit the search to the last couple of years.

- **The Directory Route**

While attending our seminar on Intelligence three days before the interview, the candidate brought up the search issue. After recognizing the candidate's well-structured and methodical work, and given her background and the scientific nature of the topic, the suggestion was to check the Web's oldest directory, the WWW Virtual Library,[120] clicking on Biosciences which appears right on the home page, and then on Cell Biology. This action quickly led to a world of relevant options, resources and learning opportunities for cell biology scientists and educators as well as basic tutorials for beginners. In less than 15 minutes, the candidate was able to locate the dozen most-pertinent documents.

As a precaution, the candidate was led to the Google Directory going through the path Health, Medicine and Directories. There was a wealth of substantive documents and scientific databases (National Library of Medicine[121] of the National Institute of Health, the Jackson Library[122] and Harding MD of the University of Iowa[123]), and a cluster of commercial sites.

The candidate was finally asked to try inserting "stem cells" and "brain stem cells" in her Internet Explorer Address bar and to her surprise, the MSN Search Engine unobtrusively delivered the bulk of the most widely published documents on the topic!

- **Human-Intelligence: The Ultimate Validity Test**

In order to corroborate the search approach, a class participant located experts on cell biology using two well-known online government directories. Using A-Z Index of FirstGov.gov, he clicked on the Science Office (Dept. of Energy) and found the Life Sciences Division of the Office of Biological and Environmental Research. He also went to the Canadian counterpart: the Cell-Biology desk at the National Research Council via the directory of the Government of Canada (.gc.ca). Contacted by phone, experts in both locations referred the caller to the National Library of Medicine and the WWW Virtual Library. The Canadian scientist added that stem-cell specialists frequently refer to Japan's Riken Brain Science Institute,[124]

Karolinska Institute in Sweden,[125] the Max Planck Institute in Germany[126] and the French CNRS network,[127] among others. It was gratifying to know that these resources were in the index page (related to cell biology) of the WWW Virtual Library discussed earlier.

- Further Tips for Intelligent Search

It is inefficient to use a directory as a search engine, yet casual Web searchers do it inadvertently. Directories are for targeted queries confined to a specific discipline, a territory or a subject area. A search string should therefore not be entered at the top of the decision tree (root level). It is often too early in the search. Most directories group web pages under selected topics and do not bother with "granular cataloguing" at the root level. In the Stem-Cell Migration case, the results would have been less focused and more time would have been wasted, had the search string been entered in Google Directory before clicking Medicine and Directories. By the same token, searching for "brain stem cells" would have been too restrictive at the top level.

In difficult situations where the information returned by search engines and directories is not satisfactory, Andrew Starling suggests to "take your best search terms and add on +*link*, or +*links*. You'll get people's link pages returned. It's a neat trick and often brings results. It's almost guaranteed to get you closer to your goal."[128] Another option is to use *Reverse Linking* (or *Backward Links* in MSN).[129] "The starting point is the best sites and pages you've found so far, the ones that came closest to meeting your needs. What you need to do with these is find out who has linked to them, because there's a good chance they'll have linked to something even better."[130]

Although the Stem-Cell Migration case study is relatively simple, it illustrates the importance of combining directories, expert referrals and multiple search-engine work. In complex intelligence issues, this task is also team-based, which makes it even more important to leverage technology with collective human intelligence.

6. Meta-Engines

Meta-engines like Copernic, Ixquick, SurfWax, MetaCrawler, ProFusion, SearchCaddy and Dogpile use several search engines to overcome the limitations of a single intelligent agent. These are capable of cost-effectively mining a large network of web sites, electronic bulletin boards, information banks and data warehouses. However, meta-engines do not have all of the features generally found in the advanced search option of plain search engines. That is why meta-engines should be used as ice breakers to identify the best engine for a given query and to move to that engine for further drilling.

Copernic is the leading meta-engine that integrates information from multiple sources, eliminates duplication and dead links produced by popular search engines and summarizes documents from e-mails, newsletters, publications and web pages. Copernic searches Google, something only a few meta-engines can do. This is a serious drawback to keep in mind in considering Copernic competitors. UC Berkeley article titled *What is wrong with relying on meta-searchers*[131] is must reading for anyone using meta-engines, even occasionally.

7. Enterprise Knowledge Platforms

Most data originating within an organization has high validity, but it is not readily available for scanning purposes. Ideally, order processing, procurement and all internal systems should be designed with scanning considerations in mind. Some companies use Google to scan their own files and documents. But searching keywords or phrases out of context is inefficient. The online edition of *The Wall Street Journal* went a step further by employing XML to facilitate accurate searching. Thus, a query about firms like Ford, Kroger or Target, yields only information about the companies rather than all instances with similar words or phrases.

The market place offers a growing number of proprietary software products to facilitate the task of collecting, cataloguing and mining business intelligence. Designated Enterprise Knowledge Platforms (EKP) are advanced tools that include The Brain,[132] Factiva[133], LexiQuest[134] or Hyperwave eKnowledge Suite.[135] Fuld (cited above) provides a current list of recommended products for this purpose.

Enterprise Knowledge Platforms facilitate sophisticated indexing, access, contextual retrieval and rule-based queries. They can be used to scan both internal and external databases. Some yield better results on Web searches than conventional search engines. Factiva provides a subscription service for clients to access the professionally indexed content of Dow Jones and Reuters archives. It also licenses its Factiva Intelligent Indexing system in-house.

8. Conclusion

Intelligence tools and platforms are improving in quality and gaining momentum. Innovative products and services are emerging to complement existing ones, fill voids in the quest for acquiring better intelligence faster and at a lower cost. Many, like the newly launched Teoma, are worthy of inclusion in the toolkit of intelligence professionals. Fundamental changes are also on the horizon; some of these could make intelligence scanning even more arduous.[136] In this context, this chapter has provided several illustrations to help readers improve the quality of queries, save time and navigate the Web with greater confidence. Although several practical features of important engines were covered, it is imperative for intelligence professionals to stay current, as the search-engine community is vibrant and rapidly evolving. Fortunately, a host of excellent resources make it possible to keep up with the future of this technology.[137] An attempt will also be made to issue periodic updates of the content of this chapter via the publisher.[138]

> "Aggregation will become part of
> our everyday information lives in the future."
> **Jenny Levine**

This chapter offers a detailed discussion of various sources of intelligence including the Invisible Web, online libraries and online education. It also addresses the importance of looking beyond the Web to get firsthand information.

1. Internal Sources of Business Intelligence

A good starting point for internal intelligence is the corporate memory, an abundant and inexpensive source of intelligence tips that is rarely exploited to its full potential. The memory is made up of digitized information banks, which include daily correspondence, corporate and local databases, hiring and termination interviews and market research buried in archives. Collected and structured for a particular operating activity, most of the digitized data has high validity, but it is not readily available for scanning purposes. In addition, there is a vast reservoir of unrecorded information held by staff members and allies that is neither recorded nor communicated to potential users and beneficiaries.

Leading companies use internal knowledge to study customer loyalty, analyze distribution patterns, recover lost clients and partners, design frequent-user programs, divest themselves of marginal activities and retain profitable customers. They study the linkages between sales fluctuations and competitive campaigns. Some, like Boise Cascade, even manage to trace customers with multiple loyalties by correlating the mean time between orders to the appearance of special offers from local competitors.

Training buyers and customer service staff to seek and capture responses to critical questions as part of their day-to-day work will significantly enrich the scanning exercise and ultimately increase margins. Systematically asking customers placing an order *"how long would the purchase last and when do they think that they may have to order again"* may help you anticipate future needs and go after the next order before the competition. A leading sales representative made it her practice to ask clients what other offers they considered before opting for her product. And in the process, she discovered dark horses emerging as competitors long before her company headquarters noticed their arrival. The cost of capturing such valuable information at the source and automatically alerting decision-makers is trivial in comparison with the benefits.

2. The Informal External and Internal Networks

Before looking far beyond the windows of your office, start with your own informal network of contacts from business, the media, professional associations, your alma mater, the public and third sectors as well as neighbors, friends, colleagues and the community at large. Even your competitors can be a valuable source of intelligence, as the following case involving Alcan demonstrates.

In fighting Dofasco and Stelco in Ontario, Alcan brought together plastic, glass and paper companies. Here, we had "glass and paper and plastics supporting aluminum, even though plastics would fight tooth and nail (against Alcan) to get their share of the market if a new plastic container is allowed."[139]

When our own company was purchasing binding materials for its Harvard Planners, we turned to Blueline, a friendly competitor, with whom we had built a relationship several years previously. Their executives did more than share intelligence. They actually proposed that we combine our orders to get better discounts. This initiative brought down the respective costs of both our firms.

The Glainard case cited in Chapter 3 offers another illustration of how the informal network can be used as a source of intelligence. In that instance, a non-competing vendor was instrumental in corroborating intelligence about a difficult customer. Small companies facing large oligopolies of buyers or sellers must work together to share whatever information they can about a difficult behemoth in order to acquire more power at the negotiating table. However, in order to gain such good standing with competitors, or anyone for that matter, you have to show discretion and nurture genuine trust in advance. By nurturing such a relationship with a non-competing vendor, the supplier in the Glainard case study learned about the credit problems of a major customer before credit agencies posted Glainard's name on their watch list.

3. External Sources: The Information Universe

There is no shortage of external sources, both **open** (unclassified and accessible to anyone) and **proprietary** (syndicated or private). The problem is where to look and how. *The New York Times*, for example, has an elaborate business section. But this leading daily has rarely broken a major business story. Available several hours ahead of the printed version, *The Wall Street Journal*'s electronic edition has a much better track record of publishing late-breaking stories about IPOs and M&As. Its cable news partner, CNBC, also has an enviable record in this area.

External information sources range from publications, printed press and electronic media (including the Internet) to conferences and survey research. Newspaper and magazine scanning should not be restricted to the most popular publications, as many do not reflect the views of change agents and tend to underestimate the potency of leaders with iconoclastic views.

Broad scanning printed media is a tedious pre-Cambrian exercise best left to powerful search engines and providers who make it their core business. Before you search electronically, take a tutorial about what is out there. You may discover that it is worth getting a subscription to an online news service, especially if the service has the know-how and means to access part of the Invisible Web using your personal folder system with customized search criteria.

4. Public Libraries and Google Answers

Despite budget cuts and a growing focus on the Internet, public libraries are still a timesaving, inexpensive and vital resource for intelligence professionals, both in terms of content, tools and search expertise.

Google has just launched Google Answers, a fee-based service of professional researchers dedicated to answer specific questions posted by clients who rate the answer. Web surfers can freely browse and comment on the questions and answers.[140] Google Answers could be a timesaver for unclassified requests with elastic deadlines, particularly for professionals in remote areas and developing countries.

5. The Visible Web Is Growing Fast.
But in the Minor League!

Two solitudes populate the Internet, namely the Visible Web and the Invisible Web. In 2002, the content of the Visible Web consisted of about 4 billion current pages plus the 10 billion pages that had been archived by the Wayback Machine. These archives covered the period 1996-2001 and used a database of more than 100 terabytes, the world's largest.[141] Even if the Wayback-Machine archives are excluded, the Visible Web is growing at a staggering rate of 8 million pages a day or about 3 billion pages a year.

In order to avoid information overload, you may get higher quality content by using engines such as Google or AllTheWeb, and by starting your search with military (.mil), governmental (.gov, .gov.uk or .gc.ca) and educational sites (.edu).

6. The Invisible Web: Mushrooming and Elusive

Search engines do NOT currently index most of the unclassified material produced by online libraries (see below) and governments. The score is worse elsewhere. It is estimated that 85% of business information from non-government sources (academia, private sector) is not indexed and the rate is much higher for military sources. This information is part of the so-called Invisible Web, "which is largely comprised of content-rich databases from universities, libraries, associations, businesses, and government agencies around the world."[142] It consists mostly of non-HTML material that is either available by subscription only or that is stored in PDF files or databases not accessible to search engines and intelligent agents. It is not only much bigger than the Visible Web; it is also growing faster. And this does not even begin to include material that is classified!

Search engines cannot conduct a search without identifying a link pointing to a web page. That is one reason for the existence of the Invisible Web: some of its material is not on a web page. However, a good deal of information on the Invisible Web is accessible to anyone who has the right web page address and who is using the engine specific to the targeted database. UCLA's Rosenfeld Library keeps an excellent up-to-date Business Database Selection Tool.[143] Another way to reach the database web page is to submit a search string to general-web directories such as Yahoo, Google, About.com, Informine or Librarians' Index with a phrase describing the subject matter followed by the term "database" such as "calcium-binding protein database", "infrared database," "venture capital database" or "current M&A database."

UC Berkeley provides a good tutorial on the Invisible Web and a reference table listing recommended directories for academic pursuits that I found helpful in business intelligence collection.[144] Gary Price, a leading authority on the Invisible Web, maintains an extensive portal of "links to the search interfaces of resources that contain data not easily or entirely searchable/accessible from general search tools like Google, or Hotbot."[145] There is even an interesting web site titled www.invisibleweb.com.

Webmasters and content providers can instruct search engines to exclude specific URLs or web pages from their search.[146] And many organizations store policy material and other information but exclude Web links either by design or by accident. As an example, the URLs to some customer-service information, delivery instructions to suppliers, driving directions to business sites and even sales-representative routes are typically given over the phone or by e-mail when the need arises.

An inadequate knowledge of search tools for the invisible Web can limit the scope of the intelligence-collection exercise, skew the analysis to what was accessed, and ultimately risk flawed decisions or policies. This is why it is important to acquire intelligence-collection skills. In the meantime, get expert advice tailored to your needs at a fraction of the cost of going the trial and error route.

7. Directories

- ### Business and Trade Directories

These notes complete the previous chapter's discussion on online directories. A number of portals can search for people and business web sites, e-mail addresses and telephones.[147] The Internet Public Library is a gateway to a wealth of online directories and resources.[148]

Trade directories can also provide information relevant to professional groups. Columbia Books of Washington, Gale Research of Detroit, Dun & Bradstreet, the Conference Board and the Chambers of Commerce compile membership statistics and planned activities of 11,000 active national trade and professional associations and labor unions.

- ### Gateways to Think Tanks and Specialty Experts

There is no shortage of published lists for this purpose. Google provides extensive links to electronic directories from its main portal, but the search can be time-consuming for beginners.[149] Kitty Bennett of the *St. Petersburg Times* compiles a useful list of "organizations that make it possible to search for experts by area of specialty, that provide contact information (phone and e-mail) and that publish the expert's credentials. This list is divided into three parts: sites that are useful for one-stop shopping for experts on a wide variety of topics; good places to look for authors and editors; and organizations arranged alphabetically by specialty area."[150] A comprehensive list of gateways to think thanks and specialty experts is also kept up to date by PDI Global Intelligence team.[151]

8. Free-Access Web Sites and News Aggregators

Executive.org/news connects to media search engines that links to thousands of newspapers, tabloids, magazines and journals, around the world. It also links to directories of live radio stations, TV channels and Web cams that permit users with streaming media to listen to audio or watch TV programs almost instantly from broadcasters worldwide. Thus, users can get "up-to-the-minute" financial, legal, political, military, scientific, technology and current affairs news, speeches, transcripts and press releases from leading North-American and foreign newswires and print media.

Currently on hiatus, *Spyonit*[152] is a free electronic tracking system driven by user-selected topics. It can track stock variations and splits, name changes, items being auctioned, theater tickets going on sale, new references to names of people, places, products, pre-defined weather forecasts and news releases with specific attributes. *Spyonit* reports via e-mail, hand-held PDAs, pagers, Web phones or a personal web page set by the user.

Ad Facts tracks advertising and publicity sponsored by organizations (competition, government, customers) targeted by its clients. Its reports provide detailed intelligence on campaign budgets, press coverage, product positioning and progress of print media and Internet advertising[153].

Cyberalert[154] scans for information and misinformation published about clients.

- **News Aggregators**

Visiting book-marked web sites and news sources is a tedious and time-consuming exercise. With freely available RSS[155] feeds and widely available web-based news-aggregator software, you can automatically get, in one single place, the latest news stories and information from your favorite Internet sources.

Jon Udell,[156] a leading authority on news aggregators, writes in an insightful article in Byte.com:

"...The built-in RSS aggregator has changed how I process information in a dramatic way. At first, my list of channels was biased towards "official" sources — that is, the RSS channels published by newspapers, magazines, and web sites in the areas of interest to me. Increasingly, though, I now rely on other people who are active in these areas, and who are publishing weblogs[157] to which I can subscribe by way of RSS.

There is a deep principle at work here. The relevance engine that powers the emerging RSS network is, very much like Google's relevance engine, decentralized and ultimately social in nature. The links that Google counts are, as Cory Doctorow has said in a beautiful essay "made by human beings, doing what they do best, link by link, drip by drip."[158] Similarly, the raw output of the online news collective is filtered for me by people doing what they do best: spotting patterns, alerting the tribe.

Years ago, I attended a seminar on advanced text processing at which Reuters demonstrated a state-of-the-art news filtering system. It used natural-language-understanding software to read through Reuters' feeds, which then amounted to some 7000 stories per day, and sorted them into bins – a classification service for which customers paid handsomely. Heuristics in the software enabled it to figure out that a story that mentioned "gold" should land in the precious metals bin – unless, that is, it mentioned Mr. Gold, in which case it probably shouldn't.

That filtering mechanism seemed unlikely to me then, and seems even less so now. If not today, then soon, we'll see weblogs written by people who professionally follow precious metals and every other imaginable field. They'll do so because they have to stay on top of these fields, and because they want to establish themselves as authoritative in them.

No single person will be completely authoritative in any one area, but that won't matter – in fact, it's better that way. In the interplay among several weblogs, the sum can be greater than the parts."[159]

9. Online Discussions: Chat, Conferences, Lists, Public Usenet and Private Newsgroups

"Journalist Alexander Wolfe broke a major story, recorded as The Pentium Papers,[160] in November 1994 by picking up on a mathematician's remark in a newsgroup that he had found a bug in Intel's Pentium™ computer chip. The story escalated when Intel admitted that it had already known about the flaw and had failed to disclose the information while at the same time continuing to sell the chip. Further controversy developed when IBM, a major customer for the chip, said that the flaw was much more common than Intel had let on. Consumers inundated Intel with complaints and queries, till the company agreed to replace chips already sold and to start shipping corrected versions."[161]

There are two kinds of newsgroups. Usenet is public. Most companies and universities host private discussion groups that require a password. Although some are frivolous, many news groups can provide valuable knowledge. "You may have trouble getting a hold of someone in the R&D department at Hewlett Packard by calling on the phone. But you may find that you can contact the head of R&D by joining a newsgroup discussion he or she subscribes to and posting a message about a technology. They may choose to stay anonymous on the newsgroup but when they see a technology they like they will contact you directly through the e-mail and reveal their company and title. You may also receive valuable feedback from technical people who know their industry and technology well. They will offer advice on who you should go to and where to look... [However,] it is often difficult to determine a person's qualifications over the Internet. Try to get some background information, company name, and position if possible with anyone you deal with so that their opinions can be qualified."[162]

Google Groups, formerly deja.com, is the best search engine for newsgroups. It indexes and provides Web-based access to the largest collection of searchable newsgroup archives comprising over a billion postings in over 40,000 subject areas![163] It provides valuable tips about navigating Usenet.[164] For the best tutorial on getting the most out of newsgroups, visit the Golden Gate University Web site.[165]

10. Tracking Discontinuity and Other Change

Corporate information is changing daily. "The advantage for competitive intelligence activities is that the updating process itself can offer important information to the alert observer. New staff appointments, the creation of new divisions, price alterations, or the opening of plants or facilities in specific locations can give important insights into the directions which competing companies are taking. Software such as Nearsite[166] will aid in automatically retrieving and filing relevant sites."[167] For less than $20 per year, *mindit.com* and *c4u.com* each provide a service and software that monitor selected web sites and notify subscribers of changes in content, keywords, objects or other criteria.[168]

11. Governments and Congress

There are several good portals for locating the web sites of foreign governments.[169] In North America, governments are by far the biggest providers of reliable material suitable for intelligence collection. But, navigating through the maze of government web sites can be a challenge. Chuck Malone, Government Information Librarian at Western Illinois University, created a valuable tutorial to help users get what they want faster.[170] Through its GPO Access site, the U.S. Superintendent of Documents provides a multi-database search engine for open-source government and congressional documents and legislation.[171]

Hosted by the U.S. Department of Energy, the Virtual Library of Energy, Science and Technology provides a worldwide gateway to refereed papers and technical reports in a variety of disciplines (biology, chemistry, energy, environmental sciences, physics, nuclear medicine and technology) as well as in multidisciplinary databases.[172]

North-American contractors can learn about the latest government procurement opportunities worldwide through GSA, its NAFTA counterparts[173] and embassy trade-mission sites. Note, however, that many agencies and departments like the U.S. Department of State[174] have their own special sites for contracting opportunities. Scientists can find about government R&D and technical publications, patent descriptions and FDA clinical trials through the U.S. FedWorld[175] portal, the U.S. Library of Congress[176] and Canada's NRC.[177] SourceCan, which can be accessed through Industry Canada's Strategis,[178] permits Canadian businesses to reach and be reached by potential importers and exporters throughout the world.

Available only through elected representatives, the U.S. Library of Congress, through the Congressional Research Service (CRS), publishes executive briefs on issues facing the nation every month. Supported by outstanding literature searches, these briefs guide Members of Congress proposing or considering various bills and legislative issues.

Several global corporations have developed effective tools for scanning and screening congressional briefs to spot emerging issues, which may affect their future. For instance, a longitudinal analysis of the volume of bills clearly indicates a constant shift in priorities. Vietnam and other foreign policy issues dominated the sixties. The seventies and early eighties were largely taken up with minority rights, unemployment and environment. The rights of the handicapped, inflation and energy then took over into the nineties. The Clinton era weathered free trade, deficit cutting, technology and ethics. The millennium began with health, genetically modified food and bioethics, education, technology and surplus allocation issues. However, the tragedies of September 11, 2001 brought security, anti-terrorism and ally building to the top of the public policy agenda.

12. Universities

The Advanced Search page of Google provides a direct link to the databases of a fast-growing number of universities throughout the world.[179] Leading university libraries (e.g., Berkeley, Caltech, Chicago, Harvard, MIT, Penn and Stanford) are extremely valuable to issue managers and technologists. As an illustration, the site of Caltech's Millikan Library hosts a general-reference page with commonly sought links that is considered a model for academic intranets.[180] The University of Chicago compiles a current directory of laws by country and topic.[181]

13. Other Public-Domain Providers

These public-domain sources include:

1. Broadcasters and cable news companies: CNBC, CNNfn, ABC business news,[182] Financial Time TV[183], the BBC and CBC Newsworld.

2. Main Portals: About.com, AltaVista, Britannica, Disney's Go.com, Excite, Groups.google.com, HotBot and Lycos of Terra Lycos, Search.com, Searchmil.com (for military sites) and Yahoo.

3. Corporate information providers: Dun & Bradstreet, Hoover's Online, Market Guide, Researchmag, Strategis (Canadian companies) and wisi.com (worldwide).

4. Public filings (10K, UCC, annual reports): Irin, from investor relations information network, 10kwizard, freeEDGAR, and annual reports of selected international companies from Global-reports, Reportgallery and Public Register's Annual Report Service (prars.com).

5. Real-time stock-price providers: bigcharts.com. Market Guide, Quote from Lycos, North-American Quotations (naq.com), Redherring, Canada Stockwatch and eSignal (includes European stock data).

6. Other resources for investors: Morningstar, The Motley Fool, Smartmoney, The Street.com, IPOcentral, InvestorGuide, Investorprotection.org, IPOexpress and ThomsonInvest.net.

7. Venture capital databases: Infon.com, Vcaonline.com, Vcprodatabase.com

8. Internet mailing-list providers: List-universe.com, Tile.net and Topica.

9. Worldwide post-office portal: Postoffice.com.

10. Electronic newsletters from banks and other financial institutions, consulting companies, associations, trade groups, research establishments, businesses, and UN agencies.

14. Proprietary Media, Databases and Online Libraries

Researchers looking to access proprietary media generally pay for the service by subscriptions, standing orders, transaction fees or site-licensing arrangements. UCLA's Rosenfeld Library is the starting point for anyone interested in searching top business databases. Its web site provides a database selection tool that describes, in a well-presented grid form, the practical features of over 70 databases[184] including Bloomberg, the Business Source, EIU Country Reports, Hoover's Online, Lexis-Nexis, ProQuest, and Standard & Poor's Research Insights.

Fee-based Dow Jones Interactive,[185] Lexis-Nexis,[186] Dialog and Profound[187] provide business intelligence on major companies and articles from thousands of business publications (newspapers, magazines, broadcast transcripts, news wires, legal reports, congressional briefs and government information). They permit customization of searches and personal investment portfolios. They provide 24-hour-a-day updates of business and geopolitical news from a vast arsenal of partners and global correspondents. In terms of the free content available on Dow Jones Interactive "…there are several well-written, step-by-step tutorials that spell out the best methods for researching companies and industries using any kind of sources."[188]

Jane's Intelligence Review (online.janes.com) focuses on global defense, aerospace, transportation, potential conflicts and security threats.

Updated weekly, *ABI/Inform* covers over 1,000 business journals with text, graphs and charts on corporate strategy, IT, finance, health care, law, taxation, marketing, banking, insurance, real estate and telecommunications.

Other sources include Bloomberg and Reuters (real-time stock quotes and financial news), Thomasregister (manufacturers), Knight-Ridder, and newswire services. Most newsrooms use Assignment Editor[189] to gain direct access to content (transcripts, archives) from major local, national and world papers, magazines and news wires (AP, Reuters, AFP, UPI). The site provides links to specialized world directories (reverse directories, schools, maps, terrorists, prisoners, child predators, fires, hurricanes, quakes).

There are a number of organizations offering syndicated services. Many of the following are already household names: Arthur D. Little,[190] Batelle,[191] the Brookings Institution,[192] the C.D. Howe Institute[193], the Conference Board[194], the Council on Foreign Relations,[195] Gallup[196], the Fraser Institute[197], Louis Harris[198], the Hudson Institute[199], MIT System Dynamics Group[200], the OECD[201], Opinion Research Corp.[202], Pricewaterhouse-Coopers[203], Rand[204], Research International[205], Roper[206], Stanford Research Institute[207], the Survey Research Center of the University of Michigan[208] and Yankelovich[209].

Most syndicated services cited above also operate throughout the Americas, Europe and the Pacific Rim. In Canada, *The National Post*[210] and *The Globe and Mail*[211] provide economic, financial and business information. Fee-based CCN Newswire[212] monitors 2,500 publications. Leading message boards like Yahoo, The Motley Fool and Stockhouse e-mail clients a daily briefing on the topics of their choice.

- **Paper-Based Publications**

Paper-based publications include books, monographs, working papers, unpublished dissertations and conference proceedings, directories and statistical abstracts. While still growing in actual number, these publications now account for a smaller percentage of the information universe. In fact, more and more are digitized to increase access, facilitate retrieval and boost sales. Leading publishers, who originally were reluctant to disseminate copyrighted material over the Web, are licensing online libraries that have a global reach and remarkable search power.

• **Online Libraries**

While the number of generalized search engines is declining, there is no shortage of online libraries providing copyrighted content from the invisible Web and known publishers. The University of Pennsylvania provides a comprehensive directory of books and publications "freely readable over Internet".[213] Private virtual libraries[214] include Questia, ebrary, Jones Knowledge and XanEdu. The leader Questia Media[215] hosts the world's largest collection of complete books and journal articles. XanEdu[216] taps into the ProQuest repository of dissertations, microfilmed print media and professional journals. Ebrary[217] permits free access to an extensive library of digitized books and journals but has a user-friendly fee structure. It only charges a minimal fee for an entire publication and much less for selected pages within a publication. Jones E-Global Library[218] is a relatively smaller library geared for distance education with librarians accessible around the clock.

HBS Working Knowledge[219] features topical information and interviews with leading professors and business executives on a host of subjects relevant to decision-makers. In cooperation with Brint,[220] the Ministry of Defense of Singapore hosts an excellent virtual library on knowledge management.[221]

• **Online Education and Digital-Campus Providers**

Educational institutions such as Cornell, Chicago, Harvard Medical School, McGill, MIT, Yale School of Medicine, Columbia Teachers College, DuPont University and Motorola University, are leveraging their core competencies in face-to-face education by developing a larger role in online learning. In the process, many are raising the quality of education, expanding their reach to new markets, improving productivity and tapping into unprecedented opportunities to license their courseware to other educational institutions and business organizations worldwide.

For businesses, e-learning is emerging as a competitive advantage rather than simply a cost-cutting intervention. It speeds up skills training. It also leverages and extends the reach of scarce professional-development resources. But e-learning requires special preparation for both the learners and the trainers. Participants must be able to focus, manage their time and be self-motivated to work either alone or in collaborative mode.

The leading e-education platforms provide customizable campus portals with extensive software for teaching and learning online plus course and campus management applications. As an example, Blackboard[222] suite features discussion boards, collaborative communication, progress tracking, calendars, e-mail, links to the Internet and direct access to all course documents, virtual libraries and multimedia archives (video, audio, flash, shockwave). It also provides an e-commerce platform for students plus billing and access to campus events and administrative services. Blackboard is also the training and development platform of choice in companies committed to lifetime learning. Other leading e-education providers include Campus Cruiser, Campus Pipeline, Jenzabar and Web Course Tools (WebCT).[223] The Center of Instructional Technology of UC in San Francisco[224] provides excellent Web-based instruction resources along with free WebCT tutorial for educators.

The Virtual-U open-source software of Simon Fraser University permits thousands of students to freely access internet-based education from participating schools and universities worldwide.[225]

In the business realm, Mentergy is a leading courseware provider with its world-class flagship product LearnLinc. It has partnered with CRK Interactive and Docent to deliver integrated sales training solutions. Other online training providers[226] include Avilar, Learnspace (Lotus) and WBT Systems.

With fragmented competition and pressure for standardization, consolidation is bound to accelerate. Already in 2002, Blackboard has acquired Prometheus, a leading competitor. Under the Advanced Distributed Learning initiative, the Department of Defense and the White House brought together major users and providers of e-learning to develop guidelines for "accessible, interoperable, durable, reusable, adaptable and affordable learning software."[227] The practical objective is to ensure that educational courseware (content) can be accessible regardless of the vendor platform. The pressure for open specifications and support for IEEE[228] standards is also echoed by IMS Global Learning Consortium,[229] the Wellspring,[230] the ARIADNE Foundation[231] and MIT Open Knowledge Initiative[232] backed by leading universities.

15. Conferences and Trade Fairs

Professional societies and governments host major conferences on the future directions of technology, biotech, education, aerospace, and health and drugs, among other subjects. These can be quite valuable inasmuch as change agents who are eager to earn the recognition of their peers occasionally (and sometimes unknowingly) use these events to disclose hard-earned intelligence.

Motorola's Chief Intelligence Officer, Jan P. Herring, insists on teamwork in conferences and trade shows as essential to ongoing competitive intelligence. "Tracking the competition is everyone's job. The more closely people work together, the better they do. For example, companies often send 15 or 20 people to a big trade show. But how often do those people bother to compare notes? Companies should do what's called 'quarterbacking'. At several points during the show, get into a huddle and ask: What have we learned? What else do we need to know? Eventually that quarterbacking mentality becomes an everyday thing".[233]

- Early-Adopter Symposia

Participating in these events can provide early warning signals on precursors' jurisdictions where national issues tend to emerge first. For example, Monsanto regularly tracks "precursor" states, which include Connecticut, California and Michigan. Intelligence agents should pay particular attention to the early adopters. To take an international example, Sweden has been at the leading edge of institutional reform, often at a pace far beyond its means. Its proposed reforms were the subject of debate at the conferences and symposia of the Swedish Employer Federation, years before they were adopted. Similarly, the Netherlands has been a silent champion of international aid. Florence (Italy) and Tokyo (Japan) are pace setters in robotics. New York took over from Milan and Paris in many segments of the fashion world. Virtual teams were using full-motion video in Silicon Valley (California) long before the establishment took notice of this technology in the aftermath of 9-11. It should be added that close observation of smaller firms can be rewarding since they tend to introduce innovations faster because they have nothing to gain by waiting.

Before making a significant investment in software acquisition or e-business development, it is worthwhile to keep up-to-date on the latest activities of the World Wide Web Consortium (W3C)[234], particularly with respect to XML, a mark-up language featuring enhanced customization and accurate searching that is bound to have a profound impact on communications and world commerce. Today's W3C discussions offer a preview of tomorrow's global Internet standards.

16. Surveys and Other Research

Another potent source of scanning material is survey research. In *The Image of the Future*, Fred Polak demonstrates that what the public thinks will happen has a definite impact on what does happen.[235] That is why opinion scanning is an important ingredient of strategy formulation.

Syndicated studies done by reputable providers can be valuable.[236] They show current public opinion on a host of issues. In some instances, it is possible to examine the views of sub-groups by income, age, geographic area, gender, ethnic or political affiliation, educational background, occupational category, buying profile and lifestyle.

General data from syndicated studies and data mining should be supplemented with special surveys to provide measures on sensitive questions that are proprietary to the organization. On critical questions, tracking studies should also be conducted frequently to monitor changes in attitudes, perceptions or behavior.

Most public surveys suffer from respondent bias. Validity and reliability tests are imperative, as a recent Gallup survey indicated. The survey found that a significant number of U.S. respondents could not define the European Union. In general, people do not know enough about the choices of the future and are only concerned with immediate personal change. Sometimes, more reliable information can be obtained by surveying policy-makers. To this end, data is available about the attitudes and opinions of influential members of society. For example, the

OECD countries systematically survey the views of business and labor leaders, government executives and legislators, experts and change advocates.

Among the proprietary providers of competitive-intelligence research, Recon CI Solutions,[237] CCS International[238] and the Phillips Group[239] have built a reputation for providing up-to-date intelligence about their clients' current and emerging competitors. They provide briefs on the competition's business plans, cost structure and sales strategies, allies and potential partners, as well as potential targets for mergers or acquisitions.

17. Best Sources of Information: Crafting Your Current List

A vibrant and mutually supportive competitive-intelligence community is stimulating a market for information that is growing at fast pace. However, keeping up to date with the latest sources of information, stakeholders and communities is still a challenging task. The web sites of Competia, Fuld and SCIP[240] have excellent links to sources of business information. Through the *Resources* feature of Teoma (discussed in Chapter 4) and Google search engines and Google Directory, you can get the latest lists of providers and emerging communities focusing on specific economic, educational, scientific, military or government sectors. Several searches are required with each engine. Enter the phrases *"sources of competitive intelligence"* and *"competitive intelligence sources"* complemented by key words related to your issue or field. Also replace the term *competitive* with words like *business, marketing, government or defense*. For non-commercial sources (governments, NGOs, UN agencies and other international organizations), restrict the search to .org, .int and government domains (.gov, .mil, .gc.ca).

It is highly recommended to build and maintain a database of intelligence sources tailored to meet your specific needs. Validate the knowledge gleaned from think tanks, networks, voluntary organizations, trade and industry associations, and keep in mind the context, perspective and vested interest of the provider.[241]

18. Mining the Internet: Some Caveats

The Internet is a unique reservoir of information with endless possibilities. There are, however, managers who rely solely on the World Wide Web for competitive intelligence[242]. Leveraging Web content is an inevitable part of the process of scanning for intelligence. But it should be one part of a far more rich and diverse set of activities that also include syndicated services, personalized research and fieldwork that combines people and various technologies. As indicated in Chapter 1, the unrecorded knowledge residing in the heads of your stakeholders is significant, even in the best run companies.

Furthermore, it is essential to validate your findings regardless of their source. Consider the panic selling due to a bogus press communiqué released through the Internet on August 25, 2000. It brought down Emulex's stock price from $110 to $45, a total loss of more than $2 billion in 30 minutes! Rather than following the bandwagon, I turned to CNBC before making a move. Listening to the cautious words of Stock Editor Joe Kernen, who prefers to validate information instead of championing spooks, I was reassured and even bought more shares. Joe's distinguished experience combines molecular biology at MIT, finance in Wall Street and over ten years of closely watching business trends.

When the stakes are high, field intelligence may be a necessity. Shiseido actually established a small perfume factory, a laboratory and a beauty salon in France's perfume-industry cluster to gain first-hand intelligence and boost its new-perfume value chain in R&D, marketing and customer service.

Fuld quotes Jan P. Herring, a 20-year CIA veteran, who subsequently led Motorola's intelligence team for more than 10 years. "Most information never gets written down – it's just floating in people's heads. The only way to access that information is to talk to people... If you find an interesting paper on the Web, don't just download it – call the author after you read it. Attending conferences is still the best way to make connections and gather intelligence. You'll hear things that never make it onto the Net. And remember: the best information on your competitors comes from your customers".[243]

- **Beware of Tipping Off Adversaries**

Mining electronic media and building virtual communities are also strategic options for your foes: unprecedented transparency, resulting from the massive volume of intelligence information available through the Internet, is attracting a greater number of both friendly and hostile stakeholders to delve deeper into business and government issues, resources and operations. Policy- and decision-makers are now under greater pressure to address issues quickly, and they frequently do so with excessive haste. They must also continually upgrade the ways in which they safeguard intellectual property and deal with a plethora of actors who are intent on applying intelligence to nefarious ends.

19. Conclusion

In most organizations, intelligence is in! Yet, many adopters still overlook valuable information by relying solely on techniques or surfing the Internet without enhancing these through intelligence gathering skills. Intuitive and common sense moves have focused on an uncritical acceptance of scanning tools and information. This narrow view falls short of dealing with the complex reality of competitive intelligence.

Smart strategists are also "channel-agnostic". They know that employees, suppliers and clients are the most undervalued intelligence hunting grounds. They use the Web extensively but cautiously, and only as a starting point. In a knowledge-driven economy, every manager should get a crash course on the peculiarities of the Invisible Web and on the power and limitations of search engines, online libraries, news aggregators, Usenet, public-domain providers, trading portals and exchanges.

This chapter built on the foundations of the intelligence road map, framework, tools and platforms covered previously to focus on both internal and external intelligence sources. It is now clear that intelligence gathering is a discipline and a skill-driven endeavor, not a hobby. Without rigorous organization and a valid framework, the effort is wasteful. With the information explosion and the plethora of growing threats, the dilemma of what to scan and what not to scan will be with us forever. Fortunately, there is a continuous stream of new developments in the weapons of competitive intelligence. Effective managers will use these to enhance their intelligence and counterintelligence arsenals.

> Selective disclosure of information
> about itself is a crucial resource the firm has in
> making competitive moves. The disclosure of any information should
> only be made as an integral part of competitive strategy.
> **Michael E. Porter**

1. A Deterrent and a Golden Shield

Unlike the ill-fated 1941 attack on the port of Dieppe, the 1944 Normandy invasion site was a well-kept secret. The consensus of expert opinion was that the Allies and the British, in particular, did an exceptional job in slipping out red herrings that pointed to Calais rather than Normandy. Without advance information on the date, scope and exact location of the attack, the Germans failed to move their armies to Normandy to counter-act the landings and prevent the Allies from gaining a foothold on the continent.[244]

- Definition

Counterintelligence is the protective multi-layered *shield* that hides your weaknesses from those who, by knowing them, can benefit at your expense. It is also used to limit the exposure of your strengths to those who ought to know them. It is the ongoing defensive process by which an organization "looks inward through the lenses of the adversary" to block its exposure to economic, cyber and industrial espionage, talent defections, fraud, terrorism, hacking, negligence, over-disclosure, illicit acquisition of proprietary information and other security risks.

Unfortunately, it is often only after things have gone wrong that counterintelligence is noticed and then only because it has been absent all along. To shield themselves from spies, intruders, hackers and thieves, organizations spend $78 billion a year on security, $7 billion of that on computer firewalls and hardware. Yet most intelligence leaks and security violations can be traced to human causes within organizations.

The previous chapters covered intelligence collection, validity, analysis, resources and organization. Counterintelligence builds on these tools. In this chapter, we will address two complementary objectives. Firstly, we will use examples to caution the reader about the actual risks that affect even the best-run companies. Secondly, we will provide a road map of specific actions that can be taken to shield an organization from exposure to such risks. Subsequent chapters will examine implementation issues associated with nurturing strong allies and steering the organization away from decisions driven by surprise events.

2. How Good Organizations Lose Intelligence

The World War II slogan "loose lips sink ships" reflects the first commandment of counterintelligence. The best scanning and competitive intelligence are worthless if your organization or its suppliers leak hard-earned intelligence and know-how to its competitors. This is a lesson learned by Microsoft, IBM and Gillette in their dealings with Oracle, Fujitsu and Bic respectively. Let us look at the predators, the sources of leaks and some real-life cases.

- ### The Predators

Some companies use spies masquerading as buyers to gather information about competitors. Others have gone as far as creating ISO-certified office-cleaning firms and non-profit associations to gain access to the laboratories of their competitors. Government-owned telephone companies throughout the world routinely intercept calls, facsimile transmissions, and electronic data interchange (EDI) information (bills, bids, contracts, pricing data). Diplomats, civil servants and business executives use carefully nurtured relationships and legitimate business transactions as a cover for clandestine intelligence gathering.

- ## Sources and Propagation Vectors of Leaks

The staff turnover and day-to-day operation of a business are bound to cause leakage of confidential information. "When done deliberately, occasional controlled disclosures can serve the corporate interests. But where disclosures are made absent-mindedly in the ordinary course of business, a company will stand to lose its competitive edge."[245] Most company secrets are obtained legally. Topping the sources is excessive disclosure to government (corporate filings), the staff (internal newsletters), the media (press releases, impromptu briefings), trade publishers, banks, credit agencies (Standard & Poor's, Dun & Bradstreet) and other third parties who disseminate these intelligence leaks. The culprits in this process can include ignorant, careless, indiscrete, disgruntled or unscrupulous employees, clients, vendors, partners and former employees.

The case of disgruntled Army private Aaron R. Eden is far from isolated. Using Back Orifice 2000 remote control hacker tool from his home, Eden managed to steal passwords and software, and alter thousands of military personnel records on computers at the Enlisted Records and Evaluation Center of the U.S. Army in Indianapolis. "In building its case against Eden, the computer crime unit showed that the private had logged on to the network as the systems administrator, deleting personnel files when the systems administrator was away from the building. The technology used to gather evidence included the law enforcement application EnCase, which enabled agents to scan hard drives... Essentially, the IT crime unit launches controlled attacks on its LAN to see how an incident took place. In addition, the investigative agents are just as concerned about insider attacks as those coming from outside hackers."[246]

"Today, no agency is immune from attack by a hacker, like Eden, who is patient, dedicated and technologically adept. And in the hands of outlaw corporations, criminal syndicates or enemy nations, techniques such as those used by Eden could bring whole departments, even cities or the nation, to their knees."[247]

- ## Dumpster Diving: How Rivals Can Intimately Map Your Business from Small Nuggets in Your Trash

Anyone who has a toll-free line gets a monthly statement detailing the phone numbers of in-coming callers plus a summary

81

and billing details on the first page. Most organizations only keep the summary sheet with the payables. The detailed list can exceed 500 pages and is generally doomed to the wastebasket given the very low cost of each call. Yet, that list can be highly informative to some competitors who will spare no effort to get at it.

In addition to providing phone numbers of your customers, the list is a snap shot of your pattern of business. Even if paper waste is destined for shredding, your staff, office cleaners and the staff of your long-distance carrier may sometimes be offered thousands of dollars to copy such lists prior to disposal.

Oracle has used undercover agents to collect Microsoft waste paper from garbage dumps. When the scheme was revealed, Oracle did not deny it. In another case, a European diplomat was caught picking up trash bags from the Houston residence of a high-tech executive.

It is even technically feasible to collect DNA samples from used paper tissues in the trash — and there is nothing in law to prevent it.

These illustrations show the extent to which everyone should be trash conscious both at work and at home!

- A Preventable But Costly-to-Ignore Trap

Counterintelligence also means keeping an eye on strategic allies and performing basic due-diligence to mitigate risks. Consider the plight of Xillix of British Columbia, which failed to do so.

"Xillix, a BC company in the medical device field, formed a strategic alliance with Olympus Optical of Japan in the early 90's and disclosed some of their trade secrets. Unknown to Xillix management, Olympus proceeded to file a number of *Japanese* patents based on the Xillix proprietary technology. Only in 1998 did Xillix discover this when a U.S. Olympus patent was issued. Although Xillix won the subsequent legal battle, the company came near bankruptcy. A little competitive-intelligence effort would have provided some early warning, since the *Japanese* patent applications were published *years* earlier."[248]

- Hotels and Meeting Places: Hot Beds for Leaks

While the hotel cleaners are preparing your room, covert agents, pretending to be guests, can access the premise and even check your luggage. The FBI advises executives to travel ultra-light and to always keep valuable documents and data in sight and within reach. They should neither receive faxes nor state their company name, particularly in foreign hotels. Other sensitive locations include bugged restaurant tables and even airline seats.

As an illustration, Hewlett-Packard accidentally found out about the launch of a new competing product from a hotel employee who was booking a nation-wide conference for a competitor. This example suggests that it may be necessary to use code names or third parties in planning strategic functions and meetings.

- **The Friendly Visitors with a Hidden Agenda**

"Companies also should limit access to areas where trade secrets are stored and where confidential processes are carried out. One company that recognized a leak in its corporate security plan is W.K. Kellogg Co. of Battle Creek, MI. It decided to stop its eighty-year-old practice of conducting public tours of its plants when security consultants discovered spies from European cereal makers taking tours of the plant. Kellogg felt certain they were observing its manufacturing methods."[249]

Peter Schweitzer describes several economic espionage cases perpetrated by U.S. allies targeting U.S. corporations.[250] Among them, a visiting chemist on a covert intelligence mission to DuPont "inadvertently" dipped "the end of his necktie in a vat of chemicals. Over his protests about the sentimental value of the necktie, DuPont officials required that the visitor surrender the necktie to the company."[251]

- **Posting Ads for Non-existent Jobs**

Fortune Magazine revealed Marriott's practice of posting ads for non-existent jobs and interviewing managers of competing hotel chains to secure intelligence about salaries and benefits, training and other management practices.[252] In their eagerness to mobilize talent, some managers even go further, as Leonard Condenzio suggests:

"You read a success story in one of the trade journals and you're impressed. Instead of waiting until the featured person is applying for a job, call and say, "Hey, by the way, I just read about you; you did a good job. How would you like to talk to us about any future possibilities?" When hearing about an organizational change, consider contacting a member of the staff... ask if they are comfortable with the change... "I met you a while ago and I was impressed. I understand there's been a change, and if it is not going as well as you expected, call me if you are interested in coming to work with us."... You learn that someone just had a new child, bought a new home, new car, is currently funding their kids in college tuition. Perhaps you feel you can offer a better quality of life, or a better benefit package, and better compensation, and you have a job opening. Call people who are already working, maybe you can offer something a little more attractive, and they'll come to you with greater enthusiasm. Whatever the case: a merger, a buyout, or a new management firm takes over. These actions present change and thus opportunity for you. This is just another way of looking for people."[253]

- A Growing Threat: Your Lap Top and PDA

In July 2001, the FBI reported the loss of 184 of its own laptops including 13 that had been stolen. "At least one of the laptops, and possibly as many as four, contained classified information. One, it was thought, might hold details about espionage cases... Over the past two years, the Energy and State departments have made similar disclosures."[254]

In London, a tabloid was offered top-secret stealth-fighter documents that were contained on a laptop left in a U.K. train station. The British Ministry of Defense (MOD) reports that an average of 50 laptops are lost every year, mostly on public transportation. As of 2002, MOD laptops with classified information will be carried in briefcases with a built-in feature that erases the machine hard drive when the lock is forced or the laptop is opened without the right code.

Moreover, "companies have reported break-ins in which laptop computers or disks were stolen, even when there were easily obtainable, more valuable items in the same vicinity. These instances are not always reported, or reported as merely break-ins, without considering the possibility that the target was information rather than equipment."[255] A GE Power Systems consultant was detained for stealing a gas turbine blade and secret information that was included in "a large quantity of computer discs, manuals, notebooks and scientific papers." [256]

In North America, over 200 palm tops and 60 laptops disappear daily in restaurants, airports, hotels, taxis and train stations. In 95% of the cases, the information contained on the hard drive can be read in a matter of seconds by using an Activex routine (among others) that bypasses the user password. Yet, there is a host of very inexpensive products and preventive measures that can prevent unauthorized disclosure. These include physical locks (Microsaver, Kryptonite), motion detectors (iSpy, SonicLock) and hidden sirens (Caveo) as well as software (file enciphering). When an unauthorized user goes online, undetectable security software such as BlackIce, Defender, LapTrak, CyberAngel and Computrace can connect the lost machine to its owner, manufacturer or software provider who can alert the police or military. Many machines fitted with these products have already been recovered from thieves.

3. Where to Find Reliable Expertise

- Government

The above examples are not isolated. Everyone knows about leaks or break-ins affecting business and government. Counterintelligence experts and the American Society of Information Security (ASIS) indicate that security breaches unknown to companies exceed reported cases by a ratio of 15 to 1 in negligent companies and they are no better than 3 to 1 even in the best-run companies.

Fortunately, the marketplace and several government agencies offer valuable assistance that can bring down that ratio, in some instances on a cost-recovery basis (particularly in the most sensitive areas such as IT).

In Canada, the Communications Security Establishment (CSE) offers state-of-the-art IT security expertise commercially. In R&D and national security, CSE teams up with the National Security Agency (NSA) and the Communication-Electronics Security Group (CESG), its British counterpart. The three are world leaders in secure connectivity – cryptography (secure telecommunications, secure Web applications, e-mail and computers) and radiation security (Tempest). Although its I.T. core mission[257] is focused on government and defense security, CSE provides consulting, training, vulnerability assessment and technical assistance in information protection and IT security to equipment manufacturers and software developers, banks and other companies.

The National Counterintelligence Executive (NCIX) reports on methods used by foreign agents to obtain U.S. corporate intellectual property illicitly. It also outlines the defensive measures applied by government agencies to counter such activities.[258] The FBI provides regular e-mails through ANSIR, a component of the National Threat Warning System (NTWS).[259] It provides awareness training on threats and measures used to protect intellectual property from illicit acquisition. Its National Infrastructure Protection Center helps U.S. companies track and prosecute intruders worldwide.

The Office of Intelligence and Threat Analysis (ITA) of the State Department maintains an unclassified electronic exchange portal (EBB) describing over 50,000 cases of foreign threats and other security-related information. The CIA and the DOD conduct risk assessments and briefing sessions on defensive travel, on intelligence-gathering practices, and on the hardware and software used by various countries and visitors targeting U.S. know-how and technology. The DOD provides security countermeasure programs and publishes the *Security Awareness Bulletin* and *Countering Espionage* videos.[260]

The Canadian Security Intelligence Service (CSIS) provides examples and a useful list of "suspicious indicators of economic espionage."[261]

MITRE is a non-profit world-class organization that serves U.S. defense, government and non-profit organizations. It provides solutions to a wide range of information security needs. Examples include security policy, training, risk analysis, secure databases, firewalls, smart cards, digital signatures, public key technology, network authentication, and Internet security. MITRE has created Felt, a language for studying the behavior of security guards. It also operates R&D centers for the Department of Defense, the Federal Aviation Administration and the Internal Revenue Service. MITRE's "rapid mapping" technology was used daily at Ground Zero to "enable rescue crews to locate fires, chemical tanks, and other dangers among the rubble" in order to facilitate safe and prompt recovery.[262]

- **Private Providers**

DuPont Consulting Solutions provides exclusive access to E.I. du Pont de Nemours global leadership and unique experience in intellectual and physical property protection. Its mission is to share with accredited clients its parent company's knowledge, best practices and skills in safety and intelligence security.[263]

IBM Global Security Solutions provides advanced safety and security software and consulting services. In addition to an extensive worldwide network of 3,000 security experts and engineers, IBM has more than 100 researchers in security-related technologies working in security labs and security competency centers.[264] IBM also partners with Kroll, a leading global provider of risk management and counterintelligence services, to assess IT infrastructure security, espionage, cyber-intrusion, business interruption risks and disaster-recovery capability.[265]

Integrated Security Solutions (ISS) is a leader in the development and delivery of integrated physical access security systems. Its installations include airports, embassies, defense establishments, high-tech companies, the New York Stock Exchange and several financial institutions.[266]

RSA Security provides e-security solutions including authentication, authorization, encryption and public key management systems. Its RSA Conference is the leading cryptography and data security event in the world.[267]

Phoenix Consulting Group tailors integrated competitive business intelligence and counterintelligence programs based on the specific needs of each client using effective, legal and ethical methods.[268]

ThunderStore focuses on threats from trusted users, be they negligent, careless or disgruntled employees or allies. It provides solutions to deal with insider threats by electronically managing access and monitoring the use of digital resources (files, applications, communication protocols) and business processes, documenting user behavior and ensuring compliance with intelligence-security policies.[269] The approach to intelligence security is multi-layered. In addition to preventing unauthorized browsing, copying and manipulation of files and documents, ThunderStore also enables document encryption, among other options.

Rpost is a new e-mail and electronic documents registration service using a patent-pending process that is invisible to senders and receivers. As an independent intermediary, Rpost offers "traceable, transparent and tamper-proof" message delivery security system to protect the sender.[270]

Timely intelligence about criminal activity and public safety can save lives. Enhanced 9-1-1 is a system that is well known to increase the effectiveness of the police and other emergency services by automatically and quickly locating callers as soon as the phone rings, even if the person dialing hangs up before making a contact with the call center. Reverse 9-1-1 is a more recent derivative system, which increases the flow of intelligence from the police and other public-safety agencies back to the community. It provides intelligence by e-mail, voice mail or fax to specific neighborhoods and subscribers with particular needs. Reverse 9-1-1 should be an integral part of the risk-prevention system of every law-enforcement agency, utility, transporter, health-care facility and any other company handling potentially harmful products (food, drugs, chemicals) or high-risk locations.

CML Emergency Services is a world leader in providing telecommunications and radio-dispatch systems to 9-1-1 call centers and other Public Safety Answering Points. Its equipment manages 9-1-1 call centers around the world. With over 900 locations installed in the United States alone, CML possesses extensive intelligence to help law-enforcement agencies and organizations with a vested interest in public safety prevent and be prepared to promptly handle emergency incidents.[271]

- Getting Inexpensive Intelligence

An independent body, the Federation of American Scientists[272], provides tips and links to government intelligence agencies throughout the world.

Several sites provide a free forum for consumers and corporate buyers to publish and view complaints about products and services.[273] Some pay a royalty based on the frequency of access to published complaints.

Used in the counterintelligence community, *Cyberalert, Spyonit* and *Ad Facts* are free electronic search services discussed in the section titled External Sources of Business Intelligence (Chapter 5).

Finally, Leonard Fuld (cited above) offers an extensive bibliography and "webliography" of both competitive intelligence and counterintelligence services.

4. Counterintelligence Road Map

- **Target Risks**

Counterintelligence scanning must cover constituencies and other risk-prone elements scattered throughout your value chain. These constituencies comprise current and lost customers, suppliers, staff, business allies and adversaries ranging from competitors who play by the rules to the underground fanatics who don't. We will learn more about them in Chapters 9 and 10.

- **20 Practical Steps to Build Counterintelligence Throughout Your Value Chain**

Ideally, counterintelligence should be embedded throughout your value chain. It means constant vigilance on the following fronts:

1. Learn about counterintelligence tools and practices. Consult the recommended web sites at the end of this book including the U.S. Secret Service : web pages titled *The Best Practices for Seizing Electronic Evidence.*[274]

2. Consult providers as well as chief intelligence officers in leading companies with an ethical track record and operating in unrelated non-competitive fields.

3. Define valuable property (physical, intellectual and virtual). Review policies for information disclosure and asset visibility. Ensure that all corporate assets, including open-source information, meet the latest policies. Systematically document tacit knowledge and subject it to intellectual-property protection rules.

4. Identify counterintelligence targets, i.e., anyone whose vested interest is to profit from gaining non-authorized access to your physical and intellectual property or damage your standing with clients, allies, staff and other constituencies. How much do they already know about you and how did they find out? Identify the current and plausible intelligence-collection goals of the above targets. How much is the dollar

89

value of your tacit and explicit intelligence assets worth to the adversary?

5. Define your structural vulnerabilities: How does your environment (i.e., location, industry, neighborhood, working climate) constitute a targeted and/or collateral risk? Vulnerability grows with employee dissatisfaction, inadequate communications and poor leadership. Without addressing the root causes of dissatisfaction and maintaining a positive working climate, counterintelligence activities will produce marginal results at best. Worse, they may backfire, particularly if they lack transparency or do not gain the staff's trust. Note that high standards of privacy and personal data protection are among the prerequisites to build credibility and trust.[275]

6. Identify human-resource vulnerabilities, i.e., risk-prone people in your own back yard and their potential motivation (greed, addictions or debt, past history, strange behavior). Identify the weakest points in your supply chain and customer relationships. Watch for well-trained intelligence agents who can apply for any job in your company and/or impersonate legitimate clients, suppliers or the media. These candidates do not exhibit the traits of risk-prone staff. They will work hard to blend with the community, gain the trust of their official employer or business contact and glean both explicit and tacit intelligence. Organizations that lead their industry sometimes unknowingly fall prey to these agents who operate undercover for the competition or other enemies.

7. Trace the exposure paths of your own staff, which may include work, private homes, planes, hotels and so on. Note that valuable intelligence was recovered by Oracle from the trash of the private homes of Microsoft staff. Also travel ultra-light and always keep valuable documents and data in sight and within reach.

8. Maintain and monitor a comprehensive log of interactions between your organization and all stakeholders, including visitors to your web sites. That is how Microsoft was able to reconstruct the incubation of "denial of service" attacks that paralyzed its portals on January 25, 2001.

9. Use security-enhanced operating systems such as SE Linux that "provide a mechanism to enforce the separation of information based on confidentiality and integrity requirements. This allows threats of tampering and bypassing of application security mechanisms to be addressed and enables the confinement of damage that can be caused by malicious or flawed applications."[276]

10. Take counter-measures to detect and prevent electronic surveillance as well as unauthorized modification, destruction or substitution of your network components and information. Note that your competitors, foreign agents and intelligence brokers may find subtle ways to enter your premises and hide powerful electronic surveillance equipment in a conference room or even a bathroom. They can also legally obtain accurate satellite imagery with less than one-meter resolution to observe your installations, parking lots, loading docks and designated trucking fleets. Pictures from the IKONOS commercial satellite and Russian DK satellites are now priced for small firms and farming cooperatives.

11. Take decisive action to prevent tampering with other assets and business secrets (e.g., competitive intelligence software, data, lists, plans, tools, know-how, systems, telecom networks, web sites, practices, technology). Keep guardians or carriers of these assets safe from hostile intelligence services and other security-risk agents (e.g., people, computer worms, viruses, Trojan horses, electronic surveillance, steganography[277]). For staff members who may be requested to provide passwords under duress, provide "alternate passwords that set off alarms."[278]

12. Seed and scatter knowledge-based assets (e.g., trade intelligence, source codes, paper waste, process methodologies) over multiple secure locations and teams to reduce risk of total access, contamination or loss. The seeding exercise should meet the legal requirements for a court order to "cease and desist" should this become necessary.

13. Consider legal and ethical deterrents, tracers and means to outmaneuver, dislocate, apprehend and seek compensatory damages from offenders. Make it particularly costly for major

competitors to intrude, rob company property or collude with insiders. The system should operate under cover to intercept predatory attacks while still in early incubation. Ideally, your organization should be able to extract a written cease and desist commitment without affidavits and be promptly paid compensation to keep the case away from courts.[279] As the noted French writer, François de la Rochefoucauld, once said, "it is a great ability to be able to conceal one's ability."[280]

If you suspect unauthorized access to your data, paper waste, fax transmissions or e-mail system, seed discarded paper, fax communications and e-mails with information traps to provoke traceable action. This is how a Swiss bank found and thwarted an insider-trading scheme. The staff of a European bureau of the *Los Angeles Times* did the same when the system logs revealed access to their e-mail at times when they were absent. The culprit, a senior foreign correspondent, read the spurious e-mail sent to his coworkers by another bureau. Unaware of the sting operation, he raised bogus issues that led to his dismissal.

14. Avoid performing sensitive transactions and communications using laptops, mobile phones and palm-held tools unless they are certified as tamper-proof. In order to ensure that confidential information remains impenetrable to unauthorized parties, use reliable encryption protocols to support transactions between storage media, caches and motherboards as well as in wired or wireless communications. Consider Fortezza-compliant cards to secure your messaging system.[281]

15. Use scenario planning, simulation, brainstorming to play the devil's advocate by scripting a series of potential moves of competitors and hostile players, disgruntled ex-employees and former partners. In high stakes cases, it is often worthwhile to ask retired executives from the competition or war room strategists, experienced trial lawyers and film-makers to shadow current and emerging opponents. In our consulting practice, we have organized script-writing contests among teams of various clients to get insights into the mind of their respective competitors, both direct and indirect.

In the 1980s, Alcan was intent on winning Ontario's $70 million market for pop cans. Alcan executives insisted on simulating not only the strategy of direct competitors such as Alcoa, Pechiney and Kaiser, but also indirect competitors such as the producers of glass, plastic and steel (Stelco and Dofasco) and even "grass-root foes" such as Pollution Probe.[282]

Created in 1999 with a five-year grant from the U.S. Army, the Institute for Creative Technology (ICT) at the University of South California (USC) is the most advanced simulation research center "incorporating virtual humans in key roles as characters, playing the roles of friendly and hostile forces".[283] In the aftermath of September 11 attacks, "government intelligence specialists have been secretly soliciting terrorist scenarios from top Hollywood filmmakers and writers."[284]

16. Train staff and close allies to cultivate a social system dedicated to building and preserving intelligence capital. Warn everyone about the lengths to which unethical firms will go in industrial espionage, including placing bogus career ads to extract competitive intelligence from innocent applicants.

17. Keep disaster recovery and contingency plans current.

18. Hedge against residual risks.

19. Ensure that the CEO frequently stresses the vital links between excellence, intelligence security and counterintelligence. Even the Department of Energy where security is paramount, "has appropriately emphasized excellence in the quality of its scientific and technical work, but only recently has begun to emphasize security, and only in recent months has articulated the importance of counterintelligence."[285]

20. Ascertain that counterintelligence is a worthwhile investment that is subject to continuous improvement. Conduct regular audits and vulnerability assessments to ensure adherence to the above guidelines.[286] Narrow the scope and the portfolio of assignments through continuous pruning to focus on high

payoff goals. Always compare the cost of counterintelligence with the damage it seeks to prevent.

- Summary

Organizations must begin by establishing counter-intelligence policies, building awareness and hiring trustworthy people who practice prevention at work and elsewhere. Practicing intelligence security means using secure-Web technology; seeding files, printed directories and confidential documents; video-recording the constant ins and outs of working areas; enforcing counter-measures; shadowing hostile activities; benchmarking response; and embedding virtual traces and auto-dialing chips on expensive plant equipment and computer hardware. It is also important to communicate strategies that can act as a deterrent to potential risk agents.

5. Conclusion

Like competitive intelligence, counterintelligence is mission-critical to every organization. Both should be an integral part of its culture and fabric. In most organizations, however, few employees have any skills in competitive intelligence and much less the skills of counterintelligence. Many only act in response to surprise events, and then do so in haste. Yet, a practical knowledge of the discipline can be significant and valuable in preventing or managing risks, as the illustrations in this book suggest.

A number of our clients in the financial and high technology sectors have discovered that relying solely on the work of best experts is costly and impractical. They found the logic of "teaching people to fish" in counterintelligence the most-effective route to leverage the time and effort of the very few experts with core competence in this domain.

PART TWO

-

INTELLIGENCE ANALYSIS AND INTERPRETATION: NEGLECTED ISSUES AND BREAKTHROUGH TOOLS

Interest speaks all sorts of tongues,
and plays all sorts of parts, even that of disinterestedness.
François de la Rochefoucauld

If you know the enemy and know yourself,
you need not fear the result of a hundred battles.
If you know yourself, but not the enemy,
for every victory gained you will also suffer defeat.
If you know neither the enemy nor yourself,
you will succumb in every battle.
Sun Tzu

CHAPTER 7
-
VALUE INCUBATION:
A PROVEN FRAMEWORK FOR EARLY DETECTION
OF THREATS AND OPPORTUNITIES

Predicting the future is nearly impossible. However, if we can pick and correctly read the early leads and know the players, we can sketch alternative pathways along which an issue may evolve. This exercise can yield dividends in a complex world where fresh opportunities and risks abound.

In business and government, every manager must learn to anticipate events before they happen. This involves predicting, tracking and orchestrating the forces at the root of upcoming issues and breakthroughs before they appear on the horizon. This chapter brings a new perspective to environmental scanning, intelligence and interpretation by examining the various phases that precede the emergence of an opportunity or threat. These phases constitute the *pre-issue life cycle* or *value incubation*. They begin with an embryo and end with the birth of a project, policy or set of objectives reflecting the consensus on issue resolution or value creation.

Even experienced decision-makers are only vaguely aware of the *value incubation cycle*. By increasing their understanding of this cycle, readers will be more equipped to scan for upcoming issues and demands relevant to their concerns. By focusing on issues and forces that lead to their objectives, they can uncover unusual threats and opportunities and assess their degree of influence before contemplating a strategy. In this context, value evolves from incubation to creation and extraction. Value incubation, the subject of this chapter, is the fuzziest and most complex of the three stages.

This chapter draws from a wide variety of real-life situations from business, science, technology, public administration, defense and geopolitics in order to demonstrate the universal nature of value incubation and its profound impact on our lives. It assumes the reader has a comprehensive understanding of business intelligence, its organization and tools.

1. Introduction

There are three certainties about the emerging global economy[287]: industrial and retail consumers will have more choices, business risks will grow globally and more dark horses than ever will emerge and challenge established incumbents. With little baggage from the past, some of these challengers will compete successfully, perhaps even changing the boundaries, landscape and fundamentals of their industry (Genentech, Conoco, eBay). Others will provoke "a lethal response"[288] and perish like so many "dotcom" companies. But in this process, both successful and unsuccessful challengers shift power further towards either the buyers or the few M&A winners. Without anticipating the effect of such challengers, organizations and individuals cannot align their strategy to survive and prosper in a merciless environment. This chapter offers a framework for acquiring further intelligence, speeding up the value-creation cycle and moving forward rapidly and confidently.

2. The Current Paradigm Trap

A clear understanding of the *value incubation period* can help you formulate policy, manage organizational change and make better decisions, both in quality and delivery time. Yet, much of the literature on *Strategic Management* neglects this "pre-birth" period. It assumes that projects and policies have a fixed start, a fixed end and clear goals. As a result, there is a widespread but false belief among decision-makers that policy, project or opportunity planning begins with the formulation of client objectives.

In reality, the roots of a project or policy can be traced back to much earlier stages. We refer to the maturing process of these roots as *value incubation* or issue *pre-life cycle*. This pre-life cycle is an evolutionary and irreversible process akin to the biological process of pregnancy and childbirth. It begins at an issue's embryo phase, often an isolated event, occurring long before the development of a mature constituency. This phase also often precedes traditional project initiation steps such as the formulation of objectives.

Being aware of the genesis of an issue and its characteristics gives decision-makers a practical framework for strategic thinking and business planning. We'll see, for example, that the fate of projects/policies and the success of work teams often depend in large measure on the work done before the formal commencement of a project.

In order to discuss the elements of the pre-life cycle precisely, we will establish a common language and working definitions in the next few paragraphs. However, caution should be used in making inferences from this chapter, since reality is too complex to model with perfect rigor. As Stephen Hawking has noted about the complexity of modeling: "One, therefore has to make simplifying assumptions and approximations – and even then the problem of extracting predictions remains a formidable one."[289]

3. Incubation of Threats and Opportunities
The Embryo Phase

- Isolated Events

Isolated events form the embryo of most opportunities and issues. An isolated event is an incident with a marginal impact on the *status quo*.[290] These events tend to go unnoticed by the majority of potential stakeholders, and result in little or no change. Indeed, resistance to change is often high after they occur because, at this stage, most decision-makers are either unaware of or unwilling to recognize the need for prompt action.[291]

This was clearly the case in the 9-11 tragedies, where a greater understanding of the linkages between isolated events, key-player profiles and issue incubation could have offered both the authorities and the airlines further insights as outlined in the Strategic Intelligence Brief researched by the author on the subject.[292] Going beyond 9-11, we must remember how even successful companies like IBM can turn complacent despite early warnings.[293]

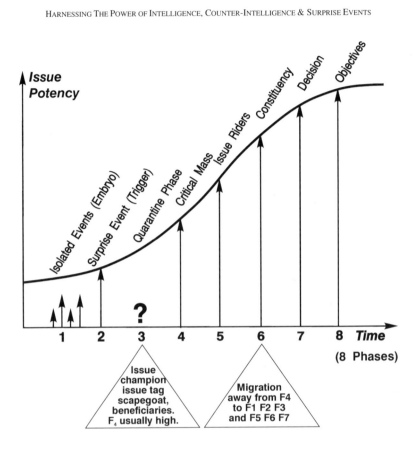

Figure 7.1. Opportunity and Threat Incubation Cycle
Note: The 7Fs of the Factional Scale™ are covered in Chapter 10.

- Case to Remember: Why the Power of Isolated Events Should Never Be Underestimated in Intelligence

Africa Watch and a special UN envoy published reports in 1993 detailing the massive distribution of arms to militia groups and the massacre of over 2,000 civilians. "From January 1994 onwards, General Romeo Dallaire, head of a UN mission in Rwanda, made repeated requests for more troops and equipment as well as for permission to confiscate known illegal arms imports to protect civilians. All these requests were denied."[294]

In April 1994, the President of Rwanda was murdered in a plane crash and, within hours, ten Belgian UN troops were tortured and killed. These "isolated events" triggered a civil war that claimed over 800,000 Rwandans in less than 100 days, and ultimately contributed, within three years, to "the overthrow of President Mobutu of Zaire by rebels backed by Rwanda and Uganda."[295]

- **The Case of Millennium Pharmaceuticals**

In the biotech field, consider the announcement in December of 2001 that COR Therapeutics was being acquired by Millennium Pharmaceuticals. The embryo of this event could be found in an interview with Mark Levin, Millennium's founder and CEO, conducted by David Champion for the Harvard Business Review. Recognizing the critical need for his company to go beyond gene and protein research, Mark Levine clearly indicated that Millennium was interested in growing downstream in the pharmaceutical value chain. It was logical to extrapolate from Champion's article that the acquisition route was preferred by Millennium as a means for fulfilling its vision of a more lucrative future by "identifying, testing, and manufacturing molecules."[296]

- **Scanning for the Future**

Foresighted entrepreneurs and decision-makers value isolated events. They build *scanners,* a socioeconomic or geopolitical version of Doppler radar or night-vision goggles. With the help of these scanners, they search for isolated events and capture data to predict the next phase in the incubation period. Top-performing investors scrutinize large insiders' sales, corporate buybacks and other precursors of major events. As an illustration, record outflows in the equity market over a one-week period (over $900 billion), combined with a soaring intra-day put-call ratio and an unusually high *Volatility Index* (VIX above 35), tend to signal that, barring a geopolitical crisis, a declining market is at least poised for a short recovery[297].

- **Watching eBay**

In October 2000, Meg Whitman of eBay talked about her company's interest in working with a TV network to develop an eBay television show. Neither Wall Street analysts nor the media have tried to chart eBay's course after Whitman's statement. Let us briefly look at the history of QVC, Intel and AOL to draw a parallel to eBay.

When QVC was launched, Wall Street analysts doubted that anyone could watch a TV-shopping channel for more than a couple of minutes, much less order goods from such an unknown broadcaster. They predicted that if a critical mass for TV shopping were reached, the leading networks (ABC, CBS and NBC) would use their franchise to split the lion's share of the market between them and defeat QVC. Today, QVC is the undisputed leader of TV shopping with over $10 billion in annual revenue.

In the eyes of the old computer establishment, Intel was consigned to a role as a junior contractor. Instead, it has emerged as a power in its own right. More than a slogan, the proud boast *"Intel Inside"* is a testimony to the growing role, functionality and value of Intel chips in the computing industry. And, watching AOL burn cash to aggressively enlist customers and build market share in the mid-nineties, many analysts could not imagine that this newcomer would survive, let alone acquire an established icon such as Time Warner.

Think about how an eBay could (a) learn from the experience of Intel, AOL and QVC, (b) lever its unique strengths and (c) partner with Microsoft (MS-NBC) or a leading broadcaster to ultimately write a success story in interactive TV. If well incubated and strategically positioned, the show could turn into a mega success. We can therefore imagine an Intel type of slogan such as *eBay Inside* [the entertainment world]. The audiences attracted by today's most successful programs would pale in comparison with eBay's. The world of strategic alliances is full of junior partners, or *rule takers*, who have the potential to turn into agenda setters, or *rule makers*.

- **Scanning at Nike, TRW, Siemens and Anheuser-Bush**

In an era where speed drives profit and market share in most companies, those who can pick out and capitalize on signs of the future will gain the upper hand. Anheuser-Busch and Nike apply the concept in advertising. TRW engineers led their field in changing the focus from closed-system phones to programmable phones and handsets as a result of attending an IEEE workshop on open logic.

Siemens and Canon credit part of their success in continuously slashing product-creation and customer-response time to the fact that they systematically scan isolated events. They find embryonic ideas from sources including the Internet, Bloomberg, CNBC, leading professional publications, conference proceedings and waves of dormant inventions registered at the U.S. and foreign patent offices.

- **$30-Million Lesson from Banking**

Overlooking a score of isolated events can be disastrous as another risk-incubation example demonstrates: Between 1985 and 1991, Julius Melnitzer, a London trial lawyer, indulged in a lavish lifestyle that was based on fraudulent bank loans. He brought his lines of credit from almost zero to over $90 million by using forged financial statements and securities. During this period, four major banks (Royal Bank, CIBC, TD Bank and National Bank) did the unthinkable by accepting Melnitzer's requests to bypass routine credit checks. They trusted his words and bogus collateral. A routine phone call in 1991 by a National Bank manager uncovered the largest multi-bank fraud in Canadian history. In the end, the banks lost $30 million when Melnitzer declared bankruptcy. As trial hearings revealed, a clear pattern of events spanning years showed that Melnitzer's questionable behavior was actually quite transparent. It is unconscionable for prudent leaders to ignore available information and to overlook a series of isolated events. A simple, routine request for audited statements or a call to a credit clearance agency, such as the one finally placed in August 1991 would have prevented the fiasco.

- **From a Cluster of Isolated Events to a Phantom Trading Scheme in Government Securities**

Even a global company like GE has been stung because it ignored isolated events. In 1994, Mr. Joseph Jett was named the employee of the year of Kidder Peabody, a GE subsidiary at the time. The event sparked the interest of the media. By looking deeper into the lifestyle of the laureate, the business press uncovered several isolated events, which were in sharp contrast to the rising-star image Joseph Jett had cultivated at Kidder Peabody. Further investigation led to the discovery of Jett's phantom trading scheme in government securities.[298] As a result, GE discharged Mr. Jett and a number of other executives and ultimately sold Kidder to Paine Webber. In a 1998 court decision, SEC Judge Carol F. Foelak concluded that Mr. Jett "exploited an anomaly in Kidder's software, in the manner of a pyramid scheme, that credited him on Kidder's books with enormous, but illusory, profits. He did this with an intent to defraud." She permanently barred Mr. Jett from trading securities and ordered him to pay a penalty of $200,000 plus a disgorgement of $8.21 million in wrongful gains.[299]

• **From Isolated Events to Stock-Market Bubbles**

In the stock market, the rules governing *issue incubation* have been at work for centuries. With some slight variations, major financial disasters have unfolded in a similar fashion, as demonstrated by a host of crashes and major corrections in England and France (1720), the USA (1819, 1837, 1873) and throughout the western world (1929, 1987, October 99, March and October 2000). Isolated events, particularly success stories, are magnified by the press and biased financial analysts, thereby attracting mass participation into the market, with the result that prices and expectations are inflated. Every wave of new entrants, mesmerized by the enthusiasm and gains of its predecessors, rushes to invest and further drives up prices. This "irrational exuberance" adds to a speculative spree and ultimately to a bubble, as was recently seen in biotech, fiber optics, wireless, Internet, defense and energy stocks. In such cases, collective wisdom is at odds with reality. Except for a very tiny minority of entrepreneurs and nervous buyers who, once warned, discreetly opt out early before the storm, the public at large is oblivious to any call for prudence or restraint – treating these calls as mere isolated events. The speculative adventure sooner or later culminates in a painful crash that has frequently been triggered by some *surprise event* – the subject of the next section.

4. The Surprise Event Phase

A *surprise event* is an incident that shakes deeply held beliefs or expectations about the status quo. It signals the beginning of the second phase of the incubation period. This is a period when established perceptions about reliability, safety, security, values, trust or other beliefs are questioned within the company or society at large.

A full chapter (Chapter 7) has been devoted to surprise events, given their growing importance and crucial role in intelligence analysis, strategy, policy formulation and decision-making in general.

5. The Quarantine Phase

Surprise events lead to a period of uncertainty termed the *quarantine phase*. Uncertainty tends to grow with the number of competing visions of the future. The quarantine period is often volatile, sometimes chaotic, and therefore complex to manage. The wildcard is the behavior of key stakeholders and changes in the power relationships between winners and losers (if any) and their respective constituencies.

Several developments are required to channel issue evolution toward a given path. Once these developments take place, we reach *the point of no return* in the incubation of issues and opportunities.

- ### The Issue Champion: A Necessary But Not Sufficient Agent of Change

One of the first requirements during the issue incubation phase is the need for an *issue champion* to get the issue on the radar screen. The champion is an individual with a high receptivity to change but often a limited ability to make it happen. The role played by the champion in advancing new ideas can be decisive. However, the mere presence of a champion, is not sufficient to launch a divergent evolutionary path. Think of the Polish monk Nicolaus Copernicus, a visionary champion whose sound ideas about the solar system were not taken seriously until Galileo, a *Conductor,* orchestrated the change a century later. Galileo had the know-how to test the theory for himself and the strategic acumen to wage an underground campaign in favor of the new paradigm while publicly acquiescing to church doctrine to avoid embarrassing his long-time friend and admirer Pope Urban VIII, an *issue rider*. He risked his freedom, but not his life. There is more on *champions, conductors* and *issue riders* in Chapter 9.

- ### The Issue Tag

Chernobyl, Tylenol, Elf and 9-11 respectively mean much more than a city, an ethical drug, an oil company and a calendar date! By referring to surprise events, these *issue tags* carry a powerful additional meaning.

Issues are usually nameless during the isolated event phase. They are haphazardly baptized by the media in the aftermath of a surprise event. Irresponsible reporters tend to dramatize in order to gain the attention of their busy audiences. They opt for titles that add to the drama and trauma of news headlines. Among their favorite targets are known brand names, company designations and institutional leaders.

Naming the issue after a company, its products, or its leaders is a practice that tends to affect corporate reputation. Therefore, the designation of the issue should not be left to the fancy of the media. For companies with high ethical standards, transparency is the best defense. With this in mind, a strategy is required to deter the media from diluting brand equity or abusing corporate names. The support of highly-respected journalists should be solicited to plead for fairness and equity. Reporters should be reminded that the company is legally a person and, as such, is innocent unless proven guilty.

The issue tag picked by the media can be seen as a libelous misrepresentation of the corporate slogan and purpose. It is often less damaging to a company to designate issues with the geographic name of the location where the surprise event occurred. Should it be the Peggy's Cove crash or Swissair 111? Contrast the Tylenol, DC-10 and Corvair issues with Three-Mile Island, Love Canal and Bhopal. A geographic tag helps to deflect the focus of attention away from the company involved. However, real-estate values in these locations often take a nosedive. Alas, in most cases, someone pays a price for the surprise event.

- **The Victims and Beneficiaries**

Although the *issue champion* may come from the universe of victims and beneficiaries, major players often emerge from elsewhere. In this context, the *beneficiaries* include people who can directly or indirectly gain from a surprise event regardless of where it occurs, even when it is unrelated to their sphere of activity.

The *victims,* if any, are the people adversely affected by the surprise event. They include *scapegoats,* i.e., anyone who is perceived to be guilty before being proven guilty. They are unjustly blamed in the aftermath of a surprise event before the real culprits are found. In this context, the *culprits* are the people who have intentionally assisted in the creation of a harmful surprise event or were able but not willing to prevent it from

106

happening. Negligent individuals who are accountable at the professional or managerial level fall into this group.

- **The Conductor:**
  A Pivotal Agent and Catalyst of Change

Issue evolution cannot go beyond the quarantine phase without a *conductor* and *beneficiaries* (or *victims* in the case of harmful surprise events). The conductor is the *architect* of change: a pragmatist, an honest broker, and a strategist with a low need for public approbation.

In summary, the existence of a conductor, a champion, an issue tag, and either victims or beneficiaries is a prerequisite for issue evolution from the *quarantine phase* to the *critical mass phase* – the subject of the next section.

6. The Critical Mass Phase

In nuclear physics, a critical mass is the minimum amount of fissionable material necessary to provoke and sustain a chain reaction.

In management, MIT's Kurt Lewin has defined the critical mass as the minimum number of people whose commitment is necessary to prevent or subdue resistance to change. This phase is reached either through orchestration or when the champions and their followers have brought the *level of dissatisfaction with the status quo* to the point where powerful fence sitters are now questioning their own attitudes. It can also be reached as a result of a tidal wave of surprise events occurring during the quarantine phase.

It is worthwhile to stress that critical mass almost never means "the majority of people". The concept of critical mass is borrowed from natural laws, particularly from the field of nuclear physics, rather than from the social science law of majority/minority as stressed by MIT's Richard Beckhard. The endorsement of a celebrity is perhaps all you need for your brand, company or charity to gain high visibility and break the resistance to change. Think how an obscure product can benefit from the leverage of image icons like Andre Agassi, Cindy Crawford, Celine Dion, Wayne Gretsky, Madonna, Jack Nicholson, Isabella Rossilini, Christopher Reid or, Claudia Schiffer. *"I give to Billy*

Graham" epitomizes the ability of TV Evangelists such as Billy Graham and Jerry Falwell to persuade large numbers of people to donate to a cause, frequently without regard to the sponsoring institution behind it! What is a celebrity trademark worth? Over one billion dollars for a Californian chef like Wolfgang Puck! Fortunately, there are other ways of getting the critical mass on board.

- ## Darwin: The Brilliant Strategist

The critical mass is frequently composed of a handful of individuals. Their commitment can be tacit, i.e., they respond on a non-objection basis. Think of Darwin, whose *Theory of Evolution* was too explosive and revolutionary for Victorian England. Knowing the tragic fate of Lavoisier and other free-thinkers across the Channel, Darwin kept his theory from the establishment and the public for twenty years until he built a critical mass by converting his professor and fewer than ten other leading scientists, transforming them from fence-sitters (or foes) into allies. Then, he wrote thousands of letters to gain *a constituency* – a journey that took another twenty years, during which he was ridiculed by the Church and the press! He was only awarded an honorary degree from his *Alma Mater,* Cambridge, when his ideas became *quasi-mainstream,* some fifty years after he first shared them with his professor.

- ## Mackenzie King at the Rockefeller Foundation

After the 1914 Ludlow Massacre, in which coal miners and their families were killed during a strike at Colorado Fuel and Iron (CFI), absentee owner John D. Rockefeller Jr. found himself on a collision course with President Woodrow Wilson, Congress, unions, the media and the public at large. Harvard-educated economist William Lyon Mackenzie King took a sabbatical from Canadian politics to join the Rockefeller Foundation and form the critical mass that helped emancipate Rockefeller Jr. from the retrograde opinions of his immediate circle. Within a year, Rockefeller was championing grievance mechanisms and better labor relations in boardrooms and in public debates to the point of being seen as a dangerous liberal by investors and industrialists.[300] Back in Canada, Mr. King went on to become Prime Minister.

- ## Dell's Linux Strategy

Compared to Microsoft's Windows, Linux was a relatively unknown operating system. Michael Dell provided the critical mass for this product when he decided in 1999, to offer a major customer, computers that were loaded with Linux. By the same token, the decision was a double-edged surprise event for Microsoft. On the one hand, it signaled the arrival of potentially-strong competition to Windows. On the other, it provided welcome ammunition for Microsoft's defense against the anti-trust case led by the Department of Justice.

- ## Ford and Toyota

The two major paradigm shifts witnessed in the automotive sector during the 20th century can be traced back to two individuals. With the introduction of the Model T in 1909, Henry Ford provided the critical mass that broke through resistance to the mass-production techniques advocated years earlier by Frederick Taylor, *a champion*. Although the concept underlying mass production was anticipated in Adam Smith's pin factory, it was Taylor who turned it into a science with *time and motion engineering*. Ford, however, demonstrated its viability on a very large scale by bringing the car production cycle down from five weeks to less than a week (89 hours)! Ford's achievement led to the concept of time-based competition that, 80 years later, has even reached the public-health system. By the same token, Engineer Taiichi Ohno's resounding success with participative management at Toyota provided the critical mass that ultimately led to the propagation of teamwork and *just-in-time* systems on the shop floors of the world.

- ## The Critical Mass for the Next Paradigm Shift

With the unprecedented support of New Yorkers and even powerful restaurant owners who have discovered that a smoke-free environment is also good for business, New York City Mayor Michael Bloomberg did not waste time to introduce a tough legislation to ban smoking from 13,000 small restaurants and bars currently exempt from the ban in the State law, passed in 1995. With Delaware, California and now New York City onboard, the critical mass for an unprecedented crusade against the anti-tobacco lobby is in place. The impact of the ban is already reverberating in city halls, state legislatures and editorial newsrooms throughout the continent.

The California Clean-Air Act (a surprise event) and the emergence of hydrogen-powered cars, new composite materials, GPS/INS[301] guidance systems and cyberspace tools are bound to provoke the critical mass for a new era in low-cost modular transportation, both above ground and underground.

On its own, however, critical mass does not result in successful change unless it secures the commitment of the *issue riders,* as demonstrated below.

7. The Issue-Rider Phase

While champions are characterized by their high readiness for change and low ability to implement it, *issue riders* are people with the ability to bring about change but low interest in making it happen. However, their behavior may be transformed once the critical mass is on board. Issue riders have the power to block or encourage the change and the shrewdness to use or abuse their power in a timely manner. The term issue rider was originally introduced in my first book on Proactive Thinking,[302] borrowing from the movie *The Easy Rider.* Fifteen years later, Gary Hamel coined another descriptive term: *rule maker.*[303]

Issue riders tend to be clever people unwilling to get involved in the absence of the critical mass. They tend either to remain quiet or walk on a tightrope while the champions struggle during the quarantine phase. Some riders position themselves on the right side of the issue when the critical mass commitment is reached. During the 1998 German elections, Gerhard Schroeder shifted his rhetoric from an anti- to a pro-European position and opposed Helmut Kohl's much needed tax reforms solely to win votes. As reported in *The New York Times*: [Schroeder] "is not someone whose heart and soul depend on a particular message. He can change, and one twist suits him as well as the next. What Schroeder likes is whatever is liked by the public he needs at the time."

For their progress, companies and society in general need champions and riders (not necessarily of Schroeder's extreme variety), as they play complementary roles. However, the champion's action is rarely the subject of public approval, much less of fair or even symbolic rewards. It is no wonder that veteran champions attempt the transition to the issue riders' group, a move that has been successful for only a very few candidates.

During the eighties and early nineties, Pope John-Paul II, a champion at heart, acted as a strategic rider on several issues. Using diplomacy, charismatic power and the moral authority of the Catholic Church in targeted countries, he engaged the Vatican in a series of well-orchestrated initiatives with the active support of the allies to help bring democracy to Eastern Europe and other regions. In a 1979 landmark address, during his first official trip to Poland, his homeland, he urged the Poles to live up to the examples set by Casimir, Stanislas and other national heroes who, by giving their lives to liberate their country, symbolized the struggle against tyranny.[304] The solemn call to action was the spark that gave the champions of liberation a new lease on life. The Pope's journeys to Haiti and the Philippines were also instrumental in removing dictators from power. Far from being symbolic and beyond its undeniable human dimension, the Pope's journey to Cuba takes on a strategic character that is already producing dividends.

In Congress, there are over 550 champions and a small number of riders. As an illustration, riders on both sides of the U.S. Senate kept a low profile during President's Clinton impeachment trial. After the 9-11 tragedies, they gave President George W. Bush a free ride for a year.

Both the New Democratic Party (NDP) in Canada and the Greens in Europe have played the role of issue champion even when they were in power, as they were in Ontario, British Columbia and Manitoba.

In business, Boeing and General Electric consolidate their lead over champions in their respective industries year after year. Until recently, IBM has acted as an issue rider around events such as the introduction of on-line terminals, database software, time sharing, word processing, personal computers, CAD/CAM networks and palm-held personal digital assistants (PDA). The list of champions forced to leave the territory to the rider is endless and includes Wang, Control Data, RCA and, more recently Digital. Thanks to Lou Gerstner and his team, IBM has regained its status and either acquired or built bridges with the most promising champions (Lotus, Dell).

Many banks have championed on-line banking and other de-regulated services but didn't seem to benefit from their lead-time advantage as one might have expected. On the other hand, issue-rider-managed CitiGroup has been able to catch and surpass the champions in insurance, investment and underwriting. In this context, the champions serve as a *de facto* testing ground for the rider.

Unlike champions, who focus on a single issue at a time, riders are multiple-issue people. Given the inability of champions to see the whole picture, the overwhelming problem for honest riders is to allocate scarce capital and resources to the endless demands and ideas put forward by the advocates of change.

Such riders are concerned with the comparative advantage of champions' ideas and their earned value. They are sensitive to a host of variables including costs, quality, risk and issue interdependence. They cannot ignore the attitudes of consumers, employees, suppliers, legislators and other constituencies. What a champion may perceive as a rider's resistance or an impediment can be a genuine effort to prevent or manage risk.

Honest issue riders fulfill a valuable role in screening issues and acting as a safety valve. However, they risk losing their status overnight if they appear to champion issues, as did President Jimmy Carter on Iran, and Senator Hillary Clinton (in her previous role as First Lady) on health. At least until the critical mass is on board, governments must appear cautious, even when they are genuinely supportive of the change.

Public-sector riders are more vulnerable in an election year. In order to survive, they have to pay greater attention to champions than they might at other times. In this context, President George Bush Sr., a powerful rider after the 1991 Gulf War, ignored the demands of grass-root champions like Ross Perot, who ultimately contributed to his defeat. Likewise, Ralph Nader, a champion, helped a foe, George W. Bush, defeat Al Gore, a pro-environment candidate!

Although each needs the other, riders and champions rarely cooperate on their own. Their interactions tend to yield greater harmony and synergy when orchestrated by a *conductor* – a sort of catalyst or mastermind in issue evolution who is apt at converting negative energy into progress. We shall see, in

Chapter 9, how the conductor works with riders and champions to achieve magic. In the meantime, let us complete our discussion of issue incubation.

8. The Constituency Phase

The commitment of issue riders signals the formation of a constituency, i.e., the majority of the people have now migrated from the fence-sitter group to become one of two other classes of players (allies or adversaries). This polarization phase is characterized by intensive surveys. It is the time when Dr. Gallup *et al* hit the streets and policy-makers are confronted by a new reality.

Prior to the surprise event, the frequency distribution of the players was single-modal and highly clustered around the center or fence-sitter group. It now evolves toward either a skewed or a bimodal distribution. A symmetrical bimodal distribution indicates a deadlock and points to the need for cautious *symptomatic* or *laissez-faire* interventions. A skewed distribution supporting the change calls for *substantive* (etiologic) action. A distribution skewed in the other direction will be used to justify the *status quo* or to *do the minimum to get by* (i.e., the compliance option).

9. The Decision and Objective-Setting Phases

The existence of a solid constituency backed by issue riders will sooner or later lead to the decision phase. This initiates a new *modus operandi*, or a new quasi-stationary equilibrium... until the next surprise event!

As illustrated by the above sections, the formulation of objectives is an outcome of issue incubation and a significant milestone in the creation of value and communication. Conventional wisdom in management theory, however, ignores value incubation by assuming that value identification, policies and business plans begin with the formulation of objectives.

10. Conclusion

This framework on issue evolution and value incubation helps decision-makers to scan for threats and identify opportunities beforehand. The objective is to gain a valuable head start. Policy and strategy are best formulated with a clear head. Managers are also in a better position to influence the volatile and unstable period following surprise events and to orchestrate their outcome.

Prudence also suggests that controversial policies and major projects should not be officially instigated without surprise events, critical mass, issue riders and a solid constituency. Otherwise, managers would be turning their corporations into second-class citizens, operating at the mercy of surprise events, budget squeezes and leftover resources (if any).

Regardless of our job and role in society, an understanding of the incubation period permits us to raise new questions about our current and forthcoming assignments and to gain further insights into the past.

As Sun Tzu wrote: "attaining one hundred victories in one hundred battles is not the pinnacle of excellence. Subjugating the enemy's army without fighting is the true pinnacle of excellence."[305] Thus, without timely, reliable and actionable intelligence — particularly during the opportunity- and threat-incubation cycle — valid decisions and implementation strategies will continue to elude us.

APPENDIX

-

MAD-COW ISSUE INCUBATION LESSONS
BY DR. J. BRIAN MORRISSEY

In an environment of frequent surprise events, the intelligence framework described in this book provides a set of tools to minimize uncertainty and understand the dynamics between events and stakeholders. While the future is indeed unpredictable, we can use information currently available to minimize surprises, and to prepare for the more probable scenarios.

The purpose of this summary is to illustrate the incubation cycle of policy issues that led to major changes in government machinery in the United Kingdom. The focus is not on the shorter incubation cycles of technical decisions and day-to-day operations. Readers interested to learn more about the chronology of events related to Mad Cow disease in the U.K. should visit www.executive.org/vCJD.

1. Mad-Cow Issue Incubation Cycle

Mad Cow (Bovine Spongiform Encephalopathy or BSE) and its human counterpart, new variant Creutzfeldt-Jacob (vCJD) disease, went through the expected phases of issue incubation outlined by Alain Paul Martin in this book. For the U.K. Ministry of Agriculture, Fisheries and food (MAFF), these arguably, were as follows:

- **Isolated event phase:** Several isolated events form the embryo of the issue in Great Britain. Citing J.W. Wilesmith, the FDA states that there are indications that the first clinical case of the disease was observed as early as April 1985.[306] The New Scientist reports "the first confirmed victim of BSE: Cow number 133 on the Stent farm in Sussex develops head tremors and a loss of coordination" on Dec. 22, 1984, to die on Feb. 11, 1985. "Other cows show similar symptoms the

115

next year... Government pathologist finds Cow 133 died from spongiform encephalopathy (SE) on Sept. 19, 1985."[307]

- **Surprise event phase:** UK laboratory identifies the first clinical case of Mad Cow in November 1986.

- **Quarantine phase:** new scientific information progressively becomes available starting in 1987, and gradually reduces uncertainty. A milestone in the Quarantine phase was reached when the EU made BSE a "notifiable" disease for animals in March 1990. It meant that EU farmers and veterinarians must notify government of animals suspected of Mad Cow disease. It did not imply any links with the human disease vCJD. That link was not established until 1996.

- **Critical-mass phase:** While the UK Minister for Health, Stephen Dorrell, maintained the status quo as late as December 1995, stating that there was "no conceivable risk of BSE being transmitted from cows to people", the CJD Surveillance Unit dropped a bombshell, in March 1996 by announcing that the "most likely explanation [for vCJD]" was "exposure to BSE." John Darnton of *The New York Times* wrote about "a total lack of confidence in what the Government or its scientific experts were saying. The suspicions that had been building up for six years suddenly reached a **critical mass** and the result was a spontaneous boycott."[308]

- **Issue rider phase:** Opposition leader Tony Blair orchestrated a smart move of the Labour Party to the political center away from the trade-union base. The move resulted in a surge in popularity. On March 7, 1997, Tony Blair commissioned Professor Philip James, Director of the Rowett Research Institute, to study the need for reform to eradicate BSE. Riding on the issue, he accused the government on March 25, 1997 "of appalling delays and incompetence in dealing with BSE."[309]

- **Constituency phase:** Opinion polls reflected the need for a major government reform in dealing with BSE and signaled the presence of powerful constituencies.

- **Decision phase:** While decisions on technical matters were made from 1986 onwards, reflecting the gradual unfolding of new knowledge, organizational restructuring decisions at the national level were only made after Tony Blair became Prime Minster on May 1, 1997. Proposed by Professor Philip James eight days later and voted by Parliament in November 1999, the UK Food Standards Agency was established in the year 2000 as an independent watchdog led by 12 commissioners. MAFF was subsequently disbanded and its duties assigned elsewhere in June 2001.

An unusual feature of this case was the long duration of the "**quarantine phase**". This is explained by the fact that Mad Cow disease was a new disease. As such, virtually nothing was known about it. There was little specific scientific knowledge on which to base informed decisions. Consequently, as new intelligence on the disease became available, the uncertainty associated with this phase was gradually removed.

By contrast, the 2001 outbreak of "Foot and Mouth" disease (FMD) in cattle that also occurred in the UK had a well-known body of science on which to base decisions. Thus, in the FMD case, the "**quarantine phase**" associated with uncertainty was much shorter. Within a year after the first FMD case was diagnosed, the UK was declared officially FMD-free. The cost to the economy (tourism and farming) was over $10 billion. For links to FMD chronology of events, policy decisions and lessons learned, visit: www.executive.org/FMD

2. Lessons Learned

The following lessons may be noted from the Mad-Cow experience in the UK. Some are drawn from this book, some from Lord Justice Phillips' inquiry report on BSE, and others from personal experience in dealing with surprise events.

1. Focus on leading. Neither the crisis nor the long term developments can wait. Both must be addressed simultaneously. At least one senior leader must devote all her/his attention to managing the crisis. That person must dramatically prune her/his remaining workload and promptly delegate what can be done by others.

2. Scan the Environment regularly. Scan the whole *value chain*, in this case from the farm to the consumer table. Focus on high-risk issues. Build, an informal early warning system with the help of sister organizations and other global allies. Train everyone to collect and submit intelligence. Validate data. Prepare a weekly roll-up of information to be shared upwards and downwards in the organization.

3. Anticipate possible surprise events. In Agriculture and Agri-Food Canada (AAFC), we frequently run simulated models of disease outbreaks.

4. Communicate with experts and policy makers. In AAFC, we held "High Visibility Meetings" twice daily in the early phases of dealing with a surprise event, and as required thereafter. For example, in the Canadian context, a surprise event involving a serious animal disease would bring together representatives from:

   – The Privy Council Office for government-wide coordination,
   – Health Canada (Department of Health),
   – Agriculture and Agri-Food Canada (AAFC) including the Canadian Food Inspection Agency, the Minister's and Deputy Minister's offices, legal and field staff,
   – The Department of Finance to explore compensation (for animals slaughtered),
   – The Treasury Board,
   – The Department of Foreign Affairs and International Trade (international impact),
   – The Department of Justice (for quick passage of new regulations), and
   – Provincial governments and other organizations, as required.

5. Communicate with other stakeholders and the public at large. Base public statements on evidence. Act as a single government, not as a collection of independent departments. Citizens don't care about government's internal structure. This is especially true in the food chain.

Provide regular public briefings with written support material (Lord Phillip's Inquiry)[310].

6. Be particularly careful to brief issue riders. Attempt to ethically move stakeholders along the Factional Scale™ from "foes" towards "friends" by listening and addressing the questions and concerns within your domain (see Chapter 10).

7. Avoid absolute statements such as "there is no conceivable risk of BSE being transmitted from cows to people." In the early stages, put emphasis on collecting evidence and facts. Information is incomplete in the early phases of a surprise event. It is important to be able to confront opinion with facts.

Misleading the media and the public is unethical and irresponsible. In this case, the Phillips' inquiry tells us the "government did not lie to the public about BSE. It believed that the risk was remote". But, the public felt betrayed when, in March 1996, the Creutzfeldt-Jacob Disease (CJD) Surveillance Unit declared that the "most likely explanation [for vCJD]" was "exposure to BSE."

8. Value prompt decision-making. Disease can spread geographically with great rapidity; thus a short, fast decision cycle is of paramount importance. In overlapping legal jurisdictions, federal, state, or provincial controls must be synchronized. Act on the suspicion of disease. Protecting human health is the first priority. Control the spread first; fight adversity afterwards. The alternative can be much worse. Armed with comprehensive intelligence about the causes and the stakeholders, AAFC has produced new regulations in a day in a crisis situation.

9. Based on Maslow hierarchy of needs, health and safety are fundamental human priorities. The precautionary principle should be used where a serious animal or human disease is suspected. This principle has been used since biblical times in disease control, e.g., the principle of quarantining suspected disease carriers.

10. Marshall adequate resources. Draw, if necessary, on all the country's resources to deal with a national crisis. Call on universities, contract employees, retired professionals and resources from other agencies and governments.

11. Consider the benefits and costs of advisory bodies. Consultative boards provide access to knowledge, a different point of view, a sense of public participation, and create a perception of openness to public participation. However, they may slow decision-making, as observed in Lord Phillips' Inquiry Report. In addition, rejecting the advice of an advisory body can lead to a serious loss of credibility.

12. Adjudicate competing priorities. The customer comes first! For government, the citizen is the customer. A farming crisis is a serious economic crisis. A food-safety crisis is a matter of grave concern. Both issues must be addressed. But, human health must be given priority over farm economics.

13. Be careful not to be contradicted by an authoritative body. Although both the UK and EU ruled on BSE, the EU can be seen as more credible if considered to be less captive to local or special interests.

CHAPTER 8

-

HITCH-HIKING ON SURPRISE EVENTS
AND TIDAL WAVES TO CREATE
UNIQUE OPPORTUNITIES

As indicated in the previous chapter, "a *surprise event* is an incident that shakes deeply held beliefs or expectations about the *status quo*. It signals the beginning of the second phase of the incubation period. This is a period when established perceptions about reliability, safety, security, values, trust or other beliefs are questioned within the company or society at large." A tidal wave is either a surprise event powerful in scope, scale and intensity such as 9-11, or a series of surprise events occurring during the quarantine period defined in the previous chapter.

A separate chapter devoted to surprise events and tidal waves is appropriate, given the growing importance of these subjects in intelligence analysis, counterintelligence and strategy formulation. Drawing from a wealth of illustrations that span many fields of business, science, technology and government, this chapter builds on the issue-incubation framework to further discuss how surprise events and tidal waves affect the emergence of threats and opportunities and frequently play a major role in policy formulation and decision-making.

1. Analogy from Thermodynamics

An interesting parallel exists between surprise events from the business world, illustrated below, and the singular points in thermodynamics described by the great physicist James Maxwell.

"In all such cases there is one common circumstance – the system has a quantity of potential energy, which is capable of being transformed into motion, but which cannot begin to be so transformed till the system has reached a certain configuration, to attain which requires an expenditure of work, which in certain cases may be infinitesimally small, and in general bears no definite proportion to the energy developed in consequence thereof. For example, the rock loosed by frost and balanced on a singular point of the mountain side, the little spark which kindles the great forest, the little word which sets the world a fighting…Every existence above a certain point has its singular points: the higher the rank, the more of them. At these points, influences whose physical magnitude is too small to be taken account of by a finite being, may produce results of the greatest importance. All great results produced by human endeavor depend on taking advantage of these singular states when they occur." [311]

Surprise events convert the equilibrium between the forces for and against change from a quasi-stationary to a fragile one. Fragile equilibrium can impede progress for years, as dramatized by the breakdown of the Soviet Bloc, the impact of September 11 on commercial aviation, and the economics of the 1970s and 80s (double-digit inflation, high unemployment and overwhelming public-sector debt). Frequently, surprise events even take us *too far from equilibrium* states.

Most surprise events are territorial. The territory could be disciplinary, socioeconomic, demographic or even confined to an entity within an organization. A surprise event in medicine could be a non-event, or, at best, an isolated event in the arts.

2. Investment Cases

For star performers, surprise events are striking moments. For shrewd investors who do not lose track of the fundamentals and dig further for insights into subtle facts obscured by the news headlines, surprise events may represent opportunities to buy on unusual dips and sell on steep rallies. We see here the opposite of Alan Greenspan's "irrational exuberance", when a massive sell-off of attractive equities bring prices of these stocks to an "irrational hand-out", as witnessed during the 1991 Gulf War and following the tragedies of September 11, 2001.

In this volatile context, the NASDAQ index can go wild for several days due to either corporate warnings or unmet earning expectations by a sector leader.

In the years 2000-2002 alone, a large number of companies faced major negative surprise events. Among the major players that became Wall Street's *disaster du jour*[312] were Arthur Andersen, AT&T, WorldCom, Enron, Ericsson, Eli Lilly, IBM, Intel, Lucent, Microsoft, Nokia, Nortel, Procter & Gamble, Qlogic, Sprint, Tyco and Vivendi. Some of these companies lost 100 to 200 billion dollars in capitalization in a single day. Furthermore, many competitor stocks were carried along in swift and unmerited downward *sympathy moves*. The shock waves experienced by Nortel, Alcatel and Lucent also hit Cisco, Corvis, AMCC, Sycamore, JDS Uniphase and Corning. These events can precipitate brief opportunity windows for traders who pick and chose among casualties featuring solid fundamentals, a reasonable price/earning ratio and high growth. In fact, the stock market offers a surprise event that creates buying or selling opportunities nearly every week!

3. The Potency of Surprise Events

Surprise events force us to learn many things. The trigger for a surprise event is frequently small in potency when compared to the enormous chain reaction it yields.

• GE-Honeywell Aborted Merger

When CNBC's David Faber reported on the final stages of secret merger negotiations between United Technologies and Honeywell, he had no idea of the stunning developments that would ensue as a result of his newscast. Alerted about the report, Jack Welch proceeded with an overnight counter offer that would bring Honeywell and GE together. The GE powerhouse was set to grow much faster than expected and without diluting its equity. Welch even had to alter his own career and retirement plans to facilitate the merger. In the end, however, the merger was vetoed by the European Union.

• American Express *Cause Celebre*

The following case reveals the potency of a marginal business activity with a huge downside risk. American Express' century-old *Field Warehousing Operations* came to an abrupt end following a surprise event – a $64 million scam involving a non-existent inventory of soybean oil in warehouses audited by American Express. This event nearly destroyed the company at a time when it was most profitable. Yet, the scam could have been prevented had the company paid attention to a score of publicly known isolated events involving a customer named Tino DeAngelis, which had been escalating for more than four years. These events included his previous bankruptcy, his multiple prosecutions by the IRS, the appearance of his name on Dun & Bradstreet's watch list and anonymous calls to American Express executives. At one point, false receipts showed that the soybean inventory at a single New Jersey farm exceeded the total quantity available in the USA! A simple reference to published data from the U.S. census would have alerted American Express to the discrepancy. Ultimately, an auditor "found that the salad oil wasn't in the tanks by drilling into the bottom of one to check for oil, instead of doing what most people did, which was to put in a dipstick from the top. Because oil rises." [313]

Rather than going after the bankrupt DeAngelis, banks like Chase held negligent American Express accountable for $64 million of loans. When they threatened to cease honoring its travelers' checks, American Express paid promptly to protect its most profitable product and salvage its reputation. It was simply unacceptable for American Express to allow Field Warehousing, a marginal activity that accounted for less than $1 million of its total earnings, to threaten the future of the entire organization.

The soybean threat to American Express opened the opportunity for Warren Buffett to buy American Express shares before they went up substantially within a year.[314]

• Public Affairs Events

Outside the business world, think of the death of Darwin's beloved daughter Ann, a tragic event that marked the end of the scientist's "faith in a moral just universe and in resurrection!" By the same token, the death of Pierre Elliott Trudeau, in the Year 2000, was a defining moment for Canadians of different beliefs and affiliations who were united in their profound respect for their late Prime Minister. Named honorary pallbearers during Trudeau's funerals, both Presidents Jimmy Carter and Fidel Castro met informally for the first time, an event that led to Carter's historic trip to Cuba in May 2002.

George Washington's unexpected military strikes prior to 1781 and Thomas Jefferson's Louisiana Purchase in 1803 are examples of surprise events with enduring value. Consider the role played by the assassination of Archduke Ferdinand in triggering the First

World War, or the scrap metal dealers' brawl that ultimately led to the battle over the Falklands. Similarly, revelations in 1999 by independent biographer Bernard Violet have tarnished the reputation of the late Oceanographer, Jacques Cousteau. The most damaging evidence, which first appeared in France-Soir, includes a 1941 hand-written anti-Semitic letter and accounts of Cousteau's secret work for the Vichy regime during World War II.

Former New York Mayor Rudolph Giuliani and President George W. Bush saw their approval ratings soar to unprecedented heights thanks to the actions they took immediately after the tragedies of September 2001. Ross Perot's surprise withdrawal from the 1992 presidential race gave Bill Clinton an unexpected boost just hours prior to his acceptance speech at the Democratic Convention in New York. Another surprise event (Monica Lewinsky) hit Clinton in January 1998, just when he was at the height of his popularity and cast a cloud over the rest of his term in office.

- Lance Armstrong's Wake-up Call

At the personal level, think of the world triathlon and cycling champion, Lance Armstrong. In October 1996, he learned that "advanced testicular cancer had spread to his lungs and his brain." A two-time Olympian, Armstrong underwent extensive surgery and intensive therapy in order to beat the cancer. He recovered and subsequently went on to win some of the toughest cycling races in the world including the Tour De France, which by the summer of 2002 he had won four consecutive times. This highly respected humanitarian and role model believes that getting cancer was "a special wake-up call", that changed his outlook on life and priorities.[315] As Lieut. Jack Cambria of New York Police Department said: "Great events do not make the heroes, they just reveal them."[316]

- Craig Kielburger's Galvanizing Event

Craig Kielburger's wake-up call came when, at the age of 12, he read about a Pakistani youngster of the same age, who was murdered for giving insider details of the harsh conditions of exploited children working in carpet factories in Pakistan. In order to eradicate the practice of child labor, Craig went on to found Kids Can Free the Children (KCFTC)[317], a global network of over 100,000 volunteer children helping children in need in 40

125

countries. "Over the past six years, KCFTC has built over 300 primary schools in developing countries, providing education to more than 15,000 children; distributed in excess of 50,000 school and health kits and $2 million (USD) worth of medical supplies to children in developing countries; and administered leadership development training programs to empower youth to become involved in social issues."[318] At the age of 19, Mr. Kielburger was the youngest nominee to the 2002 Nobel Peace Prize.

4. Surprise Events Drive Policy

Except for a few enlightened leaders, most policy-makers only pay lip service to isolated events and wait for a surprise event before considering an issue seriously. We are, unfortunately, a *surprise event-driven society* as the following illustrations demonstrate.

1. The 1994 arrest of Aldrich Ames, a senior official of the CIA, "prompted the most thorough review of U.S. intelligence needs since the CIA's founding."[319]

2. In another field, Florida election officials knew, for many years, that the 1962 punched-card system used to register votes and count ballots was outdated. It was not until the outcome of the 2000 U.S. presidential elections was decided by the interpretation of a few punched ballots that they decided to review the system.

3. In France's 2002 Elections, the surprise defeat of Prime Minister Lionel Jospin by a right-wing extremist led to massive rallies in support of President Jacques Chirac. French civil society waited for the surprise event to seriously consider the anti-immigrant and anti-Semitic messages underlying Le Pen's campaign.

4. In responding to the dreaded mad-cow disease, France had the benefit of lead-time and the experience of Great Britain. Yet, its government waited until Creutzfeldt-Jakob cases appeared on French territory before it decided to act.

5. Until 1999 neither the USDA nor the Canadian Food Inspection Agency tested for the presence of PCBs and cancer-causing dioxins in food products. Then, in Belgium, traces of dioxin were detected throughout the food chain

(from animal feed, pork and poultry to eggs, cheese, baked goods and milk chocolate). What was worse, the Belgian government remained complacent, preferring to treat the data as an isolated incident. It was not until a news leak led to a major political scandal that this surprise event began to receive significant attention.

6. Also in 1999, Coca-Cola suffered the biggest recall in its 113-year history when a small batch of Coke cans in Belgium was found to be contaminated. Governments in Belgium, France and Poland responded with demands for a prompt response. As a result, parliamentarians and regulators have crisscrossed Europe in search of more legislation to deal with the issue!

7. Other well-known surprise events that have provoked new legislation or corporate policies include 9-11 and the subsequent anthrax attacks, Watergate, Sputnik, the near crash of the stock market in 1987, the multi-billion dollar failure of Enron and WorldCom, and the Exxon *Valdez*. Still others would include the contamination of Tylenol, the DC-10 crash at O'Hare airport, the crash of TWA800 (bound for Paris), and the discovery of the HIV virus in blood banks. The French publisher Larousse had to recall more than 200,000 copies of a dictionary that inadvertently switched the labels on photographs of edible and poisonous mushrooms!

However, a surprise event need not always be negative in its consequences. It can also provide positive opportunities as illustrated by the following cases:

1. U.S. Prohibition led to the creation of a vibrant Canadian Whiskey industry led by Seagram.

2. The birth of Alcan was the result of a 1928 U.S. court decision that forced Alcoa (Aluminum Company of America) to sell its Canadian subsidiary (Alcan). Once it was independent, Alcan went on to become a world giant in its own right.

3. In another American court ruling, Western Electric was directed to sell its interest in Northern Electric (now Nortel

127

Networks) to Bell Canada in 1956. Nortel was divested from Bell in 1999.

4. The European Community ruling that prevented Boeing from selling DeHavilland to a French-Italian aerospace concern opened the door for Bombardier, which promptly seized the opportunity at a lower acquisition cost. Following a similar pattern over the past 25 years, Bombardier has been acquiring ailing aerospace companies and turning them into outstanding performers. As a result, the company has been catapulted into third position in its industry behind Boeing and Airbus. Bombardier continues to scan for such events.

5. The "Great Blackout" of 1965 in large portions of North America led policy makers to allocate funds that allowed the industry to achieve its current level of six-sigma[320] service.

6. Created in the aftermath of Bhopal tragedy, the Toxic Release Inventory (TRI) "has dramatically out-performed all other EPA regulations over the last 10 years in terms of overall toxic reductions, and… it has done so at a fraction of the cost of those other programs... The small program has eclipsed its initial goals of providing information for community planners, igniting a "right-to-know" movement in the U.S., and supporting both industry and environmentalists' efforts to reduce toxics."[321]

5. Orchestrated Surprise Events

Beyond accidents, court rulings and scientific discoveries, a host of surprise events are *orchestrated* by shrewd strategists in a conscious effort to influence public policy or expand market share.

•   Strategic Initiatives in Business

The announcement of an initial public offer, a merger and acquisition (Citigroup and Travelers, AOL and Time Warner, Pfizer and AHP, Kellogg and Keebler) or a strategic alliance (IBM and Dell) can be orchestrated as a positive surprise event. The brief withdrawal of the original Coca-Cola and its orchestrated comeback under the Coke Classic brand provided valuable free publicity for the company coupled with immediate recognition of the new flagship brand. The combination had an immediate and positive impact on the company's sales. Microsoft's notoriety and subsequent rapid growth were well orchestrated after a major surprise event: the news release announcing its first agreement with IBM on MS-DOS.

- **Provocative Advertising at Benetton**

In advertising and value communication, differentiation is the first stage in incubating value in the mind of a target audience. Inspired by Salvador Dali and Luis Bunuel[322], Olivero Toscani has, for eighteen years, achieved differentiation for Benetton by orchestrating unorthodox and controversial surprise events. Consider the provocative hard-core billboard and print campaigns featuring human hearts, newborn babies and multicolored condoms. As the chief creative director of the clothing and retail giant from 1982 to 2000, Mr. Toscani has produced eye-catching ads charged with strongly opinionated political and social messages on war, race, dying AIDS patients and the death penalty. The iconoclastic ads have always attracted strong controversy in the media, which helped immensely in drilling differentiation into the minds of the retailer's target audience. Following its differentiation ads, Benetton promoted racial harmony in selected print and TV media to inculcate brand consciousness beyond the point of no return. In advertising parlance, relevance and esteem ads are synchronized so that they piggyback on differentiation ads[323].

- **The Art of Orchestration at the Pasteur Institute**

Think of the Pasteur Institute's news release announcing its decision to publish in English only due to budget cuts from its main sponsor, the French government. The announcement was issued to coincide with the French President's arrival at a major heads-of-state summit of French-speaking countries. Rather than focusing on his delegation's agenda, the President was pressured by the press and other dignitaries to finance the Institute's publications.

The Pasteur Institute also skillfully initiated and dramatized Rock Hudson's visit to its laboratories in Paris to educate the French public about AIDS and secure unprecedented financial support. Film actor Rock Hudson "was the first celebrity to publicly announce that he had the disease. The disclosure of Hudson's condition played a catalytic role in transforming public attitudes.

Hudson's popularity and celebrity status helped to dramatize the threat of the growing epidemic within the general population, and it also stimulated greater public sympathy toward people with AIDS. Moreover, Hudson's willingness to openly publicize his condition eased the public's early sense of shame over and discomfort with the disease. Previously, many individuals had forgone testing and medical treatment rather than risk their social reputations, jobs, and housing."[324]

- **Surprise Events Fuel Social Marketing**

Surprise events are particularly potent when they relate to something we dearly value. They can be used as a stimulus for behavior modification. In the health sector, the use of a well-orchestrated surprise event can have a powerful impact on habits and life styles. Men are more likely to quit smoking if they discover the impact of tobacco on their sexual potency than if they are told about the risks of heart failure, cancer and respiratory illness.

In a study conducted by Dr. Alexandre Olchanietski of Ichilov Hospital in Tel Aviv, 80% of 886 patients quit smoking after they were told about the influence of nicotine on contraction of their blood vessels and its linkage to impotence. Contrast these results with the 15-40% of the patients who quit smoking for cardiac reasons!

Capitalizing on the findings of Dr. Olchanietski, California and several countries launched a successful advertising campaign demonstrating that smoking reduces sexual potency.[325]

In the United Kingdom, Dr. Mary Shaw at the University of Bristol found that British smokers were more responsive to positive messages. She created powerful messages by associating factual knowledge about the time gained from non-smoking with valued activities. Giving up a pack of cigarettes adds about the equivalent of 4 hours per week to life span; that is plenty of extra time to watch two great movies each week, read a short novel or have romantic sex every night!

6. Tidal Waves

An event of unprecedented consequences or a cluster of surprise events occurring within a short time is called a *tidal wave*. The tandem Enron-WorldCom is an example.

- Financial Tidal Waves

In finance, tidal-wave scenarios wipe out countless hard-earned fortunes, but they bring opportunities to the shrewd *'contrarian'* investor who takes advantage of the fears of ordinary investors who bail out of a position *en masse*.

Think about the unexpected surprises associated with the presidential election of 2000, possibly the wildest in U.S. history. During the same year, several other surprise events led to market corrections in October and November of 2000. A financial tidal wave grew out of a series of profit warnings, producing huge losses in market capitalization throughout the years 2000-2001, eventually colliding with the 9-11 tragedies. In one day (April 24, 2000), Microsoft lost over $240 billion in capitalization, the equivalent of six Amazons, two Yahoos and twenty Corels at that time!

Having already affected millions of investors as well as Andersen, Dynergy, Tyco, IBM and countless firms, the Enron-WorldCom tidal wave has not yet run its full course. It has elevated governance, transparency and full disclosure to the top of congressional and corporate agendas. A host of bills are in the legislative pipeline ushering in unprecedented regulatory initiatives.

- Boeing: Impact of F-35 Joint Strike Fighters

Coming shortly after the slump in commercial aircraft sales caused by fallout from 9-11 (among other events), the selection of Lockheed Martin to build more than 3,000 F-35 stealth Joint Strike Fighters (JSF) hit Boeing like a tidal wave. By losing this $200-billion order, the largest defense program in history, Boeing entered an era of uncertainty described previously as the *Quarantine Phase*.

Many traders sold in haste, creating a window of opportunity for those who could see a brighter future for Boeing over the long term. The optimists recognized that the time Boeing devoted to JSF was a "strategic investment" in the words of CEO Phil

131

Condit. As a result, Boeing's "team came up with new methods of manufacturing, new ways of designing".[326]

This paralleled events half a century earlier at Boeing. "The incentive for creating the giant 747 came from reductions in air fares, an explosion in air-passenger traffic and increasingly crowded skies. In addition, Boeing had already developed the design concepts and technology of such an airplane because the company had bid on, but lost, the contract for a gigantic military transport, the C-5."[327] "The knowledge that Boeing gained during the development of the C-5 was also used in the early development of the 747. Although the loss of the C-5 was a crushing blow to Boeing at the time, it turned out that pursuing the 747 was vastly more successful for Boeing than the C-5 would have ever been."[328] Managers and professionals at Boeing closed ranks to make the 747 an outstanding commercial success and the world's leading jumbo jet for more than 25 years.

- Longevity of Tidal Waves

Finally, note that time ultimately mitigates the power of surprise events and tidal waves.

The Cuban Missile Crisis of October 1962 was a major surprise event that heightened the cold-war tensions to an unprecedented level and nearly triggered a third world war. The first sign of relief came with President Kennedy's assurances against a U.S. invasion of Cuba in response to Chairman Nikita Khrushchev's offer to remove the USSR missiles from Cuba. However, a tidal wave of events, like the assassination of Kennedy by Lee Harvey Oswald who had a Russian wife, armed confrontations in the Middle East and Vietnam, the rise and death of Chilean President Salvador Allende and the 1979 Soviet invasion of Afghanistan fuelled a renewed arms race kept an immense risk of Superpower confrontation lurking beneath the surface for nearly 25 years.

7. Hitch-Hiking on Surprise Events

Conductors orchestrate issue incubation. As experienced strategists, conductors either create surprise events or relentlessly scan for upcoming events for the purpose of exploiting them, using a coincidence in timing to implement controversial decisions, announce unrelated but germane news or identify related opportunities.

This ability to *hitch-hike* on surprise events or to use them as cover is a highly valued skill. Controversial press releases are often withheld until they can be overshadowed by high-profile news stories. In a handful of countries, military strategists have perfected the art of hitch-hiking on surprise events to stage controversial interventions.

The unique attributes and crucial role of conductors is detailed in the next chapter.

8. The Surprise-Event Driven Society

This preceding chapter on issue- and value-incubation cycle confirmed the fact that objectives are the result of the interplay between surprise events, the forces for change and the forces against it. This is not to say that objectives do not respond to real needs, but externalities and changing expectations tend to play havoc with even the best plans.

In the public sector, there are always far greater needs than there are resources for addressing them. Should we devote more funds to war on terrorism, cancer therapy, AIDS research, education, aviation safety or patrolling highways? Although cost-benefits analysis can help, the conflicting interests of powerful stakeholders make selecting issues contentious. Ultimately, skills and power capitalize on surprise events to win.

All societies seem to be *surprise-event driven*, i.e., reactive in policy formulation and decision-making. Judging from the outcomes of events such as the 1965 power blackout, Three-Mile Island and the 1952 outbreak of foot and mouth disease in Canada, we can only agree with Internet pioneer Bob Metcalfe that the Web cannot improve dramatically without major surprise events.

Most surprise events originate from the vast storehouse of isolated events. Although strategists have developed reliable scanning tools to predict and probe for emerging patterns, their potential remains largely untapped by all but a few corporate and political leaders. A social scanner, the strategic equivalent of a radar, might have alerted decision-makers to the potential for surprise events as devastating as the 9-11 tragedies, the bankruptcy of Enron, the 1986 aborted takeoff of the Challenger space shuttle, the 1987 stock market crash (which was preceded by the massive entry of first-time investors), and Watergate.

It would by erroneous to conclude from these illustrations that surprise events are all bad, disastrous or accidental. At the University of Michigan in Ann Arbor, on October 14, 1960 at 2:00 a.m., presidential candidate Senator John Kennedy made the famous impromptu speech challenging 10,000 students to "serve their country and the cause of peace by living and working in the developing world."[329] A year later, "a bold new experiment" was born: the U.S. Peace Corps. Also, remember, Boeing lost the C-5 military contract but went on to apply the knowledge it had gained in preparing the bid to develop a commercial winner, the 747. When the U.S. Navy awarded EDS a $7 billion contract, it prompted a spectacular revival of EDS stock, which had been heading south throughout the summer of 2000. Thus, not only do good surprise events exist,[330] but a growing number of them are actually being initiated by a small number of clever strategists, as illustrated in several cases earlier.

- Canalsur World Premiere

The notion of surprise-event driven societies is universal. It transcends national and cultural boundaries, as illustrated throughout this publication. A powerful European example worth noting is the bold move by Canalsur of Spain to engage Nuria del Saz, a blind journalist, as anchor for their main newscast. This world premiere event brought the TV station an unprecedented audience while serving the cause of the visually impaired throughout the country.

- Crafting High-Visibility Reports and Publications

Audit reports, research papers, feasibility studies and cost/benefit analyses are generally treated as isolated events by senior executives unless they have been edited by skilled authors to bring out a surprise event. Remarkable results can be achieved by rewriting the contents of a report and then orchestrating its publication and promotion in a dramatic fashion.

Consider the profound impact of John Maynard Keynes on economic policy and modern government duties. The publication in 1936 of his comprehensive theory of employment, interest and money[331] hit policy-makers and economists of his time like a

134

shock wave. It became the prevailing orthodoxy among government leaders for the next fifty years.

Think of other influential books, such as Adam Smith's *Wealth of Nations*, Plato's *Republic*, and John Locke's *Two Treatises of Government*. Best sellers such as Ralph Nader's *Unsafe at Any Speed*, Alvin Toffler's *Future Shock* and Mao Tse-tung's *Small Red Book* have benefited from this approach. They combine a dramatic but accessible book title, short sentences, down-to-earth vocabulary, an inquisitive writing style, close-to-home illustrations and paradigms within reach of the target audience.

In this context, even a piece of research such as Tom Peters and Robert Waterman's *In Search of Excellence* can be orchestrated to reach the status of a best seller despite poor reviews. Peters and Waterman were criticized in the November-December '83 issue of the Harvard Business Review for the *"absence of any serious description of how the excellent companies were analyzed"*. But in publishing, well-presented arguments and flag-waving can give advertisers powerful ingredients with which to orchestrate a bestseller at a time when the market is longing for domestic success stories.

9. Impact on Personal Lives and Careers

What about the major decisions in our personal lives? Were they results of surprise events? Most of us believe we are planning our future in a rational fashion. In fact, this statement is only partly correct. Surprise events account for the majority of marriages, jobs, separations, divorces and other great issues of life and death. But an awareness of how surprise events operate puts us in a much better position to capitalize on them in order to pursue our dreams with a clear mission.

We know that first impressions count, be it with a potential client or a date. However, most first encounters lead nowhere because the target treats them as isolated events. By working to make targets perceive the encounter as a positive surprise event, the initiator improves the chances of building a better relationship.

- **Ivan Reitman: The Journey from a Surprise Event to a Tidal Wave of Blockbusters**

The controversial arrest and conviction of Ivan Reitman for violating Canada's morality law with his widely-acclaimed 1969 first feature movie, *The Columbus of Sex*, was among the events that catapulted the 23-year Canadian film director and producer to North-American celebrity status. Virtually every subsequent movie forged a fresh surprise event that revealed the talents of a great comedian coupled with the genius of a team leader and conductor (see next chapter). Building and retaining great allies is also second nature to Ivan Reitman.[332] His repertoire of blockbusters and great movies is nothing short of a never-ending tidal wave punctuated with a stream of distinctions and awards including recognition as a Billion-Dollar Director.

10. Conclusion

In the previous chapter, we discussed the core phases of value incubation. This chapter focused on surprise events and tidal waves, their role during the incubation cycle and their impact on policy formulation and decision-making.

If the potential for an opportunity exists, an elegant process of orchestration undertaken at exactly the right moment can create and communicate value. Each of its phases exerts a significant impact. Moreover, the best and most desirable projects and policies tend to suffer when the value incubation phases are cut short, even if backed by solid cost/benefit analyses. Their future is akin to prematurely born children.[333]

Since powerful tools can be abused, however, it is hoped that planners and decision-makers will apply this framework to create and communicate value by advancing substantive issues and finding a graceful exit from the phony ones. Unfortunately, the same instruments can be used to propel a frivolous issue to the top of the organizational agenda. Neglecting this threat is hazardous, particularly for anyone on the "receiving side" of issue management. They include auditors, judges, mediators, negotiators, members of Congress, governors, corporate board members, and other leaders whose role is rarely to initiate, but more often to approve or veto recommendations. Acquiring these skills cannot help but improve their ability to evaluate the merits

136

of the issue at hand. Even in public policy research and management literature, hidden agendas are frequent and readers should always behave according to the principle of Consumer Beware.

CHAPTER 9

THE CHANGE-MAKERS
THEIR POWER, STATUS AND ROLE

Like a chorus of performers in a modern drama, enterprising consultants are urging you to designate a champion! As we shall see, reality is unfortunately not that simple.

In the previous chapters, we briefly introduced issue champions and riders together with their respective roles in the incubation of opportunities and risk, but our focus was on business intelligence rather than on holding a community together while bringing about change. In this chapter, we shall discuss the role of change-makers at greater length, focusing on their power to stall or bring about complex change.

For our purposes, the word *community* can refer to your staff and partners, loyal patrons and clients, voters, students and faculty or other important constituencies. And the word *change* refers to the *transition state* between the present and the future. It also denotes mechanisms for achieving innovation or creating discontinuity, a break with the linear trends of the past. *Change* can be a fresh start in pursuit of business opportunities, a better personal life, a new mission or the achievement of a community's aspirations. When the transition is well orchestrated, it can unfold like a good drama written for performance on the stage of life.

For an organization or society to chart its future and change for the better, three major players are required: a champion, an issue rider (sponsor) and a conductor (maestro). They are the *pillars of change*.

1. The Champion (or the Change Advocate)

As we have seen previously, champions are individuals with a high readiness for change, but frequently with a low capacity to make it happen. They complement issue riders, who are people with a low readiness but high capacity for bringing about change. *Roget's Thesaurus* associates the verb *"to champion"* with terms including defend, stand up for, advocate, plead for, uphold, sustain, support and back up. Champions frequently emerge as a result of surprise events, i.e., incidents that shake deeply held beliefs.

Most of us were champions of some ideal, value system or product during or shortly after leaving school or university. Champions are idealists who want to change the world for the better or to change corporate practices and culture overnight.

Some champions can be *rule breakers*. They are the radicals, the malcontents, the revolutionaries.[334] Very few rule breakers, however, succeed in achieving their aims. They tend to overestimate their degree of freedom and lack the skills to accurately deal with resistance to change. Eager to lead, unskilled champions may resort to coercion when facing adversity, while those who seek a high profile may damage their aims by being indiscrete. And unlike issue riders who manage perceptions so as to appear gracious in defeat, rule-breaking champions can be bad losers. They win sporadically, but their glory tends to be short-lived because they keep using coercion to champion pet issues. The magnitude and frequency of a champion's successes determine the pace with which she reaches a wider audience or becomes a conductor or issue rider.

Champions are valuable but fragile assets of organizations and society. Even though their behavior can be misguided, it represents a check on potential abuses of power by issue riders. Think of Sharon Watkins, who blew the whistle on Enron's hedging practices, and of the role played by *The New York Times* over the Pentagon's Papers. In ruling for the right of *The Times* to publish the Papers, Judge Murray I. Gurfein supported the champion: "A cantankerous press, an obstinate press, an ubiquitous press must be suffered by those in authority in order to preserve the even greater values of freedom of expression and the right of people to know."[335] An even more dramatic example was the role of *The Washington Post* in bringing down the Nixon Administration.

As a group, champions possess tomorrow's ideas. Although champions may be unpopular today, through their commitment to innovation and change they prepare the way for development and progress in their organization. Natural survivors, they manage to stand out against the relentless pressure to conform. Although champions are often seen as threats, their individualism is a rare gift in a society that cultivates and maintains conformity with an array of reward and punishment schemes.

Champions are present in every organization. Xerox Corporation is a perfect example of a company breeding great champions. Its Palo Alto Research Center invented the personal computer, graphical user interface (GUI) and PDL page-description language (now Adobe PostScript). Frustrated, the champions left to team-up with conductors and riders who turned their ideas into successful products.

In order to become more effective and to make a lasting contribution to corporate performance, champions deserve adequate protection, genuine recognition and top management support. They also need sound training and coaching in negotiation and team-building skills. Wearing the champion's hat should be encouraged and rewarded in brainstorming, problem solving and business meetings. Each of us should learn to play the role of champion without being offensive.

- **The Training Ground For Leaders**

The world of champions is an incubator for tomorrow's leaders. At the beginning of the 21st century, the business world is entering an era that features radically different rules of engagement from those witnessed in the past. For the first time in our history, self-made entrepreneurs such as Bill Gates, Michael Dell and Warren Buffett are at the top of the world's wealthiest lists prepared by Forbes and Fortune Magazines, eclipsing royalty and inheritors. Five of the top six (Bill Gates, Larry Ellison, Steve Ballmer, Paul Allen, and Michael Dell) have made their fortunes in advanced technologies. It is also interesting to note that all five started as champions of idiosyncratic visions, and burned their hands more than once before learning to act as sponsors and architects of change.

- **Nobel Laureate Kim Dae Jung: From a Champion to a Great Architect of Change**

The world of champions is also a fertile training ground for great world leaders. For more than forty years, dissident Kim Dae Jung championed democracy, human rights and the rule of law in

South Korea while enduring torture, appalling prison conditions and forced exile. In speaking against repressive military regimes in the Koreas, Burma, Cambodia and East Timor, he faced repeated threats to his life. Coached by leading peace advocates and inspired by Confucius, Gandhi and the Dali Lama, he gradually made the transition from champion to architect of change and in doing so, earned the trust of his nation. In 1997 he was elected the first democratic President of South Korea. Kim Dae Jung admired the late German chancellor Willy Brandt, who also started his career as an ardent champion of democracy and social justice and who dared to work for détente with Eastern Europe during the Cold War. Despite the risks, President Jung went on to engage the communist dictator of North Korea and ultimately won the Nobel Peace Prize in December 2000. The role of the change agent currently espoused by Kim Dae Jung is the subject of the section on the conductor below.

2. The Issue Rider (or Sponsor)

Issue riders (or sponsors) are the *godparents of change*. Although they have a high capacity for change, they show low readiness for it prior to the critical mass stage. Since a corporation or society cannot espouse all the ideas advanced by champions, issue riders can act like safety valves or gatekeepers. They permit the allocation of limited human and financial resources to opportunities and issues that have the support of a broader constituency in their territory.

Few senior executives act like champions. Those who do are the rule makers. Most top government and business leaders are risk aversive and frequently masters of cosmetic instead of substantive change. They prefer to keep champions at bay. However, when the champions' success is imminent, shrewd *riders* applaud, take over the lead, and reap some of the benefits. Like hitch-hikers, they ride on issues without paying their dues.

Unlike prophetic champions, riders are *institutional*. Champions tend to aim at the disruption of the current state of affairs rather than the destruction of institutions, and only a small number of champions become riders down the road. Most champions blame the *status quo* squarely on issue riders who, in turn, often remain quiet.

Shrewd riders rarely limit their commitment to a single issue. In fact, their power often dissipates when they devote more than a week at a time to a problem. For example, contrast President Jimmy Carter's inability to make deals with Congress, with President Franklin Delano Roosevelt who managed to ride on several no-win issues during his prolonged mandate. President Jimmy Carter was handicapped by inexperience and inability to build staunch allies among issue riders in Washington, even within his own party.[336]

In public, issue riders prefer statesman-like behavior characterized by tact, diplomacy and compassion. In private, however, they may opt for confrontation, but only in rare cases. Their attitude toward other riders is calculated to avoid either open animosity or unlimited endorsement in public. Even when they are subject to provocation and unfair treatment, their response is restrained and usually not commensurate with the aggression they endure. It is important to note that the rider's behavior is often *intuitive rather than cognitive*. It may also be orchestrated by others, as was the case during Ronald Reagan's presidency.

Most issue riders are protected by a suite of strong loyalists or disciples. The people of this extended "family" gravitate toward one another and nurture strong bonds across corporate boundaries. Experienced issue riders *advocate restraint*, not only within the family, but also to whomever cares to listen. Zealous members of their community at large are a constant source of concern.

The best issue riders form the *ruling elite* and set corporate, economic, scientific and national agendas. They are seen as credible by virtue of their status and prestige. For influential experts, these riders are the only constituency that really counts.

Riders also behave like benevolent constitutional monarchs and are truly a scarce resource for strategists. Think of IBM's legendary executives (Thomas J. Watson, Lou Gerstner) or some other leaders of Fortune 500 companies. In fact, IBM was itself an issue rider for 30 years (1960-1990) in the computer industry where there was no shortage of champions such as Apple and Digital!

Corporate riders also resemble monarchs when it comes to their succession. Their heirs are likely to emerge from within the company and many are usually groomed for the throne. The transfer of power is well thought-out. Such orderly transition is a prerequisite for corporate stability. GE's John Welch Jr. and Toyota's Hiroshi Okuda built their reputations on being demanding but fair and generous. Contrast the compassionate way these leaders treat their staff with the notorious conduct of the mean-spirited executives you read about in the daily press!

- **The Daring Rider**

Among issue riders, there is a small group of *daring riders* – individuals with high readiness for change and high capacity to make it happen. The clever among them act like *conductors* (see below). Think of Thomas Edison (the inventor) and Admiral H. G. Rickover. At the other end of the spectrum, a few will occasionally use their clout to advance their own agendas without regard for various constituencies. These bullheaded riders can lose their power rapidly if they frequently indulge in making controversial decisions that end up failing or damaging powerful constituencies.

3. The Conductor: an Architect of Change

As the *missing link* between the champion and the rider, the *conductor* understands what makes both players tick. Conductors possess a critical mind and are blessed with intellectual rigor. "Like jigsaw puzzles, communities are difficult to hold or put together, yet the skills of community building are central to the survival of civilization."[337] Unlike the rider, who may only be concerned about stability, the conductor aims at orchestrating the change while building stronger constituencies.

Borrowed from classical music, both *conductor* and *maestro* refer to the *architect* of change: a pragmatist, an honest broker, and a strategist with a low need for public approbation. In operas and ballets, conductors play a vital role in integrating the efforts of performers; oversee protocol, control timing and decide who will do what.

Conductors are corporate stress managers. Corporate change and particularly discontinuity produce stress, which, if left unmanaged, can result in community breakdown, lost productivity, absenteeism, drugs, turnover, accidents and other problems. Like a big ship, the corporation cannot veer sharply in uncharted waters without stress management. Understanding the dynamics of stress permits the wise conductor to determine a rate of change that is humane, feasible and effective.

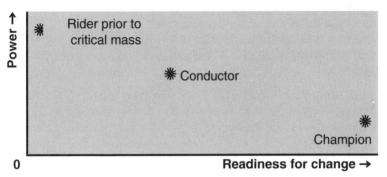

Figure 9.1. Locating the change-makers on the power scale

The conductors who chart the future are *champions at heart*. They actually emerge from a few champions who got burned several times and subsequently learned the rules of orchestrating social or technological change. They are motivated by the internal desire to do a good job and to be of service to a mission they value.

Conductors are often *pluralists*, eager to give credit to others or at least to share the rewards equitably. They frequently know how to cultivate, preserve and even channel the emotional capital of their constituents. They are willing to endure criticism and may readily accept the blame in order to protect their subordinates or an issue rider. They can be tough but fair. They demand the best from their people and set an example by doing their utmost. They motivate by empathy, role-modeling and positive reinforcement, rather than by manipulation.

Some conductors work best behind the scenes. Although conductors may not be visible (i.e., formal leaders), they exercise a profound influence on our society. Think of Chief Engineer A. Scott Crossfield who was the first person to fly at Mach 2 (about twice the speed of the Concorde airplane) and survive three times the speed of sound. Scott was the driving force behind the development of the X-15 rocket research aircraft program, which led to NASA's Space Shuttle. His aviation career spanned 50 years concluding with the U.S. House of Representatives Committee on Science and Technology. Although he has received countless honors, Scott kept a low profile always giving credit to his peers and the organizations he served. Yet, his talent, leadership and character account for his commendable contribution to the progress of his teams. Think also of the spouses behind the success of many presidents, artists or authors. Working behind the scenes like opera maestros, these conductors are almost invisible but omnipresent. Good riders dearly value their advice, without blindly deferring to their judgment.

The conductor's role is a good training ground for future riders. Unlike champions, both conductors and riders have a clear awareness of the degree of freedom within which they can operate. They tend to have a harmonious working relationship, each valuing the importance of the other's contribution to the fulfillment of their goals.

The most seasoned conductors are usually altruistic and discreet. They are most difficult to predict in their day-to-day behavior. Their experience and altruism allow them greater latitude than champions and riders in their choice of interventions. As resources, they are in very short supply.

Conductors are essential to teamwork. Conductors help team members ask the right questions, set priorities, value creativity, focus clearly on an issue and organize the thinking process to reach greater value. They are in even greater demand in a virtual-team environment. Each of us must learn to wear the conductor's hat and be prepared to assume it when a discussion drifts during a meeting, negotiation session or other important event.

Conductors are leaders. In Michael Porter's words, they "possess insights into opportunities and the tools to exploit them... They do not accept constraints and know that they can change the nature of the outcomes. They are in position to perceive something about reality that has escaped others, and have the courage to act."[338]

- Raoul Wallenberg: A Selfless Role Model Beyond Comparison

Among issue conductors, Swedish Diplomat Raoul Wallenberg stands apart as an exceptional hero and role model beyond comparison. He did not hesitate to repeatedly risk his life to save thousands of Jews from the Holocaust. Wallenberg has demonstrated that one courageous selfless person with persuasive skills and diplomatic creativity can inspire a team to make an immense difference. Motivated more by a sense of responsibility than by destiny, he was a heroic and inspiring conductor, one worth keeping in mind when thinking about serious contemporary issues.

- Greg Watson: Leading Without the Benefit of Authority

Greg Watson, an unknown 31-year old administrative assistant in Texas, epitomizes the fundamental attributes of great *maestros*. Thanks to Watson's quiet diplomacy, the 27th Amendment to the U.S. Constitution was enacted 202 years after first being tabled by James Madison. At the age of 19, Watson, a student at the University of Texas in Austin, wrote a term paper in which he argued that the Congressional Pay Amendment of 1789 should be passed. His professor disagreed and gave the paper a C. With less than $7,000 of his own money and no financial support from external sources, Watson orchestrated a 10-year campaign to have the amendment ratified by at least thirty more states to bring the total to thirty-eight as required by 75% rule for constitutional amendments. By May 1992, forty states had ratified the 27th Amendment. The achievement is no small feat. It prevents Members of Congress from raising their pay, expense allowances and benefits, both retroactively and in mid-term, as they have done in the past. Watson proved once again that with wisdom, strategic thinking and quiet diplomacy *"one person can still make the difference in this country,"* after which he went *"back to normal life."*[339]

- Nobel Laureate Jody Williams: A Lifesaver and a Shining Beacon of Hope for Civil Societies

After a solid track record in directing humanitarian relief projects and advocating change in U.S. policy toward Latin America in the eighties, Jody Williams shifted her focus to helping civil societies ban anti-personnel landmines which kill or severely injure more people than any other weapon (24,000 people every year). Most victims are innocent farmers, children and travelers in the third world. In 1992, Jody Williams coordinated the creation of the International Campaign to Ban Landmines (ICBL), originally a confederation of six nongovernmental organizations

147

(NGOs) devoted to address the humanitarian, social and economic problems resulting from landmine contamination. In less than five years, ICBL grew to over 1,200 NGOs and formed an alliance with the International Committee of the Red Cross and a small coalition of governments led by Canada. Banning landmines is not the kind of issue to win votes for candidates of the political establishment in most industrialized countries. But thanks to the tireless efforts of Jody Williams and her partners, 122 countries ratified, under the auspices of the United Nations, the 1997 Ottawa Convention, a comprehensive framework enshrining the ban in international law. Both ICBL and Jody Williams were the co-recipients of the 1997 Nobel Peace Prize. With the active participation of architects of social change like Dr. Philippe Chabasse of France, the effectiveness of ICBL has nowhere to go but up.

- ## Conductors in Business and International Organizations

- *Maurice Strong*

After a number of entrepreneurial success stories in the energy business, Maurice Strong went on to lead Power Corporation at the age of 31, then the Canadian International Development Agency (CIDA) and the International Development Research Centre (IRDC) before moving on to the United Nations. In the mid-eighties, he orchestrated a commendable struggle against the draught and famine in Sub-Saharan Africa. Promoted Secretary General of the 1992 U.N. Conference on Environment and Development (UNCED), Maurice Strong was instrumental in making sustainable development a global priority. In 1997, he spearheaded an in-depth reform of the United Nations. Strong has been a leading force behind the civil society, global governance and sustainable development movements that are now in the spotlight. Yet, like most effective conductors, he prefers the low-key informal approach.

- *Peter Uberroth and Dick Pound*

Public figures like Peter Uberroth and Dick Pound show how effective conductors can be in action. In managing the 1984 Olympics, major league baseball and numerous projects in South Central Los Angeles, Mr. Uberroth often acted as a conductor. As for Mr. Pound, he rose close to the top of the international Olympic movement by building the foundations for strategic alliances with global sponsors like Coca-Cola, IBM, Kodak and McDonald's. He "negotiated many of the sponsorship and television rights deals which poured billions of dollars into Olympic coffers. Like many great conductors, he gracefully left the position of Chief Marketing Officer, paving the way for a smooth succession by leaving a strong team and an unprecedented portfolio of long-term commitments from sponsors. When asked about his decision, he simply said: "The best time for a change is when everything is operating smoothly."[340] Mr. Pound has played an instrumental role, often behind the scenes, to eradicate corruption and establish the IOC code of ethics before moving to chair the World Anti-Doping Agency. He is concurrently leading the team mandated to make the Olympic games affordable to host countries in continents like Africa.

- William H. Gross

Considered by *Barron's* magazine, in 2001 as the most influential bond investor in the world, William H. Gross, Managing Director of the $220 billion Pacific Investment Management Fund, is a guiding light for the bond market. Gross's opinion is highly valued by his peers and by institutional investors.

- Gregory Pincus

In the pharmaceutical world, Dr. Gregory Pincus, a skilled *maestro,* led a team of distinguished scientists (John Rock, Ming-Chueh Chang and Frank Colton) to produce the first contraceptive pill (Enovid). He used his negotiation skills to gain FDA approval to pilot-test Enovid in Puerto Rico and to channel the energy of both the pill champion (Margaret Sanger) and its rider (G.D. Searle) to create critical mass in Congress. By the time the church and the Religious Broadcasting Council learned about the strategy, the critical mass was already on Dr. Pincus's side.[341]

- Mikio Sasaki at Mitsubishi

Overhauling a major global conglomerate like Mitsubishi Corporation (MC) and strengthening its essence is daunting regardless of the economic climate. But Mikio Sasaki, the conductor at the helm of Mitsubishi is no stranger to tough challenges. He is also known for addressing the toughest issues head-on with remarkable team-based solutions crafted after due consideration of value, risk and impact on the local and global

MC constituencies. Prior to being appointed President and CEO of Mitsubishi Corporation in 1998, Mr. Sasaki built a solid reputation within MC. He witnessed, first hand, civil unrest, and political violence while tracking major projects in Chile, during military siege, and subsequently, heading MC's operations in Iran during the Islamic Revolution and Iran-Iraq war. While posted in the United States during the early 1990's, he saw the worst of the economic slump of that time. In steering projects and negotiating deals, Mr. Sasaki always took the initiative to learn, forge lasting alliances, coach talent and improve productivity, wherever he worked. Recent initiatives taken by MC under Mr. Sasaki's leadership include:

1. A new approach to managing human resources focusing on a greater delegation of authority to business unit managers along with a reward system based on direct accountability for results;

2. The introduction of MVCA, a new performance measurement instrument[342] to complement the risk adjusted EVA indicator.

3. Pruning the structural layers and grouping about 180 business units into three clear categories (strategic missions), based on how they fit into MC's portfolio management strategy, and with due consideration to their abilities to progress and succeed in domestic and world markets.

4. Taking significant holdings in a leading and growing Japanese convenience store chain.[343]

Both the competition and global markets have noticed the bold and promising initiatives taken by Mitsubishi under Mr. Sasaki's leadership: leading financial analysts have raised Mitsubishi stock's rating to a Buy in the summer of 2002.

- Boeing:
From Wilson to Shrontz, Condit and Mullaly

Turning to another example, aeronautical engineer T.A.Wilson was a great conductor before turning into an issue rider at Boeing. He led a U.S. multi-company team that developed the Minuteman missile with innovative team-building ideas and unequivocal commitment to the needs of the client. Wilson preferred the use of persuasive rather than coercive power. But he didn't hesitate to use his authority to eradicate negligence, incompetence, mismanagement and hidden agendas. He returned to Boeing in the early seventies, at a time when the company was facing its worst-ever business crisis. He built a reputation as an honest broker when he successfully negotiated the reduction of nearly 100,000 jobs with the board of directors, governments and employee representatives. Wilson then orchestrated a remarkable comeback for Boeing by helping the champions simultaneously develop and build two profitable jetliners, the 757 and the 767.

Wilson's successor, Frank Shrontz, relied even more on quiet diplomacy. A former champion who successfully fought the cancellation of the B737, Shrontz quickly learned to act as a conductor and rose to the top of the Boeing hierarchy, becoming Chairman in 1986. Shrontz did not hesitate to protect and support Phil Condit and Alan Mullaly, the champions of the 777, when Boeing faced delivery problems with Lufthansa, Japan Airlines and British Airways. Shrontz also coached his succession to permit a flawless transition to Phil Condit, who gained a solid reputation as an engineer and talented communicator.

Within two years, Condit built the core team that is redefining Boeing, its markets and allies to balance its product portfolio. His succession will be even smoother with Alan Mullaly at the helm, a role model dedicated to the highest standards of ethical conduct and to the fair and best treatment of every performer. A prudent and tactful architect of change, Mr. Mullaly is bringing key riders, including customers, suppliers and even bankers, closer to the shop floor. Boeing will survive the setback of 9-11 and emerge stronger with a diversified portfolio featuring a balanced commercial, defense and space mix.

The lessons managers can learn from leading conductors are timeless. While the rider's position is to maintain the champions at arm's length to avoid controversy in public, the role of the conductor is to integrate and balance the influence of these two different types of change-makers. Unless the efforts of the champions and riders are adequately orchestrated, the management of change will suffer.

4. Synthesis

Stakeholders are organizations and individuals who have a vested interest in an issue. They include scapegoats, culprits,

151

beneficiaries and victims of change, as well as those whose vested interest is merely intellectual curiosity.

Among them, the major players are called *change-makers*. They include the champion, the issue rider (sponsor) and the conductor (maestro). Collectively, they play an instrumental role during issue incubation. Champions tend to be visible and anxious to be seen as stars, but riders and conductors are more reserved and may even opt to act behind the scenes. Although change-makers may never meet, the timing of their intervention or entry onto the scene is vital.

The rank and file consists mostly but not exclusively of people who either tacitly or actively support or oppose the change-makers. They will sooner or later form the constituency needed to legitimize either the change or the *status quo*. As such, their influence cannot be neglected. Their perceptions and vested interest will be addressed in the next chapter.

5. Conclusion

So far, we have defined the pillars of change and their characteristics. Each change-maker makes a unique contribution to charting the future and should enter the transition stage in a timely manner, as outlined in the previous chapters. It is also important to keep in mind that these change-agents are territorial and transitional. We may be a rider in the office and "a nobody" at home!

In considering change makers, our objective was not to judge these players as good and bad or as leaders and followers. Nor should we elevate maestros or riders over champions. Our intent is simply to look at the strategic roles taken by key players if the process of change is to occur. Those interested in championing change can indeed be effective, providing they act skillfully using humility, vision and logic. Those who wish to act as riders should consider whether they are sufficiently empowered to make change happen. By the same token, aspiring conductors should understand the harmony of opposites and build the talent needed to reach out to others, regardless of their beliefs. Last but not least, conductors should keep a low profile and not be motivated by a need for public approbation.

In the next chapter, we shall further consolidate our knowledge of stakeholders with the introduction of a powerful qualitative tool: the *Factional Scale*™

-

CHAPTER 10

ASSESSING STAKEHOLDERS' PERCEPTIONS WITH THE FACTIONAL SCALE™

The *Factional Scale*™ is a qualitative instrument designed to assess the perceptions of anyone with a vested interest in an objective, a project, an organization or an issue (i.e., a threat or an opportunity). Originally developed by the author for the Canadian Department of National Defence and the intelligence community, the scale helps users identify both unusual sources of risk and potential allies beyond those that intuitively come to mind. The *Factional Scale*™ is an ordinal scale that complements common quantitative approaches to risk management. Its effectiveness accounts for its acceptance in leading companies, financial institutions, utilities and defense establishments. Users, however, should exercise extreme caution and avoid stratifying individuals, particularly in the F6 and F7 categories described below, without ample evidence. Even when the analysis reveals the existence of F6s and F7s on a given issue, the data should be shredded: the sooner the better. Indiscretion in this domain could be actionable.

1. The Seven Factions

Academics tend to group stakeholders into two categories: those who support a project or policy issue and those who oppose it. Jim Sibenius calls them the "supporters" and "blockers".[344] While this simple conception of reality is better than nothing, it can lead to erroneous decisions, particularly in complex issues where numerous clusters or factions with distinct interests gradually emerge from the population of "fence sitters". The alternative is to consider the degree to which there are vested interests among the players and to rank them accordingly. At one end of the spectrum are the people needing the issue for survival. At the other end are those engaged in its systematic obstruction. Somewhere in between are the remaining fence sitters. The universe of the *Factional Scale*™ comprises the following seven generic factions as summarized in Figure 10.1.

- **F1 – Family**

This category comprises your most active and unconditional supporters, i.e., the people who see your objectives as *vital* to their own mission or objectives. They are your most valuable assets. They include your "must" customers, suppliers and staff. Most F1s want you to exceed your objectives.

The goals of F1s would be permanently handicapped unless you resolve the issue at hand and fulfill your mandate. The next chapter sheds further light on the values or glue that binds your company to its F1s, be they employees or customers.

- **F2 – Friends**

This faction actually comprises two kinds of good supporters: *friends* and *followers*.

People who deem the issue to be important, though not essential to their survival, are grouped in the friends or F2 category. They could also be seriously handicapped if the objectives are not achieved and their own performance will suffer, but unlike the F1s, they would nonetheless survive even if they had to operate in fallback sub-optimal mode.

Followers are the 'yes' people who will unquestionably support your objectives. Trust, past experience, love, tradition, reciprocity, imitative behavior, lack of confidence and fear are among the many reasons that motivate followers.

- **F3 – Fellow Travelers**

Good fellows or *fellow travelers* are your *passive supporters*, i.e., the people who see your issue as desirable but neither vital nor important. They are favorably disposed but their support is *soft* either because of the risks involved or because their interests won't be greatly affected by your decision. They can be sympathetic to the cause but will not fully commit themselves to it. They often include conditional customers, employees and suppliers as well as most of your issue riders, i.e., people with a low readiness for change and a high capacity to make it happen. They see your contribution as having marginal value and can meet their needs elsewhere. Think of customers who use your firm as a *fill-in* or contingency supplier when their favorite supplier can't do the job.

	7 Factions	Perception of Your Goals by Each Faction
F1	Family	Vital to Their Mission
F2	Friends	Important But Not Vital to Their Mission
F3	Fellow Travelers or Conditional Supporters	Nice-to-Have
F4	Fence Sitters or Foreigners	Neutral by Necessity, Choice or Ignorance
F5	Foes	Rational Adversaries (Smart Competitors)
F6	Fools	Volatile Perceptions, Erratic Behavior, Fragile Loyalty, Inconsistency of Purpose; Indiscreet, Unpredictable
F7	Fiascos or Fanatics	Systematic Obstruction Regardless of the Consequences Including Self-Destruction

Figure 10.1. Factional Scale™ Grid

- **F4 – Fence Sitters or Foreigners**

Fence sitters are neutral – neither for nor against you. Among others, intellectual curiosity can spark the vested interest of this faction. Most fence sitters ignore your existence. Others adopt the fence-sitter position by choice, preferring to remain independent or keep their options open, pending further developments. There are also individuals who adopt the fence-sitter position by necessity vis-à-vis friends or family members who are engaged in a conflict.

The F4 category includes the majority of players prior to a surprise event as discussed in Chapter 7. While often undecided, most fence sitters are susceptible to overtures and the pressure of other groups, particularly in the aftermath of a surprise event.

The potential of fence sitters, especially those who ignore your existence, remains largely untapped by managers and negotiators. Finding unknown fence sitters who can turn into allies is challenging. In the next chapter, we will see how psychographics and Brand-Cluster Analysis (BCA) facilitate the process of searching for counter-intuitive alliances, co-branding and cross-selling opportunities.

- **F5 – Foes**

People whose interests would be negatively affected by the success of your objectives are opponents or F5s. Their aim is to win at your expense. They are clever adversaries but can be open to collaboration, or even ephemeral coalitions on issues of mutual interest. It is therefore best to consider foes as temporary, territorial and situational.

There are two kinds of foes: *born foes* and *acquired foes*. Acquired foes start out as former allies and, as a result, are much more difficult to win back than born foes. Think of Ross Perot and George Bush Sr., Lee Iacocca and Henry Ford, Apple's John Scully and Steve Jobs, Jacques Chirac and Valery Giscard D'Estaing in France, Mao Tse-tung and Chang Kai-Chek in China, Paul Martin and Jean Chrétien in Canada, and most separated couples everywhere.

Even in adversarial situations, direct attacks are far costlier than other kinds of strategic intervention. Evidence from marketing, courts, labor, politics and the military suggests that there are better ways to repel F5 threats (defense) or to capture a territory or a market held by an F5 (offense). In lieu of direct confrontation, smart F5s prefer to achieve their goals by using innovations and stratagems or by covertly exploiting the potential of third parties such as the F6s and F7s. Their behavior is characterized by hidden agendas. For example, think of the customer or the supplier whose hidden agenda is really to acquire your know-how, staff, clientele or other allies.

Every neglected ally is a potential foe. Nurturing and safeguarding the alliance with genuine and ongoing cooperation is the best deterrent against the latent gravitational drift from F1, F2, F3 and F4 toward the F5 group.

Competitors who fit F5 attributes can still be great allies on issues of mutual interest (such as safety, health, the environment or education). Oil companies competing in offshore exploration (e.g., Canadian Arctic, Europe's North Sea) have been sharing air-rescue fleets for years. General Motors, Ford and Daimler-Chrysler have joined hands to implement a single environmental research organization for their industry. Alcoa, Alcan and Pechiney work hand-in-hand in expanding the applications of aluminum and strengthen its position vis-à-vis plastics, wood and other metals. Lucent works with rivals Nortel, Alcatel, Siemens and Ericsson through the Alliance for Telecommunications Industry Solutions (ATIS) to "minimize the need for regulatory or other government oversight"[345] and to develop global standards such as the UMTS single air interface solution. Competing financial institutions like CIBC, ScotiaBank and Desjardins bring down their costs by doing all of their purchasing through Procuron, a jointly owned subsidiary. Since September 2001, airlines are sharing assets and technology to improve safety.

Leaders of the music industry (Time Warner, Bertelsmann, Vivendi and Sony) fight tooth and nail against each other to extend their own share of the market. But they have also joined forces against common foes such as online music-swappers (MP3, Scour and Napster).[346]

- F6 – Fools or Fly-By-Nights

The F6 group includes a variety of types that range from those who are naïve and easily duped to those who exploit current fears to launch hoaxes, pranks or other forms of irresponsible behavior.

This group includes people with *volatile* (often erroneous) perceptions, inconsistent behavior or fragile loyalty. They are people who often unknowingly act against their own interests. F6s tend to be verbose and indiscreet. They lack foresight and rarely learn from their experiences, which abound in disappointments and *faux pas*. Covering up or rationalizing mistakes is common behavior among F6s.

F6s are most dangerous when they hold a key position in your organization and are not guided by their peers and subordinates. However, F6s tend to be dangerous by accident rather than by design. Employees who act as F6s have been used in the role of *doomed spies,* as described by Sun Tzu in *The Art of War.*[347] Fed with false intelligence calculated to thwart the aims of their employer's foes, doomed spies unknowingly act as messengers and deliver as expected. F6s are also thoroughly exploited by F5s and F7s, but almost never in an overt fashion.

The intelligence community often uses F6s as blind resources in risk management. Unlike covert and overt resources, *a blind resource* is a person serving someone's hidden objectives without being aware of it.[348] Many job candidates act as blind resources for unscrupulous companies that post bogus career ads in order to gather intelligence on their competitors. This unethical practice is especially observable in the high-tech sector.

- ## F7 – Fiascos or Fanatics

The *Fiascos* or *Fanatics* are people interested in all-out opposition, including the systematic obstruction of your issue, regardless of the consequences, even if it means self-destruction.

Included in the F7 category are individuals who see the issue as vital to their survival but will not hesitate to adopt vigilante tactics, obstruct peace or even risk their lives to achieve their aim. Many tend to be easily provoked and belligerent. Radical demagogues and ideologues tend to behave in an F7 fashion. The disgruntled employee who constantly makes gratuitous accusations and threatens others is also a typical F7. The suspended student who slanders faculty and his peers and the malicious solicitor who resorts to cheeky coercion and threatens to take formal action without validating the client's claim offer further examples of F7 behavior.

Unlike F5s (rational foes), F7s are not pragmatists. Compared to F6s who are dangerous by accident, the F7s are dangerous by choice. The strategies of shrewd F7s follow a variable ratio of intervention, as observed by B. F. Skinner, and are therefore hard to predict. They are often used by the F5s in a covert or blind manner. F6s and F7s are counter-productive and should preferably be kept at bay in any endeavor.

Our research on F7s began with DuPont thirty years ago when Vincent Meloche, a fired employee, shot and killed three managers. After analyzing similar homicides and extending the focus of the research to a host of F7s, including harsh negotiators, terrorists and other hard-core criminals, a psychographic profile of three kinds of F7s, namely ringleaders, isolated psychopaths (the Unabomber) and orchestrated F7s, has emerged.

Be they in prison, a cult or even in politics, ringleaders use heavy-handed means to control their subjects. Isolation of followers from family and community is one of their key techniques. In order to suppress resistance, ringleaders opt for group pressure, intimidation and conformism. They create fear through overt harsh treatment of dissidents; induce fatigue (physical and mental) through constant surveillance and overwork. They cause guilt by showering their subjects with pseudo-love, gifts and flattery. Such treatment breaks down the defense mechanisms of followers who can also turn into orchestrated F7s. Further research material is available to institutions engaged in dealing or negotiating with F7s.[349]

2. The Factional-Scale Road Map

- Strategic Positioning of Stakeholders

Players	F1	F2	F3	F4	F5	F6	F7	Interventions
Lyn Bud		D	←	←	C			Joint Venture
Bob Ali		D	←	C				Reciprocity
Gil Ho			D	C				Cross selling
Jo Cash				DC				Laissez-faire

Figure 10.2. Strategic Positioning of Stakeholders
Map current (C) and desirable (D) positions of key players.
Brainstorm interventions to bridge the gap.

Use the above grid to map the current and desirable F-position of your stakeholders. Brainstorm interventions to bridge the gap. For this purpose, invite suggestions; but withhold critiques. List the benefits of each suggestion, then ask each participant to present a critique of their own suggestions. Most people defy the conventional wisdom: they tend to be hard on themselves and prefer to criticize their own ideas instead of letting others do it. The collective critique should be structured in a constructive way. Thus, whoever raises a problem or an objection to someone else's suggestion must make a sincere effort to propose a solution to the stated problem in an effort to salvage the suggestion. Consider the *Harvard*™ *Strategy Grid*[350] to help you ensure complete coverage of the universe of generic choices.

3. Synthesis

The *Factional Scale*™ facilitates understanding of the dynamics of power in and around an issue, policy, project or even a day-to-day operation. It is a proven means of detecting risks associated with resistance to change and identifying no-win projects at the

161

beginning of the assignment. It points to the need for a community-building strategy coupled with preventive action.

As an example, an absence of allies (F1s, F2s, F3s) combined with the presence of adversaries (F5s, F6s, and F7s) might suggest a need for secrecy, a need for strategies to build allies, and the need for a longer pre-project timeline to deal with opposition. Potential losses perceived by stakeholders should either be removed or offset by gains elsewhere. Actions aimed at increasing the comfort level of fence-sitters are also essential for broadening the network of allies and providing the policy or project with a stable constituency in order to weather future storms.

Because F1s, F2s and F3s are considered natural allies, they are usually ignored or taken for granted in strategic thinking. As a result, some allies become adversaries of the worst kind as has been noted, former allies are much harder to please than other opponents. Therefore, ongoing efforts are necessary in order to retain the trust of teammates and current allies.

In addition to keeping allies informed earlier than others, the business plan should, whenever feasible, also include actions that will contribute to the fulfillment of your allies' own missions. This emphasis on a win-win approach strengthens the alliance. Even F5s should be considered potential allies rather than permanent adversaries.

The *Factional Scale*™ is a powerful tool. Like most potent innovations, it can be hazardous for the uninitiated. Strategists must therefore be reminded to exercise caution in applying the framework. Indiscretion and gratuitous stratification of people in the F6 and F7 groups without evidence could be actionable. As indicated earlier, once a business plan has been drafted, *Factional Scale*™ data should be shredded — the sooner the better.

Measuring stakeholders' perceptions is a mind-boggling challenge. The *Factional Scale*™ provides policy and decision-makers with another valuable lens. Its application in negotiation, competitive intelligence and national security are a fertile platform for further research.

CHAPTER 11

MINING CONSTITUENCIES
WITH DEEPER INSIGHTS, BETTER INTELLIGENCE

What do you know about your current and potential customers, your team, competitors and key players? What motivates the best talent to join your organization? Who is most likely to purchase your products and services?

This chapter focuses on additional tools to gain further insights into the mind of your clients and stakeholders, their motivations, personality traits, lifestyles, and resources. The purpose is to help you design and position products and organizations both in the market place and cyberspace, improve market share, lower customer acquisition cost as well as excel in working and communicating effectively with your constituencies (peers, bankers, suppliers, adversaries and the community at large).

1. Demographics

Logic and intuition alone are not reliable drivers of decisions. Demographics go a bit deeper. They comprise attributes such as age, gender, marital status, personal income, wealth and credit status, education, occupation, employment status, ethnicity, health and fitness status, household metrics (size, number and age of children, number of wage earners and their total income) and residence (tenure, ownership, location).

Demographics provide only a crude segmentation of your target audience. Because people with the same demographic attributes do not necessarily share similar interests, demographics are not sufficient to accurately predict behavior.

2. Psychographics

- Intelligent Targeting

Psychographics embodies psychological information that reveals much more about lifestyles, motivations, tastes, opinions, self-image and behavior, including buying and media habits[351]. While demographics count the number of potential customers with given characteristics, psychographics provides enriched profiles of homogeneous clusters of people that are most or least likely to buy a given product. Among consumers with similar demographic characteristics, psychographics reveals differences between the profiles of buyers of different brands (Pepsi versus Coke) or families of products (sports cars, station wagons and luxury sedans). That inferential-intelligence difference is vital to engineers and advertisers, among others. In this era of oversupply and global competition, knowing the nuances of what makes people tick is a competitive advantage that can lead to untapped opportunities. The sales of Revlon and Cover Girl are more sensitive to advertising messages about hope and youth than about the features of cosmetics.

Psychographics "emphasizes the relationship between people, products, and settings; examines product usage patterns and consumption constellations."[352] It facilitates targeting the right customers, throughout a product life cycle, and personalizing the value proposition. Since behavior and buying habits change over time, psychographics profiles must be kept up to date, particularly now that more mainstream consumers transact via the Internet.

Data are gathered using a variety of methods that include explicit collection (survey questionnaires, interviews), mining targeted databases, direct unobtrusive observations and electronic collection of online browsing behavior using ASP, Cookies or ISP server logs.[353]

- Psychographics in Tourism

Psychographics has been extensively applied in tourism, where culture, demographics, time and personality traits affect the choice of travel destinations and experience. Mervyn Jackson[354] assessed the impact of culture[355] on the selection of travel destinations. Earlier, Stanley Plog[356] developed a simple psychographic typology with three categories of tourists:

164

- Psychocentrics are suspicious of the new and different. They prefer travel to safe, familiar and popular destinations.

- Allocentrics are the opposite. They are adventurous, early adopters of new forms of travel, daring to explore new destinations and are not afraid of the unknown.

- Midcentrics characterize the majority of the population, which falls between the above extremes.

As we shall see below, VALS™ topology is richer. It allows for in-depth analysis and interpretation based on statistical evidence. Because of this, VALS™ is worth the investment for government agencies and companies targeting tourists.

- **Brand-Cluster Analysis**

Brand-Cluster Analysis (BCA) provides factual information about the buying behavior of your customers or any other target group by studying the content of their basket of purchases and acquisitions. By segmenting the market based on the intrinsic relationship between brands in the minds of the consumers, BCA displays a rich tapestry of opportunities for alliances, co-branding and cross selling, particularly in e-commerce. A leading airline uses BCA to select food and beverages brands for its business class passengers. A retail bank applies it to identify the best partner for locating its ATM machines.

Current BCA information is usually classified. In the following hypothetical example (Figure 11.1), our client, Alpha Group, surveys repeat buyers of its Alpha flagship products each year. The table is extracted from a brand-cluster spread sheet consisting of over 200 rows with up to 10 top brands per row. These three entries illustrate the concept.

Products	Dominant Brand	Target Brand	Psychographics Correlation
Credit Cards	41% Amex	23% Visa	High
Cars	18% GM	4% Volvo	High
Long distance	39% AT&T	32% Sprint	Low

Figure 11.1. Illustration of Brand-Cluster Analysis

Note that the psychographic profiles of Volvo car buyers and Alpha product buyers are highly correlated, but only 4% of Alpha customers own a Volvo. That difference could mean untapped opportunities for both Volvo and Alpha. It should at least trigger consultations aimed at a cross-selling alliance with Volvo. Thus, Volvo could offer Alpha products in its own gift catalog and Alpha could insert Volvo advertising material in its shipments to customers.

Likewise, the Visa market share among Alpha customers is about half the size of Amex. Visa could be approached to promote Alpha products in return for a special campaign targeting Alpha clients by Visa. This is precisely the process that led our own organization to introduce Harvard® Planners to the customers of Volvo and subsequently to millions of Visa cardholders.

In the B2B world, many of the people who exercise a profound influence on purchasing decisions tend to work best behind the scenes, like the conductors we described earlier. Learning about them is the baseline in preparation for any strategic negotiation. Knowing about their basket of favorite brands may add further insights to your current F-scale information (Chapter 10) and competitive intelligence. Note, however, that without a cultural fit and a commitment, alliances tend to be ephemeral and problematic.

- **Collaborative Filtering**

Collaborative filtering is a powerful cross-selling process that exploits a battery of statistical tools to delve deeper into the linkages between products and target audiences.[357] The simplest filtering system uses data mining engines to establish the taste affinity or correlation between different customers based on their purchases and brand preferences. A preference analysis software tracks customers with similar tastes and places a cookie in their system. Thus, a customer viewing or ordering a new product is offered additional items that were purchased by one or more buyers with similar tastes.

We know that busy professionals have less time than ever to shop. With the current migration to palm-held wireless platforms, they also have less space for browsing. Companies targeting such groups must tailor content and services to fit their needs and minimize spamming. They should consider collaborative filtering and other sound psychographic tools as an integral part of their marketing and communication toolkit.

- ## LIVES Analysis

Values do not change dramatically overnight. They influence big-ticket transactions such as buying a house or structuring a personal investment portfolio. An important business competency is to understand how values impact on behavior. LIVES Analysis[358] is a complex and powerful tool that combines values with lifestyles and demographics to identify distinct group clusters, or subcultures, with virtually identical patterns of behaviors or habits, particularly with respect to complex transactions and decisions.

- ## Technographics

Developed by Forrester Research and licensed to MRI, Technographics is a 10-category proprietary system that attempts to measure attitudes towards innovation and technology. It also develops a profile and analyzes the motivations of users of various technologies. Its typology divides target audiences into technology optimists or pessimists, correlating that with either high or low income.

High-income optimists are further divided into three segments: *Fast-Forwards* are early adopters of new software and productivity tools who fully integrate technology into their lives and careers; *New-Age Nurturers* readily invest in technology to create and extract the best value and experience for their family; and *Mouse Potatoes* are singles or couples who are captives to online sports, movies, games, chat rooms or solitary entertainment.

Paralleling these groups are three segments of high-income pessimists who will only adopt technology by necessity. *Hand-shakers* value their career and status and delegate technology-supported tasks to others. *Traditionalists* focus on family and community. *Media Junkies* include couch potatoes and are captives to traditional media.

Low-income optimists are differentiated into three segments. *Gadget Grabbers* love wireless, DVDs and computer games. *Techno-Strivers* are optimists who have a limited budget but value technology and seek online bargains and entertainment. The digital *Hopefuls* go online mostly for personal e-mail.

Finally, in the tenth segment are the pessimists or the *Sidelined Citizens* who dislike technology and would only invest in it for their children.

Technographics is attractive at a first glance. However, its North-American usefulness may diminish as more and more mainstream consumers go online.

- VALS™ Psychology of Markets

At SRI International, Arnold Mitchell's seminal work in applying developmental psychology to consumer segmentation led to the creation of Values and Life Styles (VALS™) in 1978, a proprietary breakthrough that gave psychographics considerable visibility and a well-deserved place in strategy formulation. VALS™ has been the subject of ongoing improvements that, in 1989, culminated in the current version, which migrated from values to personality traits that offer a better explanation of consumer behavior. While the system and framework are stable, the SRI Consulting Business Intelligence (SRIC-BI) team continues to calibrate the system to assure that it continues to reflect the real-world marketplace. Systems are currently available for the U.S., Canada, the United Kingdom and Japan. SRIC-BI partners with Mediamark Research Inc. (MRI) to provide consumer behavior and media usage data to analyze by VALS.

VALS is the psychographics system that is most widely used by business and government to tailor content, improve policy and decision-making around issues such as business intelligence, stakeholders' analysis, marketing, customer relationship management, product/service design and positioning, organization development, management of change, communications (corporate image) and electronic commerce.

With the iVALS pilot experiment, SRIC-BI got a head start on McKinsey and leading universities in gaining insights into the traits of Internet users of the nineties. The knowledge gained through iVALS and other initiatives have positioned SRIC-BI on the leading edge of strategic thinking in electronic commerce and virtual communities.

The best way to get a primer on VALS is to take the online survey and get immediate feedback on your personal profile before reading the detailed description of each category provided in SRIC-BI's web site[359] and reproduced in the Appendix with the permission of SRI Consulting Business Intelligence.

- Regular Users of Psychographics

DuPont is among the early adopters of integrated demo-psychographics in highly competitive markets such as fibers, process printing and crop protection. Psychographics was one of competencies that DuPont factored into consideration of its global alliance with CSC[360]. Colgate sought it to position AIM against Crest.[361] Procter & Gamble used it to gain a greater share of its customers' purse for Cover Girl, MaxFactor and other brands.[362] American Express went further, offering its members a personalized higher-margin proposition for travel packaging, insurance coverage and credit cards. Many software firms also rely on psychographics to identify the profile of early adopters, target beta sites, introduce new products and map a faster growth at a reasonable cost, even in scattered market niches.

Government agencies applied psychographics to identify and target Y2K laggards among public-sector vendors. The U.S. Army found that intuitive recruiting campaigns featuring adventure and excitement were less effective than those capitalizing on the psychographics traits of their pro-army target audience. That audience tended to be patriotic, active in the community, less interested in a swinging social life, more disciplined and work-oriented, less interested in politics and uncertain about their capacity to cope with modern life.[363]

Online vendors like Amazon.com and auctioneers like eBay keep track of click-through streams leading to each transaction for collaborative-filtering purposes. The intelligence produced is used to cross-sell books, music, movies, toys, consumer electronics, video games and travel.

3. Conclusion

With the people you meet daily, you ultimately get to know their perceptions, positions and idiosyncrasies. By using the tools described above, you can learn to do it sooner and better. Applying these instruments is even more compelling in today's virtual world where you are denied the benefit of physical proximity. Relying on intuition to understand the people that you cannot see is a far riskier proposition.

APPENDIX
-
VALS^{TM}

Adapted from www.sric-bi.com
with the permission of
SRI Consulting Business Intelligence

SRI Consulting Business Intelligence provides a wide range of services, including strategic and marketing expertise, to help its clients:

– Identify **who** to target;
– Uncover **what** the target group buys and does;
– Locate **where** concentrations of the target group lives;
– Identify **how** best to communicate with the target group;
– Gain insight into **why** the target group acts the way it does.

1. VALS Framework

The VALS^{TM} framework is comprised of eight primary groups, each with a unique position on a two-dimensional grid portraying primary motivation horizontally and capabilities (resources, innovation) vertically. These mutually-exclusive groups range from *Innovators* (center top) to *Survivors* at the bottom of the heap.

• Innovators

Innovators are successful, sophisticated, "take-charge" people with high self-esteem. Because they have such abundant resources, they exhibit all three primary motivations in varying degrees. They are change leaders and are the most receptive to new ideas and technologies. Innovators are very active consumers who favor upscale, niche products and services.

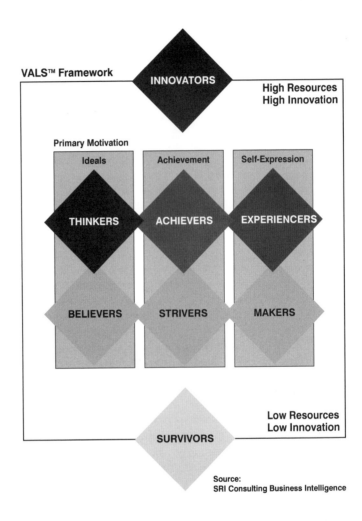

Figure 11.2. VALS^{TM} Diamond

Image is important to Innovators, not as evidence of status or power but as an expression of their taste, independence, and personality. Innovators are among the established and emerging leaders in business and government, yet they continue to seek challenges. They have a wide range of interests. Their possessions and recreation reflect a cultivated taste for the finer things in life.

172

- Thinkers

Motivated by ideals, Thinkers are mature, satisfied, comfortable, reflective people who value order, knowledge, and responsibility. They tend to be well educated and actively seek out information in the decision-making process. Well informed about world and national events, Thinkers are alert to opportunities that broaden their knowledge.

Thinkers have a moderate respect for the *status quo*, institutions of authority and social decorum, but are open-minded to new ideas. While their incomes allow them many choices, Thinkers are conservative, practical consumers; they look for durability, functionality and value in the products they buy.

- Achievers

Motivated by the desire for achievement, Achievers have goal-oriented lifestyles and a deep commitment to career and family. Their social lives reflect this focus and are structured around family, the place of worship, and work. Achievers live conventional lives, are politically conservative, and respect authority and the *status quo*. They value consensus, predictability, and stability over risk, intimacy and self-discovery.

With many wants and needs, Achievers are active in the consumer marketplace. Image is important to Achievers who favor established, prestige products and services that demonstrate success to their peers. Because of their busy lives, Achievers are often interested in a variety of timesaving devices.

- Experiencers

Motivated by self-expression, Experiencers are young and impulsive consumers. They seek variety and excitement, savoring the new, the offbeat, and the risky. Still in the process of formulating life values and patterns of behavior, they quickly become enthusiastic about new possibilities but are equally quick to cool. Their energy finds an outlet in exercise, sports, outdoor recreation and social activities.

Experiencers are avid consumers who spend a comparatively high proportion of their income on fashion, entertainment and socializing. Their purchases reflect the emphasis they place on looking good and having "cool" stuff.

- **Believers**

Like Thinkers, Believers are motivated by ideals. They are conservative, conventional people with concrete beliefs based on traditional, established codes: family, religion, community, and the nation. Many Believers express moral codes that are deeply rooted and literally interpreted. They follow established routines, organized in large part around home, family, and social or religious organizations to which they belong.

Believers are predictable and generally loyal consumers. They favor familiar products and established brands.

- **Strivers**

Strivers are trendy and fun loving. They are motivated by achievement, and concerned about the opinions and approval of others. They are striving to find a secure place in life. Money defines success for Strivers, who don't have enough of it to meet their desires. They favor stylish products that emulate the purchases of people with greater material wealth. Many lack the skills and focus to move ahead, and see themselves as having a job rather than a career.

Strivers are active consumers because shopping is both a social activity and an opportunity to demonstrate to peers their ability to buy. As consumers, they are as impulsive as their financial circumstances will allow.

- **Makers**

Like Experiencers, Makers are motivated by self-expression. They express themselves and experience the world by working on it – building a house, raising children, fixing a car, or canning vegetables – and have enough skill and energy to carry out their projects successfully. Makers are practical people who have constructive skills and value self-sufficiency. They live within a traditional context of family, practical work, and physical recreation and have little interest in what lies outside that context.

Makers are politically conservative, suspicious of new ideas and large institutions such as big business. They are respectful of government authority and organized labor, but resentful of government intrusion on individual rights. They are unimpressed by material possessions other than those with a practical or

174

functional purpose. Because they prefer value to luxury, they buy basic products.

- Survivors

Survivors live narrowly focused lives. With limited resources, Survivors believe that the world is changing too quickly. Comfortable with the familiar, they are primarily concerned with safety and security. Because they must focus on meeting needs rather than fulfilling desires, Survivors do not show a strong primary motivation.

Survivors are cautious consumers. They represent a very modest market for most products and services. They are loyal to favorite brands, especially if they can purchase them at a discount.

2. Application Examples of VALS Intelligence[364]

- Positioning New Products for Internet Delivery

An international consumer electronics firm was developing a new product to be delivered over the Internet. One of the first challenges was to identify which integrated technologies would be attractive to early adopters in the category. VALS™ was used to correctly identify the target consumer group and gain insights about how the group would react to the prototype system, delivery options, pricing, and product name. As a result, the firm was able to develop the most appropriate product features and benefits, unique product positioning, and marketing strategy. VALS was not only instrumental in helping the firm successfully launch the product but also to identify several new product opportunities.

- Fast-Tracking Development and Marketing

For planning and product development purposes, a European automotive manufacturer needed to understand U.S. consumers' needs and expectations of wireless and mobile computing services in the next five to eight years. VALS™ identified different early adopter groups and defined a variety of service concepts likely to appeal to each group. The resulting concepts were then beta tested with individuals belonging to early majority and late majority groups for comparisons. VALS provided a consumer-focused framework for the manufacturer to integrate marketing into their new product development efforts. Carrying this consumer understanding throughout all phases of the marketing process has enabled the company to more quickly identify commercialization opportunities.

- Finding and Capturing Lucrative Markets

A U.S. watch manufacturer used VALS to identify and size the market for a new product category: a blood pressure monitor for in-home health care. As an integral part of the product's development and marketing plans, VALS enabled the manufacturer to capture a 34% market share in year one.

- Tailoring Strategies For Distinct Consumer Segments

An electric utility used VALS to increase participation in its energy conservation program. By developing unique strategies for two distinctly different consumer segments and identifying ZIP codes with high percentages of each target for their direct mail, the utility reported a 25% increase in participation.

- Crafting Communications Strategy

A pension plan provider to small and mid-size U.S. companies used VALS to identify which segments of their participants could be effectively serviced electronically. By understanding the motivations of each segment, the provider was able to revise its web site and communications to better serve clients' needs.

CHAPTER 12
-
A FINAL WORD

1. From the Military Realm to the Worlds of Business and Government

Over 2,400 years ago, Sun Tzu wrote in *The Art of War*: "What enables the wise sovereign and the good general [read *leader*] to strike and conquer, and achieve things beyond the reach of ordinary men, is *foreknowledge* [read *intelligence*]". Closer to home, the U.S. Secretary of Defense, Donald Rumsfeld, was asked by CNN, on October 8, 2001, about the most important weapon to fight terrorism. His reply: "It will probably be a scrap of information rather than a cruise missile." With reliable intelligence, accountable leaders can formulate a pragmatic strategy where facts, logic and reason should prevail over the power of perceptions and the sanctity of doctrines and ideologies.

The objective of this journey was embodied in the title of this book – *Harnessing the Power of Intelligence, Counterintelligence and Surprise Events*. The focus was on human intelligence – the most important link in your value chain and, paradoxically, the least understood aspect of business intelligence and national security. The first Part (Chapters 1 to 6) covered the two key functions of intelligence: going after opportunities and shielding your organization and property from threats. We discussed intelligence talent, sources of information and validation, a structure for interpretation management and the resources needed for both functions.

In Chapters 7 and 8, we addressed some neglected aspects of intelligence analysis and saw how the genesis of major policies and projects followed a surprise-event driven path. In the process, we learned new ways to seize opportunities and anticipate threats before they appear on the intelligence radars of others.

The last three chapters focused on the most important aspect of intelligence analysis: the knowledge of clients, staff and other individuals and constituencies with a vested interest in your endeavors. Chapter 9 examined the power, status and role of the catalysts of innovation and change. Since perceptions are reality in the eye of the beholder, Chapter 10 introduced the *Factional Scale*[TM], an important tool to examine perceptions before formulating strategy. Finally, Chapter 11 introduced psychographics as a discipline to gain further understanding of your target audience and other stakeholders.

We know from experience and a large body of research knowledge[365] that those with the highest ethical standards who practice the discipline of intelligence wisely and act quickly and aggressively will frequently be rewarded. They will spawn better products, perhaps even new industries, and retain both clients and talent more effectively. Hopefully, this framework and its small arsenal of instruments will become an integral part of your toolkit for due-diligence in capturing new markets, building a sustainable competitive advantage, warding-off spies and evildoers, and accomplishing your mission ethically without needlessly protracted battles.

2. Intelligence Lessons at the Personal Level

It is appropriate to end this business publication by thinking about the importance of intelligence to our personal lives. My mentor, Herb Shepard, saw intelligence as part of a process of "discovery and creation perspectives that deepen our appreciation of ourselves in the universe."[366] About perspective, Herb went on to quote William Douglas' definition below.

> *"A person is whole when in tune with the winds, the stars and the hills as well as the neighbors, Being in tune of the community is part of the secret. Being in tune with universe is the whole secret."[367]*

Herb concluded: "In everyday experience, being in tune with the universe, or having an adequate perspective, means seeing problems from above rather than from underneath, means not getting locked in one end or the other of a presumed polarization, means being free in your situation rather than dependent on it, means owning your behavior rather than claiming someone else's caused yours."[368]

At its most fundamental, intelligence is not only mission-critical for the military and business spheres. It helps us make more transparent our opaque and chaotic world. It is a vital first step in the long journey to realize our dreams. Intelligence is therefore the foundation of one reality that conveys a sharper meaning to existence, and ultimately to a life worth living.

ABOUT ALAIN PAUL MARTIN

Alain Paul Martin coaches executives and intelligence analysts and teaches strategy, risk management, negotiation and leadership. His experience includes the turnaround of a national financial institution and the management of projects ranging from airport security, and e-business strategy for a multi-billion dollar client, to the evaluation of TV coverage of major news events at the CBC. He has advised the Director General of UNESCO on restructuring and renewal, and has served as executive member of the non-partisan Committee of The Prime Minister of Canada on Government Reform. His presentation titled *"Building a Great Nation and Governing in a World of Surprise Events"* was attended by the Prime Minister of Canada, Cabinet ministers and legislators, among others. Mr. Martin's clients include Boeing, Boliden, Bombardier, EDC, GE, Cap-Gemini, GM, Hilton, MetLife, Procter & Gamble, Skanska Cement of Sweden, The Association for Science and Technology in China (CAST), the Swedish Employers Council, The Engineering Advancement Association of Japan, telecom companies, governments and NGOs.

An alumni of Harvard Business School and a recipient of patents and innovation awards, Mr. Martin is the architect of *HUMINT*™ *Contact*, a human-intelligence software to map relationships between various players. He has invented the Harvard Business Planner and developed Harvard University Global System™ – a practical framework comprising management tools and road maps on human intelligence, issue analysis, strategy, risk and project management. He has also been recognized by the Project Management Institute (PMI) for "his outstanding contribution to the state-of-the-art of project management".

For more information on Mr. Martin's background, publications and public seminars, visit www.executive.org/martin.

ABOUT DR. J. BRIAN MORRISSEY

Brian Morrissey has an outstanding track record in managing research teams and complex issues, as Assistant Deputy Minister (ADM) of the Research Branch in the Department of Agriculture and Agri-Food, and as ADM for Science at the Department of Fisheries & Oceans. In Agriculture Canada, Dr. Morrissey was ADM for Food Production & Inspection Branch (now the Canadian Food Inspection Agency), Director General of its Food Inspection Directorate, and Director of Canada's Animal Health Division, where he was responsible for Canada's animal disease control programs. For three years, Dr. Morrissey has lectured in the Executive MBA program of the University of Ottawa. He provides expertise to the World Bank (IBRD) and the Canadian International Development Agency (CIDA) in China and other countries.

Dr. Morrissey was received as a member of the Royal College of Veterinary Surgeons, London, England in 1965. He holds a Master of Business Administration degree from Warwick University, England, and a diploma in Public Policy and Public Administration from the University of Guelph, Ontario.

In October 2001, Dr. Morrissey was presented with Canada's "Outstanding Achievement Award". This is the highest award given by Canada to its public servants. Furthermore, Dr. Morrissey is a recipient of the French Ministry of Agriculture's professional designation known as "Chevalier dans l'Ordre du Mérite Agricole" for advancing Franco-Canadian cooperation in research.

Dr. Morrissey and Alain Paul Martin work together as a team to deliver advanced workshops on policy and strategy formulation, and risk and project management in a turbulent environment. For more information, visit www.executive.org/morrissey.

197

BIBLIOGRAPHY

-

BOOKS AND WEB SITES IN ENGLISH AND FRENCH

For the latest list, refer to www.executive.org. Visitors to this site can also connect to Web links listed in this document.

1. Suggested Readings on Intelligence and Counterintelligence

1. M. Abrams and M. Joyce: New Thinking About Information Technology Security, Computers & Security, 1995, Vol. 14, No. 1, pp. 69-81.
2. Karl Albrecht: Corporate Radar: Tracking The Forces That Are Shaping Your Business, AMACOM, New York, 1999.
3. Glenn Spencer Bacal: Law of Trade Secrets, Non-competes, and Anti-piracy Agreements - A Practical Guide for Business and In-House Lawyers, 1996.
    www.azlink.com/lawyers/articles/secrets.htm#conc
4. Nick Bontis and Chun-Wei Choo (Editors): The Strategic Management of Intellectual Capital and Organizational Knowledge, Oxford University Press, New York, 2002. ISBN: 019515486X.
5. Steve Burnett and Stephen Paine: RSA Security's Official Guide to Cryptography, McGraw-Hill, New York, March 2001, ISBN: 007213139X
6. Helen Burwell, Carl Ernst, Michael Sankey: Online Competitive Intelligence: Increase Your Profits Using Cyber-Intelligence, Facts on Demand Press, Tempe, AZ, 2000. ISBN 1-889150-08-8
7. Chun-Wei Choo: Information Management for the Intelligent Organization: The Art of Scanning the Environment, American Society for Information Science by Information Today, Medford, NJ. 2001.
8. Alan F. Dutka: Competitive Intelligence for the Competitive Edge, NTC Business Books, Lincolnwood, IL, 1999, 320 pages, ISBN 0844202932.
9. Liam Fahey: Outwitting, Outmaneuvering and Outperforming Competitors, Jossey-Bass, San Francisco, CA, 1999.
10. Richard J. Foster: The S-Curve: Profiting from Technological Change, Simon & Schuster, 1986. ASIN: 0671509187.
11. George Friedman, Meredith Friedman, Colin Chapman, John Baker: The Intelligence Edge: How to Profit in the Information Age, Crown, New York, 1997.
12. Leonard M. Fuld: The New Competitor Intelligence: The Complete Resource for Finding, Analyzing, and Using Information About Your Competitors, John Wiley & Sons, 1995.

13. Leonard M. Fuld: Monitoring the Competition, John Wiley & Sons, 1988.

14. Benjamin Gilad: Business Blindspots: Replacing Your Company's Entrenched and Outdated Myths, Beliefs and Assumptions With the Realities of Today's Markets, Infonortics, Tetbury, UK, 1996, ISBN 1-873699-33-6.

15. Benjamin Gilad and Jan Herring (Editors): The Art and Science of Business Intelligence Analysis: Intelligence Analysis and Its Applications (Advances in Applied Business Strategy, Supplement), JAI Press, New York, 1996, ASIN: 076230159

16. Maurice R. Greenberg, Richard N. Hanse: Making Intelligence Smarter: The Future of U.S. Intelligence, U.S. Council on Foreign Relations, 1996

17. Barrie Gunter, Adrian Furnham: Consumer Profiles: An Introduction to Psychographics, International Thomson Publishing; Cambridge, MA. 1992. ISBN 0-415-07534-3. www.thomson.com,

18. David E Hussey, Per Jenster: Competitor Intelligence: Turning Analysis into Success, Jossey-Bass, San Francisco, CA, ISBN: 0-471-98407-8, Jan. 1999.

19. Larry Kahaner: Competitive Intelligence – How to Gather, Analyze and Use Information to Move Your Business to the Top, Simon & Schuster, 1997, 300 pages, ISBN: 0684844044.

20. Lynn R. Kahle (Editor), Lawrence Chiagouris (Editor): Values, Lifestyles, and Psychographics, Lawrence Erlbaum Associates, Mahwah, NJ. 1997, ISBN: 0805814965. www.erlbaum.com

21. Lynn R. Kahle (Editor): Cross-National Consumer Psychographics, International Business Press, New York, NY, 2000. ISBN: 0789009625.

22. Christopher M. King, Curtis E. Dalton and T. Ertem Osmanoglu: Security Architecture: Design, Deployment & Operations, McGraw-Hill, New York, July 2001, ISBN: 0-07-213385-6

23. John J. McGonagle, Carolyn M. Vella: The Internet Age of Competitive Intelligence, Quorum, Westport, CT, 1999.

24. John J. McGonagle, Carolyn M. Vella: Protecting Your Company Against Competitive Intelligence, Quorum, Westport, CT, 1998.

25. Jerry Miller and the Business Intelligence Braintrust: Millennium Intelligence: Understanding and Conducting Competitive Intelligence in the Digital Age, CyberAge Books Medford, NJ. 2000. ISBN 0-910965-28-5.

26. J. Nolan: Confidential: Uncover Your Competitor's Top Business Secrets Legally and Quickly–and Protect Your Own, HarperBusiness, New York, 1999.

27. Adam L. Penenberg, Marc Berry: Spooked: Espionage in Corporate America, Perseus Publishing, Cambridge, MA, 2000. ISBN: 0738202711.

28. Michael Porter: Competitive Strategy: Techniques for Analyzing Industries and Competitors, Simon & Schuster, New York, 1998, ISBN: 0684841487.

29. Michael Porter: On Competition, Harvard Business School Press, Boston, 1998, ISBN: 0875847951.

30. Michael Porter: The Competitive Advantage of Nations, The Free Press, New York, 1998, ISBN: 0684841479.

31. Michael Porter: Competitive Advantage: Creating and Sustaining Superior Performance, The Free Press, New York, 1998, ISBN: 0684841460.

32. John Prescott: Proven Strategies in Competitive Intelligence – Lessons from the Trenches, John Wiley & Sons, New York, 2001.

33. Sandra Seagal and David Horne: Human Dynamics: A New Framework for Understanding People and Realizing the Potential in Our Organizations, Pegasus Communications, Williston, Vermont 05495 USA, 2000. ISBN: 1883823072.

34. M. Shaker, M.P. Gembicki: War Room Guide to Competitive Intelligence, McGraw-Hill, New York, 1999.

35. Chris Sherman and Gary Price: The Invisible Web: Uncovering Information Sources Search Engines Can't See, CyberAge Books, 2001, ISBN 0-910965-51-X. www.cyberagebooks.com

36. Simon Singh: The Code Book: The Evolution of Secrecy from Mary, Queen of Scots to Quantum Cryptography, Doubleday, New York, 1999. A history of the scientific breakthroughs in cryptography and the role codes play in intelligence, warfare and politics. "At the end of *The Code Book*, the author has included *The Cipher Challenge*, ten separate messages encrypted using a series of different codes and ciphers, some ancient, some modern. Each of the ten messages contains a code word, and the first person to crack all ten stages and send in all ten code words will win a prize of £10,000." For more information and the current status of *The Cipher Challenge*, visit www.4thestate.co.uk/cipherchallenge

37. John Thorp: The Information Paradox, MacGraw-Hill, New York, 1998.

38. Kirk Tyson: The Complete Guide to Competitive Intelligence, Kirk Tyson International, Lisle, IL, 1998, ISBN 0966321901, www.kirktyson.com.

39. Sun Tzu: The Art of War, Edited and a Foreword by James Clavell, Bantam Doubleday Dell Publishing Group, 1988, ISBN 0-440-55005-X. There is also a bibliography on new books and translations of The Art of War at: http://vikingphoenix.com/public/SunTzu/stbiblio.htm

40. Art Weinstein: Market Segmentation: Using Demographics, Psychographics and Other Niche Marketing Techniques to Predict and Model Customer Behavior, McGraw-Hill, New York, NY. 1993. ISBN: 1557384924

41. Christopher West: Competitive Intelligence, Palgrave Macmillan Press, 2001. ISBN: 0333786696.

42. Yoram Wind, Robert E. Gunther and Vijay Mahajan: Convergence Marketing: Strategies for Reaching the New Hybrid Consumer, Financial Times-Prentice Hall, 2001. ISBN: 0130650757.

2. Courtesy of CIA Web Site

43. Mark M. Lowenthal: Intelligence - From Secrets to Policy, Congressional Quarterly Press, Washington DC, 2000. A sweeping look at intelligence and the intelligence community (comment from CIA web site).

44. David C. Martin: Wilderness of Mirrors, Bantam Books, New York, 1980. A controversial yet thought-provoking treatment of some well-known intelligence cases from a counterintelligence perspective (comment from CIA web site).

45. Norman Polmar and Thomas B. Allen: Spy Book - The Encyclopedia of Espionage, Random House, New York, 1997. A reference book of the people, the agencies and the equipment in intelligence history (comment from CIA web site).

46. Abram N. Shulsky: Silent Warfare, Brassey's, Washington, D.C. 1991. A basic textbook of intelligence work describing all levels of intelligence collection and analysis (comment from CIA web site).

3. Recommended Web Sites

47. Gateways to Think Tanks and Specialty Experts:
   – Google Directory: http://directory.google.com
   – Google links to universities:
     www.google.com/options/universities.html
   – PDI Global Intelligence Team: www.executive.org
   – The Virtual Library of Energy Science and Technology,
     U.S. Department of Energy. www.osti.gov
   – Intelligence think tanks:
     www.intelforum.org/resources.html#think
   – Kitty Bennett: Sources and Experts, St. Petersburg
     www.ibiblio.org/slanews/internet/experts.html
   – Intelligence about Japan expressed in English by
     Japanese scholars, business leaders, mass media and
     government officials: www.glocom.org

48. Excellent Business Database Selection Tool, Rosenfeld Library, Anderson School, UCLA. www.anderson.ucla.edu/resources/library/libdgrid.htm

49. The best online dictionary and search engine for computer and Internet terminology www.pcwebopedia.com

50. **BioSpace, Inc.** is a specialized supplier of web-based products and information services to the life sciences. Updated daily, its Clinical Competitive Intelligence System (CCIS) "tracks more than 7,000 clinical trials in the USA and Europe sponsored by more than 1,000 companies focused on 350 disease targets." Its BioSpace Glossary defines the most current biotechnology terms. The glossary also provides links to companies doing research in fields related to a specific term.

51. DuPont Consulting Solutions is a subsidiary of E. I. du Pont de Nemours: www.dupont.com/consulting

52. American Society of Association Executives (ASAE): With 25,000 individual members, the ASAE is the association of non-governmental organizations (NGO), i.e., associations, trade groups and professional societies. It provides valuable up-to-date information about the membership, finances and leadership of 12,700 associations "serving more than 287 million people and companies worldwide." www.asaenet.org/Gateway/OnlineAssocSlist.html

ASAE publishes electronic and paper-based directories with insights into the $60 billion market of products and services for meetings and conventions. It also provides a forum for scanning: www.asaenet.org/environmental_scan.

53. ASAE partners offering information and links to associations, trade organizations and marketing intelligence products worldwide:

54. - The Virtual Community Association (VCA) provides a free listing of associations and web search by association name or key words: www.vcanet.org/vca/assns.htm
-Association Central provides association-related products and services: www.associationcentral.com

55. Assignment Editor is a site used by most newsrooms to gain direct access to content (transcripts, archives) from major local, national and world papers, magazines and news wires www.assignmenteditor.com

56. Baker Library of Harvard Business School: Selected List of Search Engines, Internet Portals and Web Guides: www.library.hbs.edu/genref/netguide.htm

57. The Brain provides two powerful and patented knowledge organizers. The BrainEKP is a collaborative enterprise knowledge platform and the Personal Brain is a personal organizer. Both help users organize and facilitate access to documents, contacts, e-mails, Web pages, databases, and other applications. www.thebrain.com

58. Carleton University:
Center for Security and Defence Studies (CSDS): www.carleton.ca/csds
Canadian Centre of Intelligence and Security Studies (CCISS): www.carleton.ca/npsia/new_npsia/research_centres/cciss.html

59. The Canadian Association for Security and Intelligence Studies (CASIS): www.sfu.ca/igs/CASIS

60. The worldwide portal for chambers of commerce: www.worldchambers.com

61. CIA web page on *The Intelligence Cycle:* www.cia.gov/cia/publications/facttell/index.html

62. Competia hosts symposia and courses, publishes a magazine and papers, and manages a virtual community for competitive intelligence professionals. www.competia.com

63. The Conference Board provides excellent research material and tutorials about business cycles and economic intelligence in general: www.conference-board.org

64. The Council on Intelligence promotes and provides advice and information on ethical intelligence reform worldwide. Its mission is "to change the predominant culture of international intelligence agencies, to encourage a shift in spending from spies and satellites to analysts, analytic tools, and open sources." www.council-on-intelligence.org

65. Corporate Strategy Board: Strategic Intelligence: Providing Critical Information for Strategic Decisions, Corporate Executive Board, Washington, D.C., 2000. Corporate Strategy Board publications are available exclusively to clients of the Corporate Strategy Board, a membership-based research program of the Corporate Executive Board serving heads of corporate strategy at leading institutions worldwide. Non-members interested in obtaining more information about the Board should contact the firm's headquarters in Washington, D.C., on 202-777-5000. www.corporatestrategyboard.com

66. Defense Intelligence Agency: www.dia.mil

67. Delphion (formerly available at ibm.com/patents) archives over 2.3 million patent citations. It provides access to patent research, IP management and other analytic tools www.delphion.com

68. Directory of Information Brokers: www.burwellinc.com

69. Executive.org provides seminars, tools and a list of books and web sites on competitive intelligence, mission-setting, strategic thinking, risk management, e-business, project management, time management and leadership www.executive.org

70. Factiva is a Dow Jones and Reuters company providing a proprietary indexing system used to search Dow Jones and Reuters documents. Its Intelligent Indexing system is also available under license for corporate intranets and portals. Click products at www.factiva.com. Factiva also provides a white paper on document indexing worth reading: www.bestofboth.com/infopro/indexingwhitepaper.pdf

71. The Federal Emergency Management Agency: www.fema.gov

72. The Federation of American Scientists: Intelligence on the web: www.fas.org

73. Federation of International Trade Associations (FITA): www.fita.org

74. Florida State University: List of Internet links by crime type including intellectual property crimes: www.criminology.fsu.edu/cjlinks/killers.html

75. Global Entrepreneurship Institute: www.gcase.org

76. GPO Access: Multi Database Search, U.S. Government Printing Office & Superintentendent of Documents, 2002. www.access.gpo.gov/su_docs/index.html

77. IBM Global Security Solutions provides advanced safety and security applications software and consulting services. In addition to partners like

Kroll, IBM has an extensive worldwide network of experts, engineers and researchers in security-related technologies. www.ibm.com/security

78. The Intelligence Forum is a not-for-profit organization dedicated to the scholarly study of intelligence history, theory, and practice www.intelforum.org

79. The International Journal of Intelligence and Counter Intelligence http://search.epnet.com

80. The International Security Management Association (ISMA) groups senior-level security executives of global companies with an asset base exceeding $500 millions: www.ismanet.com

81. Johns Hopkins University: Center for Strategic Education (CSE) www.sais-jhu.edu/cse

82. Kentucky State University Competitive Intelligence Web Page www.kysu.edu/library/CompIntell/compete.htm

83. Knowledge Management Benchmarking Association: www.kmba.org

84. Kroll is a leading provider of risk management and counterintelligence services. It partners with IBM Global Security Solutions to assess IT infrastructure security, espionage, cyber-intrusion, business interruption risks and disaster recovery capability: www.krollworldwide.com

85. Management First is a vertical portal specializing in management issues. Membership is free. Its weekly articles are worth reading. www.managementfirst.com

86. MIT Plasma Science & Fusion Center: Major Search Engines, Tips & Hints, Jason Thomas, Cambridge, 2002. www.psfc.mit.edu/library/search_engines.html www.psfc.mit.edu/library/search_engines_tips&hints.html

87. National Counterintelligence Executive (NCIX): www.ncix.gov

88. News worldwide portal links: www.executive.org/news

89. NSA on information security: www.nsa.gov

90. The Open Source Intelligence (OSINT) Conference is the world largest meeting of over 6,000 government all-source intelligence professionals. It focuses on a "new form of national intelligence that requires the fullest possible exploitation of open sources of information, new forms of web-based multi-lateral information sharing arrangements, and new forms of directed open source support to classified activities and analysis." www.oss.net

91. One Source provides business and financial information on one million public and private companies www.onesource.com

92. The Parliamentary Library of the Future William Robinson, Library of Congress www.ifla.org/IV/ifla61/61-robw.htm

93. John L. Petersen: Out of the Blue: Wild Cards and Other Big Future Surprises: How to Anticipate and Respond to Profound Change, The

Arlington Institute, Washington DC, 1997. ISBN:0-9659027-2-2
www.arlingtoninstitute.org

94. Phoenix Consulting Group: Competitive Intelligence & Counterintelligence
Services: www.intellpros.com

95. The Privacy Association organizes the Annual Privacy and Data Security
Summit, a "leading forum on confidentiality, security, regulatory
requirements and technology tools." www.privacyassociation.org

96. RSA Security provides e-security solutions including authentication,
authorization, encryption and public key management systems. Its RSA
Conference is the leading cryptography and data security event in the
world. www.rsasecurity.com

97. Security Technology & Design Magazine:
www.simon-net.com.

98. The Society of Competitive Intelligence Professionals (SCIP) has a global
membership in over 50 countries. It "provides education and networking
opportunities for business professionals working in the rapidly growing
field of competitive intelligence. Many SCIP members have backgrounds
in market research, strategic analysis, or science and technology." For SCIP
publications, discussion groups and professional development activities,
visit www.scip.org.

99. University of California – Berkeley: Recommended Search Engines: Table
of Features; How Do Search Engines Work? Joe Barker Tutorials, UC
Berkeley, 2002
www.lib.berkeley.edu/TeachingLib/Guides/Internet/SearchEngines.html

100. University of Nevada in Reno: Interesting web page on Competitive
Intelligence (Page 100): http://unr.edu/homepage/jstrauss/prenhall/Ch03--
research.doc

101. U.S. National Archives and Records Administration: www.archives.gov

102. U.S. Secret Service on The Best Practices for Seizing Electronic Evidence:
www.ustreas.gov/usss

103. Washington Researchers publish a weekly paper on Competitive
Intelligence Tips and Tools: www.washingtonresearchers.com

104. The Williams Inference Center has developed proprietary techniques to
spot early signs of change. It "monitors a broad spectrum of global
information" and provides state-of-the-art training in inferential scanning.
It is the oldest and most-established provider of competitive intelligence
services. www.williamsinference.com

105. The World Future Society: www.wfs.org

106. The World Trade Centers Association: http://iserve.wtca.org

4. Books in French

107. L'Assemblée des chambres françaises de commerce et d'industrie (ACFCI):
Le Livre blanc sur l'intelligence économique, AFCI, Paris, 1997

108. Bernard Besson and Jean-Claude Possin: L'audit de l'intelligence économique. Mettre en place et optimiser un dispositif coordonné d'intelligence collective, Dunod, 1998.

109. Alain Bloch: L'Intelligence économique, Editions Economica, Paris, 1999.

110. Franck Bournois and Pierre-Jacquelin Romani: L'Intelligence économique et stratégique dans les entreprises françaises, Economica, Paris, 2000, IEC Award 2000.

111. Henri Dou: Veille technologique et compétitivité – l'intelligence économique au service du développement industriel, Dunod, Paris, 1995.

112. Pierre Fayard, Christian Marcon and Nicolas Moinet: La Maîtrise de l'interaction – La stratégie réseau, Zéro Heure, Paris, 2000.

113. François Jakobiak: L'Intelligence économique en pratique, Éditions d'organisation, Paris, 1998.

114. François Jakobiak: Pratique de la veille technologique, Éditions d'organisation, Paris, 1991.

115. Humber Lesca: Systèmes d'information pour le management stratégique de l'entreprise, MacGraw-Hill, 1996.

116. Jean-Marie Lepeule and Yves-Michel Marti: Benchmarking et intelligence économique, Eurostaf & Les Echos, Paris, June 1999. www.egideria.com

117. Thibaud du Manoir de Juaye: Intelligence économique: utilisez toutes les resources du droit, Eyrolles, Paris, 2000.

118. Bruno Martinet and Yves-Michel Marti: L'intelligence économique, Éditions d'Organisation, Paris, 1995.

119. Bruno Martinet and Yves-Michel Marti: L'Intelligence économique et concurrentielle : les yeux et les oreilles de l'entreprise, Éditions d'Organisation, Paris, 1996, 2001, six reprints, Booz Allen Hamilton and Financial Times Award "Best European Management Book" of 1996. Sample Chapter: www.egideria.com/cyndiniques.html

120. Henri Martre (Commissariat Général du Plan): Intelligence économique et stratégie des enterprises, La Documentation française, Paris, 1994.

121. Pierre Pelou (Editor): La documentation internationale, ESF, Paris, 1991. ISBN 2-7101-0908-5.

122. Patrick Romagni and Valerie Wild: L'intelligence économique au service de l'entreprise, Presse du Management, Paris, 1998.

123. Robert Salmon and Yolaine de Lineares: L'intelligence compétitive : une combinaison subtile pour gagner ensemble, Economica, Paris, 1997.

124. Daniel Rouach: La veille technologique et l'intelligence économique. PUF, Que-sais-je?, Paris, 1999.

125. Serge Vincon: Intelligence économique: enjeu stratégique pour l'économie française, ECL Communication, Paris, 2000.

126. Sun Tzu: L'Art de la guerre, Jean Lévi (Translator), Hachette Littérature (Pluriel), Paris, 2000, ISBN: 201278917X.

5. Web Sites in French

127. *ADBS (Association des Professionnels de l'Information et de la Documentation)* is an economic-intelligence professional society based in France. It is the French equivalent of SCIP. The site is currently available in French only: www.adbs.fr

128. CEFRIO: Le Centre francophone pour l'informatisation des enterprises is predominantly a network of organizations and government agencies operating in Quebec. Its focus is performance improvement via information technologies. The CEFRIO performs a daily scan of news and issues related to information technologies including security, virtual communities and electronic commerce. www.cefrio.qc.ca

129. *Egidia* is a leading French holding of 10 companies specialized in the field of intelligence acquisition and information management in France, the United Kingdom, Germany and the USA. www.egideria.com

130. *Espionage Économique* is a series of French newspaper clippings and testimonies about industrial espionage: http://strategique.free.fr/archives/textes/ie/archives_ie_16.htm

131. *Inforama* provides economic and international development intelligence and houses the web site for the French Academy of Economic Intelligence (L'Académie de l'intelligence économique): www.alogic.fr/inforama

132. *Intelligence Online:* www.intelligenceonline.fr

133. Science et Avenir: Moteurs de recherche: En quête de pertinence. No: 652, Juin 2001. www.kartoo.fr/fr/presse/2001/sciences-et-avenir.htm

134. *Strategie.org* provides economic, geopolitical and military intelligence including economic and information warfare www.frstrategie.org

135. *Teaming* provides expertise and intelligence on best practices and partnership opportunities: www.teaming.fr

136. The University of Montreal provides a bibliography on strategic intelligence with a focus on technology: www.fas.umontreal.ca/EBSI/varia/veille/veille.htm

137. *Veille* site provides a comprehensive list of professional societies and associations www.veille.com

For the latest list, refer to www.executive.org. Visitors to this site can also connect to Web links listed in this document.

Chapter 1: Rethinking Intelligence in Business and Government

[1] The Global Method is currently known as *Harvard University Global System* (HUGS). Harvard and Harvard University are registered trademarks of the President and Fellows of Harvard College. *Harvard University Global System* was developed independently of Harvard University and is distributed under trademark license. For more on HUGS, visit www.executive.org.

[2] The removal of trade barriers fosters competition, offers consumers more choice and provides exporters with new opportunities. In less than ten years, the market for consumer product companies like Colgate-Palmolive, Procter & Gamble and Unilever went from one to five billion potential customers.

[3] Intellectual capital comprises the collective knowledge of the workforce, available intelligence, information and other intellectual property plus, within limits, the knowledge held by allies.

[4] HUMINT is an important element of C4I (Command, Control, Communications, Computers and Intelligence).

Signals intelligence (SIGINT) is the set of competencies and processes to intercept and decipher electronic emissions, telemetry, voice and data communications transmitted on wireless, cable, fiber optic, copper wires and microwaves using ground sites and airborne collectors including satellites. Using similar platforms, imagery intelligence (IMINT) is the set of tools and competencies used to collect, analyze and interpret photographic, infrared and radar images and other objects. Satellite images with a high resolution of a couple of meters are now available from private providers, making it possible to track activities on loading docks, parking lots and testing grounds.

Measurements and signatures intelligence (MASINT) is focused on remote measurement of device signatures using radar, infrared and other multi-sensor means to identify the presence and functional attributes of devices and systems.

The objective of the recent Human Identification at a Distance (HID or HumanID) is to "develop automated biometric identification technologies to detect, recognize and identify humans at great distances". The current research focus is on "multi-modal surveillance technology using different biometrics techniques such as face and body parts identification, infrared and hyper-spectral imagery, gait and temporal human dynamics, non-imaging physiological based-biometrics, and remote iris scan."

[5] Michael E. Porter: Competitive Advantage: Creating and Sustaining Superior Performance, Free Press, New York NY, 1998. ISBN: 0684841460

[6] As an illustration, Wal-Mart entered Canada with stores too close to the competition for comfort. It launched an ad campaign that forced Zellers and Canadian Tire to acquire new product lines and invest in major renovations. While both competitors were busy repelling these direct attacks, Wal-Mart opened stores in strategic growth areas that were off-limits to the Canadian chains and loaded them with high-volume goods that earned respectable margins.

[7] An agile enterprise is "capable of operating profitably in a competitive environment of continually, and unpredictably, changing customer opportunities... The agile enterprise provides solutions to its customers, not just products. It works adaptively, responding to marketplace opportunities by reconfiguring its organization of work, its exploitation of technology, its use of alliances. It engages in intensive collaboration within the company, pulling together all of the resources that are necessary to produce profitable products and services regardless or where they may be distributed. And it forms alliances with suppliers, customers, and partnering companies. And finally, it is a knowledge-driven enterprise." Edited excerpts from Steven L. Goldman, Roger N. Nagel, Kenneth Preiss: Agile Competitors and Virtual Organizations: Strategies for Enriching the Customer, Van Nostrand Reinhold, New York NY, 1995. ISBN: 0442019033.

[8] The value chain consists of three generic phases. The first, value identification and incubation, covers the pre-life cycle of opportunities, threats, risks and other issues. The second, value creation and communication, starts with policy formulation, project and product development and ends with the launching and commissioning phases. The third, value extraction (or harvesting), is the profit-making and revenue-generating phase in business. It includes the management of both client and distribution-channel relationships (satisfaction, retention, quality and profitability). Governments prefer value or service delivery to designate this phase, which covers day-to-day operations. Harvesting value is also the best prelude for incubating future value.

[9] Alain Paul Martin: Harnessing the Power of a Clear Mission, Vision, Values, Goals & Priorities, Sept. 2004. Executive.org Press. For excerpts, visit www.executive.org

[10] Quotation of Prof. John E. Prescott, University of Pittsburgh in E. B. Baatz: Competitive Intelligence: The Quest for Corporate Smarts, CIO

Magazine, Sept. 15, 1994. Reprinted through the courtesy of CIO/Darwin. Copyrights © 2002 CXO Media, Inc. All rights reserved. www.cio.com/archive

[11] Skip Kaltenheuser and Keith Epstein: Spies Like Us, Strategy, CIO Insight Magazine, Ziff-Davis Media, August 1, 2001. Reprinted through the courtesy of CIO/Darwin. Copyrights © 2002 CXO Media, Inc. All rights reserved. www.cioinsight.com

[12] Gary Anthes: Competitive Intelligence: IT is Helping Companies Dig Up Vital Information on their Archenemies, Computer World, July 6, 1998. Reprinted with the permission of Computerworld Magazine. Copyrights © 2002 Computerworld, Inc. All rights reserved. www.computerworld.com/news/1998/story/0,11280,31674,00.html

[13] Skip Kaltenheuser and Keith Epstein: See above.

[14] Gary Anthes: See above.

[15] Adapted from Skip Kaltenheuser and Keith Epstein: see above.

[16] Gary Anthes: See above.

[17] I wish to thank Mr. Yoshi Komatsu of Nippon Roche in Tokyo for kindly validating the background information about this case.

[18] Nippon Engineering Academy of Japan: EAJ News, Number 83, December 2001. www.eaj.or.jp/eajnews/news83/news83-e.html

[19] Alan-Burton Jones: Competing with Knowledge: How to Gain and Retain a Knowledge-Based Competitive Advantage, 2001. www.burton-jones.com/articles/Competing_with_Knowledge-Nov01.htm.

[20] IBM: NBA Coaches Score Big With IBM Data Mining Application, IBM, San Jose CA. 2001. www.software.ibm.com/casestudies

[21] IBM: see above.

[22] For centuries, Japan had approximately 16 major conglomerates such as Mitsui, Sumitomo, Sanwa and Mitsubishi which were termed Zaibatsu (i.e., large families). Each Zaibatsu consisted of a cluster of companies with major cross-ownership holdings. It always included a family bank at the center, which owned a web of *sogo shosha* (trading houses), insurance companies and other financial institutions plus heavy and light industries. In the aftermath of the Second World War, General McArthur pressed Japan to promote competition and Tokyo declared the Zaibatsu illegal. However, with the reality of the Korean War, the allies enlisted the help of Japanese business leaders, who possessed valuable intelligence about their new adversary. In the meantime, the Government of Japan softened its position on the revival of the Zaibatsu; thus, permitting each former conglomerate member to regroup with looser ties, forming a tacit syndicate. The politically-correct word Kiretsu (i.e.,

217

informal family) has replaced the term Zaibatsu since the mid-fifties. The main bank is less obtrusive in these new arrangements, acting almost like the German Haus-Bank, but intelligence sharing permeates each Kiretsu. As for Honda, it is a relative newcomer to the Japanese manufacturing scene. Founded in 1946 to make motorcycles, it entered Formula-1 car racing and won its first victory in the mid-sixties. It is not a member of the Kiretsu establishment.

[23] Alain Paul Martin: The Salvation Army: An Agile Intelligent NGO, The www.executive.org/salvationarmy.

[24] R. Subramanian et al: The Scanning of Task Environments in Hospitals: An Empirical Study, Journal of Applied Business Research, volume 10 No. 4, Western Academic Press, Littleton, Colorado, 1994.

[25] ASAE: www.asae.org

Chapter 2: Building A High-Performing Organization. Focus on Talent, Teams and Culture

[26] Excerpts from Science at Its Best, Security at Its Worst, Report by a Special Investigative Panel, U.S. President's Foreign Intelligence Advisory Board, June 1999.

[27] Corporate Strategy Board: Strategic Intelligence: Providing Critical Information for Strategic Decisions, Corporate Executive Board, Washington, D.C., 2000. Corporate Strategy Board publications are available exclusively to clients of the Corporate Strategy Board, a membership-based research program of the Corporate Executive Board serving heads of corporate strategy at leading institutions worldwide. Non-members interested in obtaining information about the Board should contact 202-777-5000 in Washington, DC. www.corporatestrategyboard.com

[28] Interview notes prepared by Alain Paul Martin for Procter & Gamble *Strategic Thinking Seminars* delivered in Chicago IL and New York NY.

[29] This is a reference to culture as defined by Arthur Henry Rolph Fairchild: "The most distinctive mark of a cultured mind is the ability to take another's point of view; to put one's self in another's place, and see the life and its problems from a point of view different from one's own. To be willing to test a new idea; to be able to live on the edge of difference in all matters intellectually; to examine without heat the burning question of the day; to have imaginative sympathy, openness and flexibility of mind, steadiness and poise of feeling, cool calmness of judgment, is to have culture."

[30] Alain Paul Martin: Focus on Accountable Leadership with Competence, Commitment and a Conscience, Sept. 2004. Executive.org Press. For excerpts, visit www.executive.org

[31] Human Dynamics "involves identifying fundamental distinctions in the way people function as whole systems – distinctions in how people innately process information, learn, communicate, problem-solve, contribute to teams, become stressed, maintain health, and advance along their path of development." www.humandynamics.com/pages/Dbt_Cert.html

[32] The electronics industry provides a good example of fuzzy boundaries that can be easily overlooked in intelligence collection and analysis. It "has grown rapidly to include semiconductors, connectors, office equipment, measuring and testing tools, office automation, audio and video products, electronic games and toys, home computers, and home automation products. Each field can be viewed as a segment of an industry or a distinct industry in its own right. When companies compete in an industry similar to the electronic industry, the chances for errors in misjudging boundaries increase because the segments are related and participants in one segment may opt to penetrate others, almost without being detected." Excerpts from Sherry S. Chaples and Shaker A. Zahra: Blind Spots in Competitive Analysis, The Academy of Management Executive, Briarcliff Manor, NY10510-3020, Volume 7, No. 2.

[33] For more about matrix organizations, refer to Alain Paul Martin: Shifting Gears to Matrix, in J. Meredith's Project Management, John Wiley & Son, 1985 (1st Edition). A new version of this document will be available in Alain Paul Martin: Focus on Accountable Leadership with Competence, Commitment and a Conscience, Sept. 2004. Executive.org Press. For excerpts, visit www.executive.org/matrix.

[34] James H. Thomas specializes in counterintelligence: www.mindspring.com/~jt-group/default.htm

[35] Society for Competitive Intelligence Professionals: Competencies for Intelligence Professionals, www.scip.org/education/module2.asp

[36] Based on FIRO-B and SDI scores administered by the author to clients including professionals and managers from the intelligence community attending PDI World Seminars since 1980. Walter Schultz pioneered compatibility theory with the Fundamental Interpersonal Orientation-Behavior™ (FIRO-B) instrument originally developed for the U.S. Navy. Currently used in the public and private sectors worldwide, FIRO-B validity has been the subject of countless Ph.D. dissertations.

"The FIRO-B instrument is a powerful tool that assesses how personal needs for *Inclusion*, *Control* and *Affection* affect an individual's behavior toward other people. Each item is measured in two dimensions: the expressed behavior of your client, and the behavior he or she wants from others.

The FIRO-B™ instrument offers insight into an individual's compatibility with other people, as well as into his or her individual characteristics. Use it in any situation that requires interpersonal behavior measurement, including management development, team building, employee development, and individual or couples counseling." Excerpts from Consulting Psychologists Press site www.skillsone.com/firo.html

Created by Dr. Elias H. Porter, the *Strength Deployment Inventory*® (SDI) is "a motivational assessment tool as opposed to being a behavioral assessment. The SDI goes below the surface of the behaviors into the motivations and the values that underlie and influence those behaviors. By understanding what motivates us in our lives to do the things we do, we can better manage our behaviors, and in turn, our relationships with others. Additionally, the SDI integrates going-well and conflict motivations into one easy-to-administer tool that has immediate and lasting results." Excerpts from Personal Strengths Publishing site www.personalstrengths.com

[37] Alain Paul Martin: Strategic Thinking Simplified with Harvard Road Maps, 2005. Executive.org Press. For excerpts, visit www.executive.org

[38] Bruce D. Berkowitz and Allan E. Goodman: Best Truth: Intelligence in the Information Age, Yale University Press, 2001.

[39] E. Baatz: Competitive Intelligence: The Quest for Corporate Smarts, CIO Magazine, Sept. 15 '94. Reprinted through the courtesy of CIO/Darwin. Copyrights © 2002 CXO Media, Inc. All rights reserved. www.cio.com/archive.

[40] Alain Paul Martin: Focus on Accountable Leadership with Competence, Commitment and a Conscience, Sept. 2004. Executive.org Press. For excerpts, visit www.executive.org/matrix.

[41] Bill Gates: Business @ the Speed of Thought: Succeding in Digital Economy, Collins Hemingway (Contributor), Warner Books, New York, 1999, ISBN: 0446525685.

Chapter 3: Intelligence Capital and Road Map

[42] Bank Rate Monitor: www.bankrate.com

[43] The Economist Intelligence Unit: www.store.eiu.com

[44] The Conference Board provides excellent research material and tutorials about business cycles and economic intelligence in general. www.conference-board.org

[45] Ron Insana: The Message of the Markets: How Financial Markets Foretell the Future--And How You Can Profit from Their Guidance, Harper, New York, 2000, ISBN: 0066620457.

[46] U.S. Census Bureau: www.census.gov
U.S. Bureau of Economic Analysis: www.bea.gov
Dan L. Crippen: The Budget and Economic Outlook: Fiscal Years 2003-2012, Congressional Budget Office in cooperation with the Department of Commerce, Bureau of Economic Analysis, the Department of Labor and the Federal Reserve Board, January 23, 2002.
www.cbo.gov/showdoc.cfm?index=2517&sequence=0

[47] Chris Sherman: The Invisible Web, Aug. 6, 2000
www.freepint.co.uk/issues/080600.htm#feature

[48] As an illustration, the Commercial Service of the U.S. Consulate General in Hong Kong compiles and e-mails to its subscribers, twice per week, valuable information about the latest business developments and opportunities in Hong Kong. U.S. companies, retailers, import/export houses and government officials have subscribed. But they represent a tiny fraction of the U.S. firms interested in doing business in Hong Kong. Most prospects don't even know about the existence of the service. Just searching for the URL or e-mail subscription address (comm-service@usfcs-hk.org) can be difficult because it is buried under a ".org" rather than the standard U.S. Government ".gov" domain registration. The URL for the U.S. Embassy in Beijing provides one of the best commercial briefs on China, except that the web site is more than 80 characters long at the time of this publication. The author has asked the Embassy to use a shorter URL to facilitate recording, book marking, retention and access. http://www.usembassy-china.org.cn/english/commercial/english/products/china_commercial_brief.html

[49] Main U.S. Government Portal: www.firstgov.gov. Search for either "business intelligence" or "competitive intelligence."

[50] U.S. Embassies portal: www.usembassy.state.gov

[51] Excerpts from the site of Export Development Canada (www.edc.ca): "EDC is a Canadian financial institution devoted exclusively to providing trade finance services to support Canadian exporters and investors in some 200 markets, 130 of which are in developing markets. These markets offer a wealth of opportunity for Canadian exporters and investors, but also involve greater risk. EDC helps them assess the long-term potential and manage the increased complexity and risk."

Other export promotion and trade financing organizations:
U.S.: www.export.gov, www.sba.gov and www.usatrade.gov,
Australia: www.efic.gov.au
U.K.: www.ecgd.gov.uk.

[52] CBC National News, January 16, 2002.

[53] Michael Porter: Competitive Strategy, 1980, The Free Press.

[54] Excerpts from SCIP web site at www.scip.org

[55] Leonard M. Fuld: The New Competitor Intelligence: The Complete Resource for Finding, Analyzing, and Using Information About Your Competitors, John Wiley & Sons, 1995. Also of interest: The Fuld War Room™ is an interactive multimedia training, reference and application software developed to help you and your organization harness the power of competitive intelligence (CI). The Fuld War Room™ provides instruction, tools and resources from CI fundamentals to advanced analytical techniques. To order the Fuld War Room or for the latest on Leonard M. Fuld's work, visit www.fuld.com.

[56] CIA: Intelligence Cycle, Factbook on Intelligence, CIA Publications. www.cia.gov/cia/publications/facttell.

[57] Alain Paul Martin: Harnessing the Power of a Clear Mission, Vision, Values, Goals & Priorities, June 2004. Executive.org Press. For excerpts, visit www.executive.org

[58] Borrowing from hydrocarbon exploration, we can say that scanning is the intelligence analog of offshore prospecting and focused scanning corresponds to drilling. Prospecting consists of satellite-produced gravity and magnetic surveys that provide clues about where to drill. It requires an understanding of the underground geometry of the rocks (plate tectonics). Neither intelligence scanning nor hydrocarbon prospecting offer sure bets. Well drilling, the second task, is the only way to know whether and what kind of hydrocarbons are actually there. Focused scanning is its equivalent in intelligence production.

[59] The Williams Inference Center "starting point is the search for anomalies: irregularities, surprises and the unusual. These early indications of change may easily be missed in today's morass of obsolete and meaningless data. Inference Center maintains a staff of readers who monitor a broad spectrum of global information and select the anomalies. Sources include over 200 publications, financial markets, popular culture and demographic shifts. Although apparently unrelated on the surface, these clues often reveal a pattern of change. Recognising these patterns and exploring their implication is the essence of the service." www.williamsinference.com

[60] Gerald M. Ostrov, Company Group Chairman, Johnson & Johnson in an e-mail to the author, August 11, 2002.

[61] Darwin Nickel: Intelligence & the "Net": Managing the Mayhem, 26 Sept 2001, www.intelligenceexperts.com

[62] Cyberalert News Monitoring Service: www.cyberalert.com

[63] CCN Newswire Monitoring Service:
www.cdn-news.com/ccnnewswire/clients-netcurrents.html

[64] Frank Benford was the GE scientist who confirmed Simon Newcomb's discovery of the frequency of any digit from 1 to 10 to appear in a set of random numbers. Benford has demonstrated the application of the frequency distribution in areas ranging from telephone numbers and street addresses to finance and physics. Mark Nagrini has applied the Law to tax evasion, fraud detection and suspicious clinical trials. http://mathworld.wolfram.com/BenfordsLaw. www.nist.gov/dads

[65] Fuzzy-set theory is among the potent tools recently used in high-stakes intelligence production. Since perceptions can, at first glance, differ and perfect information is rarely available, particularly when time is of the essence, intelligence analysts and mathematicians work together to fill the void in available data and see some truth behind the veil of contradicting perceptions, observations and testimonies. They can also provide a richer interpretation of a message in the context of the sender, codify the known behavior and mimic or obtain a psycho-graphic profile of an individual. Cutting-edge actuarial work increasingly relies on fuzzy-set theory to account for uncertainty and risk (Jean Lemaire: Fuzzy Insurance, ASTIN Bulletin, April 1990) www.casact.org/library/astin/vol20no1/

Law-enforcement investigators resort to fuzzy-set mathematics to model and simulate the most difficult crime cases (Earl Cox: A Fuzzy System for Detecting Anomalous Behaviors in Healthcare Provider Claims, Intelligent System for Finance and Business, IFRR-201, 1995, p.111-134). A growing number of cases have been resolved thanks to this emerging discipline. Professor Lofti Zadeh is among the leading authorities of the theory and practice of fuzzy sets. www.cs.berkeley.edu

[66] Note that the FBI has recently developed keystroke-monitoring software, named Magic Lantern, capable of reading scrambled databases by gaining access to encryption keys.

[67] For a discussion on these options, read the section titled The Fast-Cycle Competitor (pages 18-19) in Steven C. Wheelwright and Kim B. Clark: Revolutionizing Product Development: Quantum Leaps in Speed, Efficiency, and Quality, The Free Press, 1992.

[68] Cross-impact analysis studies show how a change in one part of a social system might impact on others. The method was instrumental in the development of new pharmaceutical products at Monsanto.

[69] Future Wheels describe the possible immediate and long-term implications that might occur both directly and indirectly as a result of a

decision, an event, an innovation and a new policy or information disclosure. It is a network of circles. Starting from the central node describing the event, each generation of circles outlines the immediate implications that would result from the previous order of events.

Future Wheels are developed as a team effort. The description of each event or implication should be succinct, to facilitate communication with other decision-makers and also for future reference. The team should indicate the probability, desirability and time horizon of each implication, then differentiate among the possibilities under organizational control, and identify the stakeholders controlling the remaining events and their relationship to the company using the Factional Scale® discussed in Chapter 10. Interventions could be explored at this point or developed later in strategy formulation.

[70] For an excellent coverage of strategic maps, mapping and development funnels for new product or process development, read Steven C. Wheelwright and Kim B. Clark: Revolutionizing Product Development: Quantum Leaps in Speed, Efficiency, and Quality, The Free Press, 1992.

[71] I am indebted to Deputy Commissioner Eva Kmiecic of the RCMP for the addition of this paragraph on S-curves. The responsibility for errors and omission is completely mine.

[72] Mohanbir Sawhney: Patterns of Progress, CIO Magazine, Dec1, 2001. Reprinted through the courtesy of CIO/Darwin. Copyrights © 2002 CXO Media, Inc. All rights reserved.

[73] Excerpt from Topic 6: Product Concepts in Danielle McCartan-Quinn, Mark Durkin and Kate Stewart: Fundamentals of Marketing, University of Ulster. E-mail: ERU@ulst.ac.uk www.busmgt.ulst.ac.uk/manage/marketing/notes_6.html

[74] Most leading companies and service organizations have a tendency to ignore the power of disruptive technologies and either go downhill or end up playing catch up with newcomers who see its potential early. There are many examples of winners who turned into losers, from satellite communication and disk drive makers to transportation and heavy industries. Harvard Business School Publications produced an outstanding video on the topic: Disruptive Technologies: Catch the Wave featuring Profs. Joseph L. Bower and Clayton M. Christensen. Harvard Business School Publishing, Boston MA; www.hbsp.harvard.edu

[75] Excerpts from: www.fuld.com/softwareguide

[76] Paul Hession: Adding Value through Knowledge and Information, Canadian Government Executive, Issue 6, pages 2-4, November 2001. www.cangovexec.com

[77] Alain Paul Martin: Strategic Thinking Simplified with Harvard Road Maps, 2005. Executive.org Press. For excerpts, visit www.executive.org

[78] Long lead times were normal during the telecom bubble.

Chapter 4: Intelligence Tools, Platforms and Sources

[79] Joe Barker: Recommended Search Strategy: Analyze Your Topic & Search With Peripheral Vision, UC Berkeley - Teaching Library Internet Workshops, 2002.
www.lib.berkeley.edu/TeachingLib/Guides/Internet/Strategies.html

[80] Gary Price: Web Search Engines FAQs: Questions, Answers and Issues, Searcher, Volume 9, Number 9, October 2001.
www.infotoday.com/searcher/oct01/price.htm

[81] Joe Barker: Begin With Pre-Searching Analysis, UC Berkeley - Teaching Library Internet Workshops, 2002.
www.lib.berkeley.edu/TeachingLib/Guides/Internet/form.pdf

[82] Pandia Advanced Search Query Syntax and Rules
www.pandia.com/goalgettera
http://pandia.com/q-cards

[83] Rosenfeld Library: Searching for Online Information, Anderson School, UCLA. www.anderson.ucla.edu/resources/library/online.htm

[84] Google Directory: http://directory.google.com

[85] Joe Barker: The Best Search Engines, Teaching Library Internet Workshops, UC Berkeley, 2002
www.lib.berkeley.edu/TeachingLib/Guides/Internet/SearchEngines.html

[86] Anita Hamilton: Gaga over Google, Online Advice from TIME Technology Columnist Anita Hamilton, Volume 155, No. 10, March 13, 2000. Time Magazine web site.
www.time.com/time/personal/20000320/tech.html

[87] Corey Kilgannon: Teacher Is Sentenced for Hijacking Past, New York Times, June 16,2002, Late Edition - Final, Section 14WC, Page 7, Column 1

[88] Teoma Search Engine: www.teoma.com

[89] Richard S. Huleatt: AllTheWeb: The Search Engine That Can – And More, Online Newsletter, Information Intelligence, Database Plus, March 2002.
www.fastsearch.com/press/press_pdf/IIMarch-2002.pdf

[90] www.google.com/webmasters/faq.html#nonindex

[91] Teoma Search Engine: www.teoma.com

[92] Teoma: Search With Authority: The Teoma Difference:
http://static.wc.teoma.com/docs/teoma/about/searchWithAuthority.html

[93] NEC ResearchIndex Search Engine and Digital Library:
www.neci.nec.com/~lawrence/researchindex.html

[94] Jason Thomas: Major Search Engines, Tips & Hints, MIT Plasma
Science & Fusion Center, Cambridge, 2002.
www.psfc.mit.edu/library/search_engines.html
www.psfc.mit.edu/library/search_engines_tips&hints.html

[95] SciNet Science Search Engine and Directory: www.scinet.cc

[96] CERN Library: http://weblib.cern.ch//Home/index.php

[97] PhysLink Search Engine and Directories:
www.physlink.com/Directories/Index.cfm
www.physlink.com/search.cfm

[98] NASA Astrophysics Data System: http://adsabs.harvard.edu

[99] Biolinks Directory: www.biolinks.org

[100] Biology Directory (in German): www.biologie.de

[101] Chemie Search Engine and Directory: www.chemie.de

[102] iCivilEngineer Search Engine: www.icivilengineer.com

[103] IT, Computer Science and Statistics Research Papers:
IT and Computer Science: http://cora.whizbang.com
Statistics: http://cora.whizbang.com/sara

[104] SciSeek Directory: www.sciseek.com

[105] National Library of Medicine: www.nlm.nih.gov/hinfo.html

[106] The Health On the Net Foundation MARVIN search engine:
www.hon.ch

[107] Medical Matrix Directory: www.medmatrix.org/reg/login.asp

[108] HealthAtoZ Directory: http://healthatoz.com/atoz

[109] Achoo Health Directory: www.achoo.com

[110] Legal Research Guide: www.ilrg.com

[111] FindLaw Directory: www.findlaw.com

[112] LawGuru Directory: www.lawguru.com

[113] Company Finder: www.searchbug.com/companyfinder

[114] CanadaOne Business Directory: www.canadaone.com/business

[115] Ditto Visual search engine: www.ditto.com

[116] Music robot search engine: www.musicrobot.com

[117] Vivisimo Search engine & Advanced Search page: www.vivisimo.com
http://vivisimo.com/form?form=Advanced

[118] Top 10 of 5,800 Web pages returned by Google for a query on "stem cells" + brain + (migrate OR migration):
1. www.ninds.nih.gov/news_and_events/ pressrelease_neural_stem_cells_060799.htm?type=archived
2. www.sciencedaily.com/releases/2002/03/020319075419.htm
3. www.eurekalert.org/pub_releases/2002-02/uomh-nsc021202.php
4. www.sciam.com/1999/0799issue/0799scicit4.html
5. http://accessible.ninds.nih.gov/news_and_events/ pressrelease_neural_stem_cells_060799.htm?type=archived
6. www.today.uci.edu/releases/00releases/171ap00.htm
7. www.wired.com/news/medtech/0,1286,45599,00.html
8. www.psycport.com/stories/medinews_2002_03_27_eng-medinews_eng-medinews_044950_1781116302651929502.xml.html
9. www.stemcellresearch.org/info/quotes2.htm
10. http://unisci.com/stories/20021/0326026.htm

[119] Additional Web pages that were not returned in first the top 10 of 5,800 pages (see above) but part of the 10 out 192 Web pages returned by Google for a query on "brain stem cells" + (migrate OR migration):
11. www.ninds.nih.gov/news_and_events/pressrelease_bloodtobrain_11 3000.htm?type=archived
12. www.newswise.com/articles/2002/3/SCHIZO.UIC.html
13. www.ucihealth.com/News/Releases/StemCells.htm
14. http://home.no.net/troruud/nytt/extra/spost-xtra3-content.html
15. www.family.org.au/bioethics/docs/bestadultstemcells.html

[120] The WWW Virtual Library is an initiative of Tim Berners-Lee, the inventor of the World Wide Web: http://vlib.org

[121] National Library of Medicine: www.nlm.nih.gov/hinfo.html

[122] The Jackson Library: www.jax.org

[123] Hardin MD, the medical directory of the University of Iowa: www.lib.uiowa.edu/hardin/md

[124] Riken Brain Research Institute of Japan: www.brain.riken.go.jp

[125] Karolinska Institute, Stockholm, Sweden: www.ki.se

[126] Max Planck Cell Biology Institutes in Martiensried, Heidelberg and Dresden, Germany: www.biochem.mpg.de/gerisch/home.htm www.mpg.de/english/institut

[127] French Centre National de la Recherche Scientifique (CNRS) Network: www.cnrs.fr/Chimie/Annuaire/TABLEAUEXCEL.htm

[128] Andrew Starling: Tips on Using Search Engines, Tin Hat www.tinhat.com/internet_basics/effective_internet_searches.htm

[129] Reverse linking syntax. In MSN Search, use the pull-down menu and click on Backward Links. In Google, enter a string comprising the word

link, a colon and the complete URL signature (without spaces in between) such as *link:www.executive.org*

[130] Andrew Starling: see above

[131] Joe Barker: What is Wrong With Relying On Meta-Searchers? Tutorials, UC Berkeley, 2002 www.lib.berkeley.edu/TeachingLib/Guides/Internet/MetaSearch.html

[132] www.thebrain.com

[133] Factiva is a Dow Jones and Reuters company providing a proprietary indexing system used to search Dow Jones and Reuters documents. Its Intelligent Indexing system is also available under license for corporate intranets and portals. Click *products* at www.factiva.com. Factiva also provides a white paper on document indexing worth reading: www.bestofboth.com/infopro/indexingwhitepaper.pdf

[134] LexiQuest is a powerful text mining software. www.spss.com/events

[135] Hyperwave eKnowledge Suite available from: www.hyperwave.com

[136] With the proliferation of hand-held platforms and other devices on the Internet, the 20-year old Domain Name System (DNS) is bound to change, not necessarily for the benefit of those in favor of maintaining a unique generic URL across geopolitical boundaries. Currently supported by most Asian countries, the September 6, 2001 Proposal submitted by RealNames to integrate language and country in each domain name (URL), if adopted, would make intelligence scanning more arduous. Furthermore, it would be a backward step in the establishment of a truly global and democratic Web. It is worthwhile to note, however, that RealNames Keyword Web Registration is a valuable service. For proposal details see: Internet Naming for the Next Generation, www.realnames.com/media/tech_internetNamingNextGen.pdf

[137] The Future of search engines: Bookmark the following resources: Prof. Tom Mitchell: Carnegie Mellon University, www-2.cs.cmu.edu/~tom
Columnist Detlev Johnson: www.adventive.com/lists/isearch/summary.html www.searchengineguide.com/detlev/2002/0213_dj1.html
Charlie Malouf: The Future of Search Engines, www.techeditorial.com/browse.php/category/articles/id/7/index.php

[138] For periodic updates of Chapter 4 on Intelligence Tools, Platforms and Sources, visit www.executive.org

Chapter 5: Internal and External Sources of Business Intelligence

[139] Jennifer Hunter: Lobbies Aim to Make Dent in Can Market, The Globe and Mail, B1 (Business Section), January 21 '84.

[140] Google Live Researcher Answering Service: www.answers.google.com

[141] The Wayback Machine is a web service allowing users to surf web pages from the past by simply specifying a web address and a date. It is ideal to monitor and investigate changes in domain content www.archive.org/news

[142] Chris Sherman and Gary Price: The Invisible Web: Uncovering Information Sources Search Engines Can't See, CyberAge Books, 2001, ISBN 0-910965-51-X. www.cyberagebooks.com

[143] Eloisa Gomez Borah and Rita Costello: Business Database Selection Tool, Rosenfeld Library, Anderson School, UCLA. www.anderson.ucla.edu/resources/library/libdgrid.htm

[144] Joe Barker: Recommended General Subject Directories: Table of Features; Tutorials, UC Berkeley, 2002 www.lib.berkeley.edu/TeachingLib/Guides/Internet/SubjDirectories.html
www.lib.berkeley.edu/TeachingLib/Guides/Internet/InvisibleWeb.html

[145] Gary Price: Direct Search, www.freepint.com/gary/direct.htm

[146] Search Engine Exclusion Protocol: A Web author can indicate if a page may or may not be indexed, or analyzed for links, through the use of a special HTML META tag. www.robotstxt.org/wc/exclusion.html

[147] Portals to search for people or business web sites, e-mail addresses and telephones include: www.411.com, www.whowhere.lycos.com, www.switchboard.com, www.whitepages.com and www.anywho.com E-mail addresses: http://mesa.rrzn.uni-hannover.de

[148] Internet Public Library: www.ipl.org

[149] Google Main Portal: http://directory.google.com

[150] Kitty Bennett: Sources and Experts, St. Petersburg Times, www.ibiblio.org/slanews/internet/experts.html E-mail: bennett@sptimes.com

[151] PDI Global Intelligence Team: Gateways to Think Thanks and Specialty Experts, Executive.org, 2002. Updated regularly. www.executive.org/experts

[152] Spyonit web site: www.spyonit.com

[153] Adapted from web site www.adfacts.com

[154] Cyberalert News Monitoring Service: www.cyberalert.com

[155] The Rich Site Summary (RSS) is the most widely used XML-based content syndication format to share news headlines and exchange documents over the Internet. Content providers create an RSS channel to feed content to interested parties. News-aggregator software programs

use the RSS feeds to deliver web site updates to users. The following Web Site offers tutorials on RSS syndication and provides a list of domains where you can submit your own feeds for redistribution: www.webreference.com/authoring/languages/xml/rss

[156] Jon Udell (http://udell.roninhouse.com/) was BYTE Magazine's executive editor for new media, the architect of the original www.byte.com, and author of BYTE's Web Project column. He is the author of Practical Internet Groupware, from O'Reilly and Associates. Jon now works as an independent Web/Internet consultant. His recent BYTE.com columns are archived at www.byte.com/tangled

[157] Weblogs (or blogs) are webpages created by Internet users to log webpages they find interesting. Ryan Kawailani Ozawa: Jounal versus Weblog, August 4, 2002. www.diarist.net/guide/blogjournal.shtml

[158] Cory Doctorow: How I Learned to Stop Worrying and Love the Panopticon, March 8, 2002. Cory is an award-winning science fiction writer, a regular contributor to Wired magazine and a columnist for the O'Reilly Network.
www.oreillynet.com/lpt/a/network/2002/03/08/cory_google.html

[159] Jon Udell: Personal RSS Zggregators, May 27, 2002. Excerpts with permission from the author October 1, 2002.
www.byte.com/documents/s=7181/byt1022183228615/0527_udell.html

[160] The Pentium Papers:
www.mathworks.com/company/pentium/Nicely_1.txt
www.mathworks.com/company/pentium/index.shtml

[161] Guy Berger: Finding Information on the Net, Excerpts from The Internet: A Goldmine for Editors and Journalists, World Editors Forum, Washington, 1996
http://journ.ru.ac.za/goldmine/INFO.HTM

[162] Engineering Technology Transfer Center: Guide to Using Newsgroups, University of South California, Los Angeles CA 90007.
http://ettc.usc.edu/reports/newsgrp.htm

[163] Google Groups: www.groups.google.com

[164] Google Groups: Basics of Usenet
http://groups.google.com/googlegroups/basics.html

[165] Golden Gate University: Online Discussions: Chat, Conferences, Lists, and Usenet Newsgroups
http://internet.ggu.edu/university_library/conf.html

[166] Nearsite software: www.nearsite.com

[167] Cavan McCarthy: Internet as a Source of Competitive Intelligence – A New Field of Activity for Special Libraries and Information Centers, 6th

Annual Conference, Special Library Association, Nov. 1998, mingo.info-science.uiowa.edu/mccarthy/index.html

[168] Change detection and notification software: www.c4u.com, www.mymindit.com

[169] List of portals for locating foreign governments by country: www.executive.org/news

[170] Chuck Malone: The "Agency Approach" to Locating Government Information on the Internet, W. Illinois University, 1999, wiu.edu/users/mfcem/agency.htm

[171] GPO: www.access.gpo.gov/su_docs/aces/aaces002.html

[172] The Virtual Library of Energy Science and Technology, U.S. Department of Energy: www.osti.gov

[173] Sites for North-American contractors: www.GSA.gov, www.contractscanada.gc.ca, www.mac.doc.gov/nafta

[174] U.S. State Department's site for procurement opportunities: www.statebuy.gov

[175] The FDA site also links to other health organizations and drug agencies: www.fda.gov. The U.S. patent Office provides patent descriptions and links to intellectual property agencies: www.uspto.gov. FedWorld is a portal to locate U.S. Government information including job ads and scientific and technical publications sites: www.fedworld.gov

[176] U.S. Library of Congress: www.loc.gov

[177] National Research Council of Canada: www.nrc.ca

[178] Industry Canada: www.strategis.ic.gc.ca

[179] Google links to databases of various universities: www.google.com/options/universities.html

[180] Caltech's Millikan Library: General Reference Portal http://library.caltech.edu/reference/default.htm

[181] Lyonette Louis-Jacques: Foreign Law: Legal Research Resources on the Internet, University of Chicago. www.lib.uchicago.edu/~llou/foreignlaw.html

[182] ABC business news: www.moneyscope.com

[183] Financial Time Television: www.ft.com

[184] Eloisa Gomez Borah and Rita Costello: Business Database Selection Tool, Rosenfeld Library, Anderson School, UCLA. www.anderson.ucla.edu/resources/library/libdgrid.htm

[185] Dow Jones Interactive: http://askdj.dowjones.com

[186] Lexis-Nexis provides news, business and legal information solutions to corporate, academic, legal and government markets. Its services combine searchable access to over three billion documents. It is owned by Reed International PLC. www.lexisnexis.com

[187] Dialog and Profound are products of Thomson Company: www.dialog.com, www.profound.com

[188] Adapted excerpts from: Corporate Intelligence, www.secondarydata.com/secdata/CorpIntel.htm

[189] Assignment Editor: www.assignmenteditor.com

[190] Arthur D. Little: www.adlittle.com

[191] Batelle: www.batelle.org/conferences

[192] The Brookings Institution: www.brook.edu

[193] C.D. Howe Institute: www.cdhowe.org

[194] The Conference Board: www.conference-board.org

[195] The Council on Foreign Relations: www.cfr.org

[196] Gallup: www.gallup.com

[197] Fraser Institute www.fraserinstitute.org

[198] Louis Harris: www.harrisinteractive.com

[199] Hudson Institute: www.hudson.org

[200] MIT System Dynamics Group: http://sysdyn.mit.edu/sd-group/home.html

[201] OECD: www.oecd.org

[202] Opinion Research Corp.: www.opinionresearch.com

[203] PriceWaterhouse-Coopers: www.pwcglobal.com

[204] Rand Corporation: www.rand.org

[205] Research International: www.research-int.com

[206] RoperASW: www.roperasw.com

[207] Stanford Research Institute: www.sri.com

[208] Survey Research Center of the University of Michigan: www.isr.umich.edu/src

[209] Yankelovich: www.yankelovich.com

[210] The National Post sites: www.financialpost.com and www.infomart.ca

[211] The Globe and Mail: www.theglobeandmail.com

[212] CCN Newswire Monitoring Service: www.cdn-news.com/ccnnewswire/clients-netcurrents.html

[213] Online books freely readable over the Internet: http://digital.library.upenn.edu/books

[214] Important online libraries provide content from publishers like Oxford University Press, Academic Press, Cambridge University Press, Harvard University Press, John Wiley & Sons, McGraw-Hill, OECD, Palgrave, Paragon Press, Penguin Classics, Rand Corporation, Random House, Sage publishing, University of Chicago Press and Yale University Press.

[215] The leader www.questia.com partners with 250 publishers. A subscription to Questia costs less than $20 per month. Questia also distributes XanEdu materials.

[216] www.xanedu.com develops and provides print and electronic course materials to educators and students worldwide directly or via AOL, Barnes & Nobles, Gateway and Microsoft. It also distributes content materials from AMA, INSEAD, Richard Ivey School of Business and Harvard University, among others. Subscription is $10 per month. Questia also distributes XanEdu materials.

[217] www.ebrary.com is a collection from over 100 publishers including the World Bank and the United Nations.

[218] Jones International is a multimedia conglomerate. It includes a fully accredited online university and a virtual library www.egloballibrary.com.

[219] Harvard Business School Working Knowledge portal: http://hbswk.hbs.edu

[220] Brint is a knowledge management and technology portal: www.brint.com

[221] Library on Knowledge Management of the Ministry of Defense of Singapore: Bookmark www.executive.org/news for an easier way to access the library. Otherwise, use the site actual identifier as follows: http://openacademy.mindef.gov.sg/OpenAcademy/Learning%20Resourc es/Knowledge%20Mgmt/know_mainmenu.htm

[222] Online e-education platforms: www.blackboard.com

[223] Other leading e-education platforms: www.webct.com, www.campuscruiser.com, www.campuspipeline.com

[224] CIT of the University of California in San Francisco: http://cit.ucsf.edu/classes http://cit.ucsf.edu/webct/designerlinks.php

[225] Simon Fraser University Virtual U: http://virtual-u.cs.sfu.ca/vuweb.new/new.html

[226] Online training providers for business: www.mentergy.com, www.crkinteractive.com, www.avilar.com (for WebMentor), www.lotus.com/home.nsf/welcome/learnspace, www.wbtsystems.com

[227] Advanced Distributed Learning (ADL) initiative: www.adlnet.org

[228] IEEE Learning Technology Standards Committee (LTSC) is the official body responsible for developing "standards, recommended practices, and guides for software components, tools, technologies and design methods that facilitate the development, deployment, maintenance and interoperation of computer implementations of education and training components and systems." http://ltsc.ieee.org

[229] IMS Global Learning Consortium: www.imsproject.org

[230] A partnership of Columbia University and Instructional Systems Inc., the Wellspring is a community of distance educators: http://wellspring.isinj.com

[231] The Alliance of Remote Instructional Authoring and Distribution Networks for Europe (ARIADNE) is a non-profit foundation created by the European Union. www.ariadne-eu.org ARIADNE partners with IEE LTSC (see above) and the European Committee for Standardization www.cenorm.be/isss

[232] MIT Open Knowledge Initiative: http://web.mit.edu/oki/

[233] Leonard M. Fuld: see above.

[234] World Wide Web Consortium (W3C): www.w3.org

[235] Fred Polak: The Image of the Future, Oceana Publications, 81, Main Street, Dobbs Ferry, NY 10522, 1961. Two Volumes.

[236] Vibert Conor: Web-Based Analysis for Competitive Intelligence, Quorum Books, Westport, CT, 2000

[237] Recon Competitive Intelligence Solutions is a division of Aurora WDC: www.aurorawdc.com

[238] CCS specializes in electronic surveillance counter-measures, wireless digital communications, computer intrusion and personal protection. www.spyzone.com

[239] The Phillips Group specializes in CI for the telecom sector. www.phillips-infotech.com

[240] www.competia.com, www.fuld.com, www.scip.org

[241] I am indebted to Deputy Commissioner Eva Kmiecic of the RCMP for the addition of this section to guide readers in their ongoing search for new sources of information. The responsibility for errors and omission is completely mine.

[242] C. Klein: Overcoming Net Disease: The Risks in Depending Solely on the Internet for Competitive Intelligence Research. FID Review 1(4/5), 27-30, 1999.

[243] Jan Herring quotation cited from Leonard M. Fuld: The New Competitor Intelligence: The Complete Resource for Finding, Analyzing, and Using Information About Your Competitors, John Wiley & Sons, 1995.

Chapter 6: Counterintelligence and Intelligence Security in Business and Government

[244] Based on private conversation with Mark Thompson, currently President of Equity Resources Group Inc. September 4, 2002.

[245] Glenn Spencer Bacal: Law of Trade Secrets, Non-competes, and Anti-piracy Agreements - A Practical Guide for Business and In-House Lawyers, 1996. www.azlink.com/lawyers/articles/secrets.htm#conc

[246] Bill Murray: Army Debuts IT Crime Unit, Government Computer News, 2000-07-24, Volume 19, No. 20, Page 48. www.nlectc.org/justnetnews/08172000.htm

[247] Joshua Dean: Risking IT, Information Management, Government Executive Magazine, 2001-04-01. www.govexec.com/fpp/fpp01/s4.htm

[248] Ron Simmer: Using Intellectual Property Data for Competitive Intelligence, University of British Columbia, Vancouver, 2001, www.library.ubc.ca/patscan/CH4-CompIntelRevB.pdf

[249] Rene Zentner: When Competition Crosses Legal Limits, College of Engineering and Computer Science, Portland State University, 1997. www.cecs.pdx.edu/~herm/capstone/mee9899/design/qfd/zentner.htm

[250] Peter Schweitzer: Friendly Spies: How America's Allies Are Using Economic Espionage to Steal Our Secrets, Atlantic Monthly Press, New York, 1993. ISBN: 0871134977.

[251] Ernest M. Teagarden: James Bond and George Smiley Go Into Business — Teaching About Business Espionage, Volume 72, Issue 4, pp. 250-252, Journal of Education for Business, Washington, March-April 1997. ISSN 08832323.

[252] Linda Klebe Trevino, Gary R. Weaver: Ethical Issues in Competitive Intelligence Practice: Consensus, Conflicts, and Challenges, Competitive Intelligence Review, SCIP, Volume 8, no. 1, Spring 1997, www.scip.org/Library/8(1)ethics.pdf

[253] Excerpts from Leonard Condenzio: Best Practices for Retaining and Hiring Employees, www.nacufs.org/resources/condenz.asp

[254] Joshua Dean: Lost Laptops Compromise Secrets, October 21, 2001, www.govexec.com,.

[255] Excerpts from the Annual Report to Congress on Foreign Economic Collection and Industrial Espionage: www.fas.org/sgp/othergov/indust.html

[256] The Wall Street Journal: Ex-Consultant to GE Charged with Theft of Secret Information, Feb. 7, 1996.

[257] CSE's other critical mission is signals intelligence. CSE is a member of the Echelon Alliance, a global surveillance network that includes signals-intelligence agencies of the United States, Canada, the U.K., Australia and New Zealand.
- Communications Security Establishment (CSE), DND, Ottawa, Canada, K1G 3Z4. www.cse.gc.ca
- National Security Agency, Fort George G. Meade, Maryland 20755-6740, USA, www.nsa.mil
- Communications-Electronics Security Group (CESG), Cheltenham, GL52 5UE, U.K., www.cesg.gov.uk
- Defence Signals Directorate (DSD) Kingston ACT 2604, Australia, www.dsd.gov.au
- Government Communications Security Bureau (GCSB) Freyberg Building, Aitken Street, Wellington, New Zealand

[258] The new mission of the National Counter-Intelligence Executive (NCIX) is to provide the U.S. Government with "policy-driven, and accountable leadership by creating new and enhanced counter-intelligence capabilities, ensuring coherent programs, strategies, cooperative approaches, and conducting effective oversight." The NCIX accomplishes its mission "through the identification of the nation's most critical assets (tangible and intangible), production of strategic CI analysis, development of a national threat assessment, formulation of a national counter-intelligence strategy, creation of an integrated counter-intelligence budget, and an agenda of program reviews and evaluations. This approach requires direct interaction with policymakers and the private sector and the adoption of a new philosophy that embraces cooperation, coordination, and collaboration among the intelligence, law enforcement, security, and counter-intelligence communities." www.ncix.gov

[259] FBI: Awareness of National Security Issues and Response (ANSIR) Program: www.fbi.gov/hq/nsd/ansir/ansir.htm

[260] The Annual Report to Congress on Foreign Economic Collection and Industrial Espionage (see above) provided background information for this section. For the latest on the subject, consult Government

Documents on Secrecy and Security Policy at www.fas.org/sgp/othergov/

[261] The Canadian Security Intelligence Service (CSIS): www.csis.gc.ca

[262] Adapted from MITRE web site: www.mitre.org

[263] DuPont Consulting Solutions is a subsidiary of E. I. du Pont de Nemours and Company: www.dupont.com/consulting

[264] IBM Global Security Solutions www.ibm.com/security

[265] Kroll web site: www.krollworldwide.com

[266] ISS Security web site: www.issinc.ca

[267] With offices around the world serving nearly 10,000 clients, RSA Security of Bedford MA provides e-security solutions including authentication, authorization, encryption and public key management systems. www.rsasecurity.com

[268] Phoenix Consulting Group: www.intellpros.com

[269] Insider threat prevention software from ThunderStore: www.thunderstore.com

[270] Registered e-Mail Delivery Provider: www.rpost.com

[271] CML Emergency Services Inc. provides public-safety solutions that integrate telephone, radio and data management in 9-1-1 and other emergency service call centers. www.cmles.com

[272] Federation of American Scientists: www.FAS.org

[273] Free forums for consumers and corporate buyers to publish and view complaints about products and services: www.ecomplaints.com, www.epinions.com and www.fightback.com

[274] U.S. Secret Service: The Best Practices for Seizing Electronic Evidence. www.secretservice.gov/electronic_evidence.shtml

[275] I am indebted to Jean-Claude Theurillat, Vice President, Schindler Management Ltd (Switzerland) for reminding me about the importance of working climates, employee satisfaction, privacy and personal data protection.

[276] Excerpts from Security – Enhanced Linux, Information Security, National Security Agency, www.nsa.gov

[277] Steganography permits users to transmit a secret message concealed in an object or in other messages. The object can be a text or graphic document, a digital picture, a filmstrip, audio work, an unused sector of a floppy disk or a physical object. Steganography enabling software includes S-Tools, White Noise Storm, Stego Dos, EzStego, Mandelstag and Hide and Seek. www.jjtc.com/stegdoc/index2.html

[278] Robert D. Steele: Virtual Intelligence & American Enterprise: Ensuring the Security & Competitiveness of America, www.oss.net

[279] General Motors used its audit-trail system to force Volkswagen to pay over $1 billion in an out-of-court settlement after GM discovered that a purchasing manager who left Adam Opel AG, a German unit of GM, provided VW with stolen plans for a new GM car.

[280] François de la Rochefoucauld: Maximes, 1665-1678.

[281] The Fortezza crypto card uses public key technology and a special card reader. It provides secure interoperability in network communications. It is an integral part of MISSI, an initiative of the National Security Agency. MISSI stands for Multilevel Information System Security initiative. MISSI's goal is to provide dependable and affordable security services necessary to protect information from unauthorized disclosure or modification and to provide mechanisms to authenticate users participating in the exchange of information. www.chips.navy.mil/archives/95_jul/file6.html

[282] Based on several sources, such as the Ontario Ministry of the Environment, and press articles including Jennifer Hunter: Lobbies Aim to Dent in Can Market, The Globe and Mail, January 21, 1984, Dow Jones & Company, 1998.

[283] Adapted text from the web site www.ict.usc.edu

[284] "A unique ad hoc working group convened at ICT at the behest of the U.S. Army. The goal was to brainstorm about possible terrorist targets and schemes in America and to offer solutions to those threats, in light of the twin assaults on the Pentagon and the World Trade Center. Among those in the working group based at the Institute for Creative Technology are screenwriter Steven E. De Souza, TV writer David Engelbach, and Joseph Zito, who directed the features *Delta Force One*, *Missing in Action* and *The Abduction*. But the list also includes… David Fincher, Spike Jonze, Randal Kleiser and Mary Lambert, as well as feature screenwriters Paul De Meo and Danny Bilson." Adapted and summarized from Variety Magazine excerpts reported by James Der Derian: 9.11: Before, After and In Between, Essays, Social Science Research Council, New York, 2001.

[285] Excerpts from: Science at Its Best, Security at Its Worst, Report by a Special Investigative Panel, U.S. President's Foreign Intelligence Advisory Board, June 1999.

[286] John A. Nolan, III: Competitive Intelligence, Journal of Business Strategy, November/December 1999.

Chapter 7: Value and Threat Incubation

[287] Most people identify the new economy with the Internet and dot.com companies, while ignoring other IT areas and important sectors like microelectronics, new materials, robotics, biotechnology, preventive health and wellness, optical networking and telecommunications, education, aerospace, environment sciences and alternative energy sources.

[288] Phrase borrowed from David B. Yoffe and Michael A. Cusumano: Judo Strategy: The Competitive Dynamics of Internet Time, Harvard Business Review, January-February 1999.

[289] Stephen Hawking, A Brief History of Time, From the Big Bang to Black Holes, Bantam Books, June 1990 edition, New York, p.137. This citation by Hawking referred to the complexity of any model attempting to describe the universe.

[290] The status quo is defined as the state of quasi-stationary equilibrium between the forces for and against change.

[291] As an illustration, major casualty insurers knew about the unprecedented cluster of claims involving Firestone tires and Ford Explorers. But most institutional investors kept buying Ford stock. Seduced by the acumen of former Ford's President Jacques Nasser, they closed their eyes to the disaster waiting to happen.

[292] Alain Paul Martin: Managerial Lessons Learned From 9-11 Tragedies, Strategic Intelligence Briefs, 2003. www.executive.org/9-11

[293] Alain Paul Martin: IBM: Then and Now, Strategic Intelligence Briefs, 2003. www.executive.org/ibm

[294] Peter Uvin: The Failure of the International Community to Prevent Genocide in Rwanda. Excerpts from Peter Uvin: Aiding Violence: The Development Enterprise in Rwanda, Kumarian Press, West Hartford, 1998. www.globalpolicy.org/security/issues/uvin.htm

[295] http://news.bbc.co.uk/1/hi/world/africa/820827.stm

[296] David Champion: Mastering the Value Chain: An Interview with Mark Levin of Millennium Pharmaceuticals, Harvard Business Review, June 2001, Product Number: 0106G.

[297] Based on interviews of John Bollinger by CNBC's Ron Insana. John Bollinger's Acme Analytics provides an arsenal of weapons for the skilled investor at virtually no cost. Acme Analytics' instruments include a proprietary rating engine that "uses 54 rules to determine a stock's potential return". Using fuzzy logic, the engine offers a potent tool for making wise investment decisions by mining information about

some 3200 stocks. For more information on Acme's products and search engine, visit www.equitytrader.com

[298] Terence Pare: Jack Welch's Nightmare on Wall Street, Fortune Magazine, 1994-09-05

Laurie Cohen and Alix Freedman: How a Kidder Trader Stumbled Upward Before Scandal Struck, Wall Street Journal, June 3, 1994

Leah Nathans Spiro: What Joseph Jett's Defense Will Look Like, Business Week, June 13, 1994

[299] SEC: Administrative Proceeding File No. 3-8919 in the Matter of Orlando Joseph Jett, Initial decision Release No. 127, United States of America Before the Securities and Exchange Commission, Washington, D.C., July 21, 1998. www.sec.gov/litigation/aljdec/id127cff.htm

[300] Ron Chernow: Titan – The Life of John D. Rockefeller, Sr., Random House, New York, 1998.

[301] Integrated Global Positioning System (GPS) and inertial navigation systems (INS). "The GPS produces precise positions that are subject to errors arising from loss of satellite lock and resolution of phase ambiguities. Information from the INS can be used to correct these errors while the GPS data are used to continuously calibrate the INS." Richard D. Sanchez and Larry D. Hothem: Positional Accuracy of Airborne Integrated Global Positioning and Inertial Navigation Systems for Mapping in Glen Canyon, Arizona, Open-File Report 02-222. http://mac.usgs.gov/mac/isb/pubs/openfile/OFR02-222ss.pdf

[302] Alain Paul Martin: Think Proactive: New Insights into Decision-Making, Executive.org Press, 1983, U.S. Library of Congress Catalog Number: 83-670057. www.executive.org

[303] Gary Hamel: Strategy as Revolution, Harvard Business Review, July-August 1996, pages 69-82. Although this paper contains several good ideas, it is worthwhile noting that Gary Hamel's approach is reductive. It focuses on companies rather than the people who lead them. Also, the principle of removing intermediaries advocated in Hamel's road map is neither prudent nor universally sound. It should be assessed on a case-by-case basis. For ten years, I was privileged to guide John Harbour, who led the dis-intermediation of casualty insurance in North America by eliminating the brokers from his supply chain and tripling his income within three years. But our experience in electronic commerce has demonstrated the value of mediation, particularly in the realm of Business-to-Business (B2B). We are even witnessing *hyper-mediation* in the supply chain of Inktomi, eBay and AOL. As for Xerox staging a revolution to get rid of intermediaries, one may argue that the company has been dis-intermediating itself out of business for over ten years! Its downfall incubated over a two-year period during which Xerox was

restructured to focus undue energy on winning the Malcolm-Baldridge Quality Award. Even worse, the award facilitated the disclosure of Xerox's most coveted trade secrets to Canon, Hewlett-Packard and IBM. It has also inflated the reward expectations of senior professionals, many of whom ultimately left Xerox.

[304] The reference to the 1979 landmark address by Pope John-Paul II was added after a private communication with Dr. André Potworowski who traveled with the Pope throughout Poland as a journalist.

[305] Sun Tzu: The Art of War, Doubleday Publishing Group, 1988, ISBN 0-440-55005-X. Bibliography: http://vikingphoenix.com/public/SunTzu/stbiblio.htm

[306] U.S. Food and Drug Administration: BSE Contingency Plan, Version 1.0 – February 15, 2001 quoting J.W. Wilesmith et al.: Bovine Spongiform Encephalopathy: Epidemiologic Features 1985 to 1990. Veterinary Record 130:90-94. 1992. www.fda.gov/oc/bse/contingency.html#background

[307] New Scientist: Timeline: The Rise and Rise of BSE, undated. Consulted August 25, 2002. www.newscientist.com/hottopics/bse/bsetimeline.jsp

[308] John Darnton: The Logic of the "Mad Cow" Scare, The New York Times, March 30, 1996. www.mad-cow.org/96mar.html

[309] Reuters Newsmedia. www.ita.suite.dk/alreuter.htm

[310] BBC News: BSE Report: The Main Points, BBC, October 26, 2000. http://news.bbc.co.uk/1/hi/uk_politics/992435.stm

Chapter 8: Hitch-Hiking on Surprise Events and Tidal Waves to Create Opportunities

[311] James C. Maxwell, Science and Free Will cited in The Life of James Clerk Maxwell by L. Campbell and W. Garnett, Macmillan, London, 1882.

[312] Wall-Street analysts use the phrase "disaster du jour" to refer to the stock-market loser of the day. Established search engines provide over 200 references to the expression.

[313] Marty Sass: Finding Bear Market Opportunities, ListeningIn, volume 3, i. 21, November 9, 2001. www.weedenco.com/welling/archive/all/v03i21lilogo.asp

[314] Marty Sass: See above.

[315] Michael Sterling & Associates: Lance Armstrong – A Biography, edited and updated in Dec. 2001by Chris Brewer. www.lancearmstrong.com

[316] Melanie Roush: Voices from Ground Zero, RCMP Gazette, Page 33, Volume 64, Number 2, 2002.

[317] Children Can Free the Children: www.freethechildren.org

[318] UniverCity 2002 Keynote Speaker Graig Kielburger, Ball State University, September 25,2002. www.bsu.edu/univercity/speakers/kielburger_craig.htm

[319] *Mary H. Cooper:* The Clinton Administration Plan for Reforming the CIA, The CQ Researcher, Volume 6, No. 5, Feb. 2, 1996, pp. 109-112, www.cqpress.com.

[320] Sigma, designation σ in statistics, represents one standard deviation from the arithmetic mean. One mistake per hundred transactions translates to 99% efficiency or 3.8 Sigma. Over the long term, any service, product, process, transaction or complete network that is delivered with less than 3.4 non-conforming parts (or occurrences) per million is 99.99966% conformance or virtual perfection equivalent to six standard deviations (or 6σ). Spearheaded as a benchmarking instrument by Motorola's President Bob Galvin, Six Sigma was the theme for a company-wide quality initiative in the eighties that subsequently earned Motorola the Malcolm Baldridge National Quality Award. Created by Galvin to share Motorola's experience, the Six-Sigma Research Institute (SSRI) is a cooperative network that has permitted companies like GE to adopt the method and gain billions through improved productivity and benefits to customers.

[321] Archon Fung and Dara O'Rourke: Reinventing Environmental Regulations from the Grassroots Up: Explaining and Expanding the Success of the Toxic Release Inventory, Environmental Management, Springer-Verlag, New York. February 2000, Volume 25, No. 2 pp. 115-127. For other excellent publications of Professor Archon Fung: www.archonfung.net/docs

[322] Luis Bunuel: An Andalusian Dog is a legendary surrealist movie produced in 1928.

[323] Titled "We, On Death Row" and featuring 26 death-sentenced inmates, Benetton's $20 million global anti-capital punishment campaign launched in the Year 2000 was the last to be crafted by Toscani. Its billboards and 96-page brochure brought the controversy to an unprecedented plateau. Pressure from City Hall in Sears' hometown of Chicago, forced Sears to sever its long-standing relationship with the Italian company. Within a year, CEO Luciano Benetton apologized about the adverse consequence of the campaign and terminated the long tenure of Toscani.

[324] Gregory Gibert: Artists and Entertainers, from The Encyclopedia of AIDS: A Social, Political, Cultural, and Scientific Record of the HIV Epidemic, Raymond A. Smith, Editor, Fitzroy Dearborn Publishers, 1998. www.thebody.com/encyclo/artists.html

[325] The smoking rate among the youth in California dropped from 11 per cent to 6.9 per cent in 1999. This 35 per cent reduction in one year is partly attributable to the quality of California's anti-smoking campaign. Tobacco Youth Protection Bill, Hansard, Canadian Senate, Sept. 21, 2000. David Briscoe: Smokers Stopping: Government Data Shows Americans Smoking Less, Associated Press, May 22, 2000.

[326] Boeing: Chairman and CEO Phil Condit on the JSF Decision, Washington, D.C., Oct. 26, 2001, www.boeing.com/news/breakingnews/2001/011026n.htm

[327] Excerpts from Being web site: www.boeing.com/companyoffices/history/boeing/747.html

[328] I am indebted to Boeing Corporate Historian, Michael J. Lombardi, for the background information on Boeing 747.

[329] www.peacecorps.gov

[330] Examples of good surprise events (www.executive.org/events): unexpected surges in demand, new sources of supply, unsolicited good customers, the surprise election of your favorite candidate, the repeated triumphs of Lance Armstrong in the *Tour de France*, the first official trip of Pope John-Paul II to Poland, the liberation of Nelson Mandela, the rise to power of Mikael Gorbachev and the 1997 Nobel Peace Prize awarded to Jody Williams and her NGO confederation namely the International Campaign to Ban Landmines (ICBL).

[331] John Maynard Keynes: The General Theory of Employment, Interest and Money, Harcourt Brace Jovanovich, New York, 1936.

[332] Ivan Reitman's great allies include Billy Crystal, Harrison Ford, Daniel Goldberg, Anne Heche, Sheldon Kahn, Joe Medjuck, Gordon Webb and Robin Williams.

[333] That is why the long incubation of democracy in the West took over one thousand years, with democracy emerging long after endless struggles, embryonic interventions and major surprise events that covered the period from the fall of the Roman Empire to the fall of communism.

Chapter 9: The Change-makers - Their Power, Status and Role

[334] The term *Rule Breaker* is borrowed from Gary Hamel: Strategy as Revolution, Harvard Business Review, July-August 1996, pages 69-82.

[335] The Pentagon Papers: Secrets, Lies and Audio-Tapes, The National Security Archives, George Washington University, www.gwu.edu/~nsarchiv/NSAEBB/NSAEBB48/nixon.html

[336] From the book Jimmy Carter: Keeping Faith: Memoirs of a President, University of Arkansas Press, 1995. ISBN 1557283303 and several

interviews, it is clear that President Carter spent endless days and sleepless nights on one issue: the Iranian hostage crisis.

Fred Greenstein [The Presidential Difference: Leadership Style from FRD to Clinton, Princeton University Press, 2001. ISBN 0691090831], quotes a 1982 interview in which President Carter states: "As an engineer and as a governor, I was more inclined to move rapidly and without equivocation and without the interminable consultations and so forth that are inherent, I think, in someone who has a more legislative attitude, or psyche, or training, or experience."

Ruthless rulers like Soviet President Leonid Brezhnev and Ayatolla Khomeini, may have taken advantage of Carter's difficulties.

Since leaving the Oval Office, Mr. Carter has learned to reach out to powerful constituencies and has lead a life of dedication to public good. He has frequently played the instrumental role of an honest broker and promoter of justice and human rights, acting either as a wise champion or conductor, depending upon the issue. On October 11, 2002, Mr. Carter was awarded the Nobel Peace Prize.

337 Borrowed from an excellent book by Jamie McKenzie: Parenting for an Age of Information: Preparing Your Daughter or Son for the Next Century, Chapter 3: Puzzling, Educational Technology Journal, Bellingham, WA98225. Tel. (360) 223-0255. www.fno.org/parenting/outline.html

338 Michael E. Porter: The Competitive Advantage of Nations, The Free Press, New York, 1990.

339 Notes based on July 29 1993 phone conversation with Mr. Gregory Watson and more recent research including Ruth Ann Strickland: The Twenty-seventh Amendment and Constitutional Change by Stealth, PS: Political Science and Politics 26, no. 4, pp.716-722, December 1993. Quotations in italic from People Magazine, June 1993. www.usconstitution.net/constamnotes.html#Am27

340 Associated Press (AP): Canadian Dick Pound Replaced by Heiberg as IOC Marketing Chief, Lausanne, Switzerland, December 20, 2001

341 Seymour Brody: Dr. Gregory Goodwin Pincus: Father of The Pill, Jewish Heroes in America, Florida Atlantic University Libraries, www.fau.edu/library/br138.htm
Sanger's Role in the Development of Contraceptive Technologies, Margaret Sanger Papers Project Newsletter, #6, Winter 1993/4, New York University, Revised 1998.
www.nyu.edu/projects/sanger/techno.htm.
Claudia Goldin: The Power of the Pill: Oral Contraceptives and Women's Career and Marriage Decisions, 2001.
www.economics.harvard.edu/~goldin/papers/pillpaper.pdf

Betsy Hartmann: <u>Reproductive Rights and Wrongs: The Global Politics of Population Control</u>, South End Press, Cambridge, MA, 1995, pp. 173-187 <u>www.hsph.harvard.edu/rt21/race/HARTMANNCh10.html</u>

[342] Derived from the EVA concept, the Mitsubishi Corporation Value Added (MCVA) "clearly shows whether businesses are able to cover the cost of capital associated with a given level of risk... With MC's 694 subsidiaries and affiliates, this is clearly significant... MCVA forces MC business groups to take a long, hard look at cross-shareholdings." Adapted excerpts from <u>MC2003 Blueprint</u>; Mitsubishi Corporation, 2002. <u>www.mitsubishi.co.jp/En/investor/company/mc2003/company_e06.html</u>

[343] Mitsubishi Monitor <u>www.mitsubishi.or.jp/e/monitor/2k06/interview.html</u>

Chapter 10: Understanding Your Constituencies
Their Perceptions and Vested Interests

[344] David A. Lax, James Sibenius: <u>The Manager As Negotiator: Bargaining for Cooperation and Competitive Gain</u>, Free Press, New York, 1986, ISBN: 0029187702.

[345] Peter Hoffman: <u>Alliance for Telecom Industry Solutions Launches Post Deregulation Network Interoperability Effort</u>, ATIS, 1200 G Street, NW, 500, Washington, DC 20005, Sept. 12, 1996,

[346] Rather than maintaining solidarity with the coalition against Napster on the online-copyright lawsuit, Bertelsmann broke ranks with the plaintiffs in order to enter into a partnership with the defendant and exploit the synergy of content, technology and market power. With this move, Bertelsmann was hoping to gain access to Napster's technology and fast-growing market of music fans (45 million in the 2001). Napster was on its way to gaining a global ally with unparalleled content and far-reaching capabilities. However, a court order blocked Napster from offering major-label songs for free and the opportunity to settle out of court was rejected by the plaintiffs.

[347] Sun Tzu: <u>The New Translation (The Art of War)</u>, J.H. Huang (Editor), Quill, 1993, ISBN: 0688124003.

[348] In underground organizations (terrorism and organized crime), *blind resources* are often used as *doomed spies*. Borrowed from Sun Tzu in <u>The Art of War</u>, a doomed spy acts "openly for the purpose of deception". Also, watch for doomed spies in global markets where 'guerrilla' marketing and cutthroat competition are a way of life.

[349] Alain Paul Martin: <u>Dealing with Fanatics</u>; <u>Hostage Negotiation</u>, 2003. <u>www.executive.org/F7</u>

245

[350] The *Harvard™ Strategy Grid* facilitates strategic thinking. Its content and applications are discussed in Alain Paul Martin: Strategic Thinking Simplified with Harvard Road Maps, 2005. Executive.org Press. The *Harvard™ Strategy Grid* is currently available. For book excerpts, visit www.executive.org.

Chapter 11: Knowing the Players
Deeper Insights, Better Intelligence

[351] Since direct mailing and media channels (TV, radio, Internet and printed media) are prime vehicles for reaching target audiences, media habits are essential to marketers and advertisers. They include TV channels watched, radio stations tuned to, program and subject preferences, consumption time, web pages visited and newspaper sections read. A Canadian veteran in media audience measurements, the BBM correlates attitudes and lifestyles (leisure activities) with media habits (radio listening, magazine and newspaper readership, Internet activity), home and vehicle ownerships, electronic product purchases, long-distance expenses, insurance and other financial expenditures. The BBM stratified sampling approach makes it possible to identify target groups and clusters with similar characteristics both at the national and local levels. www.bbm.ca

[352] James R. Bettman: Segmentation, BA362, The Fuqua School of Business, Duke University, Fall 2000. http://faculty.fuqua.duke.edu/~jrb12/ba362/segmentation.pdf

[353] Dragica Jovanovic: A Survey of Internet Oriented Information Systems Based on Customer Profile and Customer Behavior, Republic Job Market Bureau, Gundulicev venac 23-25, 11000 Beograd, Serbia. www.ssgrr.it/en/ssgrr2001/papers/Dragica%20Jovanovic.pd

[354] Mervyn Jackson: Cultural Influences on Tourist Destination Choices of 21 Pacific Rim Nations, 2001 CAUTHE National Research Conference, RMIT University. www.btr.gov.au/conf_proc/cauthe/Jackson.pdf

[355] Culture is a set of beliefs, values, attitudes, habits, and forms of behavior that are shared by a society and are transmitted from generation to generation. Excerpts from Peter D. Bennett, Harold H. Kassarjian: Consumer Behavior, Prentice-Hall Foundations of Marketing Series, 1972. ISBN: 0131693832

[356] Stanley C. Plog: Understanding Psychographics in Tourism Research, in Travel, Tourism & Hospitality Research, Edited by R. Ritchie and C. Goeldner, 1987. New York: Wiley.

[357] Research on collaborative filtering indicates "that incorporating temporal aspects of user preference histories can greatly improve predictive accuracy. Bayesian models provide a natural mechanism for

integrating explicit user preferences (user profiles) with user histories to yield a more robust representation of usage patterns." Excerpts from Andrew Zimdars: Recommender Systems for Data Caching and Prefetch, Electronic Research Laboratory, UC Berkeley, CA. 2001. http://db.cs.berkeley.edu/papers/ERL/erl01.html

358 American LIVES or Lifestyles, Interests, Values, Expectations, and Symbols: www.americanlives.com

359 VALS™ framework: www.sric-bi.com/VALS/types.shtml

360 Computer Sciences Corporation: CSC/DuPont Alliance, June 1997. Use CSC search engine for the background of the alliance at www.csc.com

361 Hugh Cannon: Segmentation and Marketing, Reading 05, Marketing 7430, Winter 2002, School of Business Administration, Wayne State University, Detroit, MI 48202. www.cis.wayne.edu/cannon/mkts/7430/R5.pdf

362 Interview notes prepared by Alain Paul Martin for Procter & Gamble *Strategic Thinking Seminars* delivered in Chicago IL and New York NY.

363 Hugh Cannon: Segmentation and Marketing, see above.

364 VALS™ Cases were kindly provided by Patricia Breman, SRI Consulting Business Intelligence, pbreman@sric-bi.com

Chapter 12: A Final Word

365 Mark Halligan and Richard Horowitz: Five Years After the EEA, 2001 Annual Conference Proceedings, and Navigating through the Gray Zone: A Collection of Corporate Codes of Conduct and Ethical Guidelines, SCIP Publications, 1997 and 2001.

366 Herbert Shepard: Essence of a Proactive Life: Two Practical Essays on Life & Career Planning, 30 pages of an unfinished landmark book published post-mortem. 1994. ISBN 0-86502-050-7. An MIT alumnus, a former President of the Gestalt Institute of Cleveland, a professor at Yale, Case Western Reserve, Herb Shepard was a pioneer in the Organization Development movement. Book available from www.executive.org

367 Summarized and edited by the author to bring into focus the central point of William O. Douglas's message. This passage was quoted in Herbert Shepard's Essence of a Proactive Life (see above)

368 Herbert Shepard: Essence of a Proactive Life (see above).

Managing Important Projects Today

Some of our success in becoming a world-class manufacturer can be attributed to A. P. Martin's leadership and abilities both as project management practitioner and instructor.

Don Mallory, Manager, Training & Development, Boeing

Coached by a leader in the field of project management, you will learn cutting-edge skills to maximize clients' benefits in small and large or complex projects. You will apply the best available framework and *Harvard University Global System*™ *(HUGS)* road maps. You will take home practical tools, not available elsewhere, to define projects, negotiate, coach teams, forge alliances, mitigate risk, allocate scarce resources and control quality, cost and time .

WHO SHOULD ATTEND

Project and functional managers, executives and professionals who play a key role in project teams and in risk management.

PRACTICAL OBJECTIVES

At the end of this course, you will be able to:
- Select projects; validate goals & priorities
- Define the project strategy & deliverables
- Identify the critical success factors
- Secure the commitment of stakeholders
- Inspire and retain talent; build, motivate and lead high-performing teams
- Define clear role and strict accountability
- Influence without the benefit of authority
- Enlarge the pie; negotiate win-win deals
- Forge lasting alliances; widen your lead
- Estimate and allocate the best resources
- Schedule and budget multiple projects
- Establish mechanisms to control change
- Anticipate and manage risks and conflicts
- Act on early signs of delays, cost overruns
- Control and communicate progress
- Evaluate project impact

COURSE MATERIALS

Participants receive a practical workbook, HUGS road maps, templates for defining projects, formulating strategy, managing risk, charting responsibility and evaluating performance as well as the latest Harvard Planner and Boeing Case Study.

"I found the course content, your presentation and the group interaction discussions simulating, and the real-life cases very enlightening."
Noel Mailvaganam
Principal Research Officer
National Research Council

OUTLINE: 5 DAYS, 3.75 CEU

1. Tools to Scope and Define Projects
- The Global framework and road maps
- How to select projects and validate goals
- Practical tips from project incubation
- How to set priority and validate deadlines
- People skills for high-performing teams
- Six acid tests to discard flawed objectives
- Balancing multi-project portfolios
- Project scope definition and charter
- Translating strategy into deliverables
- The art of crafting the right deliverables

2. Practical Road Map to Manage Risk
- How to identify neglected risks
- Estimating original and residual risks
- Proven tool to manage transition risk
- Case study: Complex risk management

3. Responsibility and Accountability Skills
- Exercise: Global responsibility charting
- Leading without hierarchical authority
- Responsibility, accountability and power

4. Estimating, Scheduling and Budgeting
- Developing a work-breakdown structure
- Best practices in estimating time and cost
- New tools to allocate scarce resources across multiple projects: real-life cases
- Sound scheduling with the Global Method
- Techniques to accelerate project duration
- How to budget under uncertainty
- Frequency of control: new practices

5. Implementation and Control
  Tools, Demonstration and Practice
- Best tools to manage inelastic deadlines, critical milestones and constant change
- Deviation domino effects: surprise events
- Global tools to assess project progress
- Final delivery and phase-out issues

6. Boeing: Advanced and Practical Case

7. Synthesis: Proactive Leadership

For the dates and locations of upcoming sessions, contact PDI at
1-800-HARVARD or (613) 730-7777 *www.executive.org*

Strategy, Risk, Negotiation and Leadership

In every good organization, there is an acute shortage of talented team leaders with four competencies: (i) sound **strategic thinking** to craft a bold vision of change, (ii) skills to create and extract value without undue exposure to risk, (iii) business **negotiation** acumen to secure commitment, and (iv) exemplary **leadership** skills to pull it all together and fulfill the mission with minimum friction and adverse consequences.

WHO SHOULD ATTEND

This practical workshop focuses on above competencies for managers, team leaders, negotiators, executives and professionals who play a key role in crafting policy or strategy, or in managing projects and risk.

PRACTICAL OBJECTIVES

This intensive workshop will provide you with the skills, competencies and tools to:
- secure advanced intelligence
- analyze the stakeholders in any issue
- craft important policies and strategies
- anticipate and manage complex risks
- inspire and retain talent; build top teams
- define clear roles and accountabilities
- orchestrate change under tight deadlines
- enlarge the pie; negotiate lasting deals; finance projects; buy or sell property; weigh intricate pricing and soft money;
- arbitrate disputes; manage conflicts
- forge lasting alliances to widen your lead and retain long-term leadership.

COURSE MATERIALS

Participants receive a practical workbook, road maps (Harvard University Global System™), templates for defining change, formulating strategy, managing risk, charting responsibility and evaluating performance as well as the latest Harvard Planner, and an advanced case study on multi-partite multi-issue negotiation.

"An outstanding course on how-to's of strategy, leadership and negotiation skills. This course would be beneficial for all levels of management."
Mark Farmer, Director, Engineering
General Motors

Our strategy sessions with Mr. Martin's method were a resounding success.
A. Deschesnes, Executive Vice-President
Desjardins Casualty Insurance Group

COURSE OUTLINE: 4 DAYS, 3 CEU

1. Intelligence to Anticipate Issues
- Intelligence tools and organization
- Scanning for threats and opportunities

2. People Skills - Team Competencies
- Proven ways to empower talent
- Instruments to analyze stakeholders

3. Skills for Charting a Clear Vision
- Tests to discard questionable goals
- How to define change: tools, practices

4. How to Invent Innovative Strategies
- Strategy Grid to brainstorm options
- From strategy to work plan: practice
- Translating strategy into deliverables
- How to build lasting alliances
- How to test the validity of a strategy

5. Management Road Map on Risk
- How to identify hidden risks
- Instrument to manage transition risks
- Case study: Complex risk mitigation

6. Leadership and Accountability
- Using power and authority ethically
- Teamwork: Responsibility charting
- Exercise: Accountability balance sheet
- Characteristics of effective leaders

7. How to Prepare for Negotiation
- Detailed road map for negotiation
- Exercises: Critical success factors
- Crafting mutual-gain opportunities

8. Pricing, Bidding and Other Terms
- Bidding, auctioning, concessions
- Escalation, soft money, other tactics

9. Hands-on Negotiations: Practice
- How to forge lasting agreements
- Subtleties that make or break deals
- How and when to act as mediator
- Complex multi-partite negotiation
- Fleeting coalitions and framing issues
- High-stake labor negotiation: UAW
- How to deal with harsh 'negotiators'
- Closing a deal or exiting gracefully
- Ten steps to avoid deadlocks

10. Synthesis: Proactive Leadership

For the dates and locations of upcoming sessions, contact PDI at
1-800-HARVARD or (613) 730-7777 www.executive.org

New-Manager and Team-Leader Workshop
Mastering the Skills, Techniques and Tools

"This course was a great experience and has armed me with proven methods that apply to either public or private industries."

Alex Quijano, JSI Shipping, Burlingame, CA

This intensive workshop focuses on what works in real life. Whether you are new or aspiring to management, we want you to excel in the difficult transition to team leader and manager. You'll take home the skills, tools and know-how to get the very best of every employee and make a real difference in the effectiveness and productivity of your organization. You will learn to set and accomplish objectives, coach, delegate and motivate, solve problems, review performance, communicate and give feedback including unpleasant news without impairing self-esteem ... and much more.

WORKSHOP BENEFITS

At the end of this hands-on workshop you will acquire the proven skills to attract; empower; reward and retain talent; get commitment to a shared vision; delegate; bring out the best in others and lead your team to success. You will learn to recognize true priorities; assume responsibility and accountability; manage risks; resolve problems and conflicts; respect diversity; build a culture based on trust and mutual respect; inspire; mentor and serve as a role model for others. And you will take home new ideas, proven tools and sound timesaving skills, most of which are unavailable elsewhere.

DETAILED OUTLINE - 3 DAYS - 2.25 CEU

1. Neglected Issues in Team Leadership
• How to validate goals and prevent errors
• Exercise: How to set priority and urgency
• How to lead without the benefit of authority
• How to get and apply collaborative power
2. Profession Team Leader
• Beyond situational leadership: Acting with a conscience, competence and commitment
• Most-valuable leadership knowledge (not necessarily diplomas)
• Interpersonal skills; behavior of leaders
• Attitudes conducive to effective leadership
• Essential team-management skills
3. Effective Coaching and Mentoring
• Critical success factors for new managers
• Model coaches and mentors for managers
4. How to Prepare Your Team to Succeed Beyond Measure
• 5-stage journey to a high-performing team
• Team & leader: roles; keys to compatibility
• Charting responsibility and accountability
• Exercise: How to assign clear roles
5. Best Practices to Motivate, Delegate and Empower your Team
• The current theories: Schein, Katz et al
• The best practices on motivation
• Motivating former peers and newcomers
• How to delegate and get results
• How to empower your team members

6. Management of Change
• What should change and in what sequence
• Changing attitudes and behavior
7. How to Conduct Effective Reviews
• Exercise: Sensitive performance review
• Performance review steps
• Tips for successful review meetings
• How to praise, reward and discipline
• Managing various staff reactions
8. Managing Conflict
• How to discuss complaints with employees
• Conflict diagnosis: 8 early signs; causes
• Conflict resolution road map
9. Managing Difficult and Hostile People
• Film: Dealing with team members who are passive resistant or openly hostile
• How to discipline or terminate
10. Managing Time, Organizing the Team
• How to set priority and schedule your time
• How to get and stay organized: tools; tips
• Effective ways to manage interruptions: Demonstration and practice
• Key secrets to higher productivity
• 25 tips to effective e-mails
11. Ongoing Improvement: Best Sources
• Best resources for cutting-edge leadership
• Non-commercial Web references
• Formal and informal networks
13. Exercises, Teamwork and Synthesis

For the dates and locations of upcoming sessions, contact PDI at
1-800-HARVARD or (613) 730-7777 *www.executive.org*

Management road maps and other practical tools available
on laminated posters. For the latest, visit www.executive.org
Turn Strategy into Value: Executive Checklist (Code: Z1)

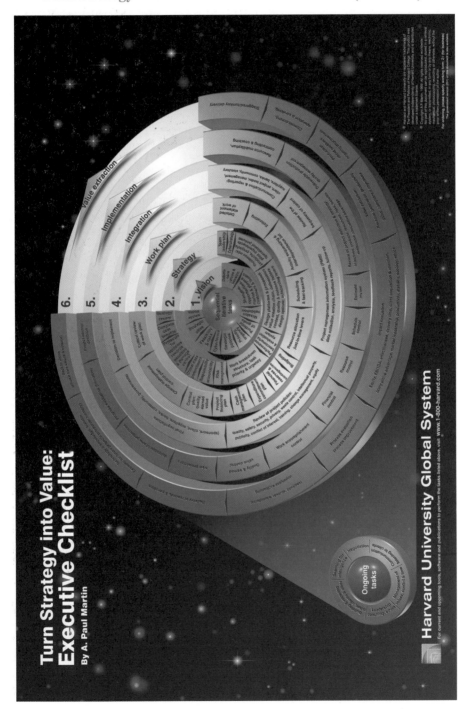

Management road maps and other practical tools available on laminated posters. For the latest, visit www.executive.org.
Risk Management Road Map (Code: Z16)

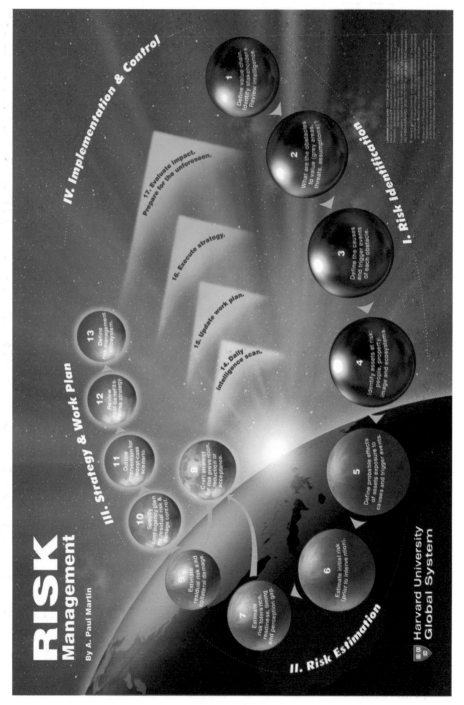